Letters to the Editor

CFI Book Division
Gordonsville, Tennessee USA

Letters to the Editor

A conversation between the author and a
newspaper editor on the life of Abraham

Adrianne Asheburton

Copyright © 2019 by CFI Book Division

Cover and interior design by CFI Graphic Design

All Rights Reserved. No part of this book may be reproduced in any form or by any electronic or mechanical means including information storage and retrieval systems without permission from its publisher, CFI Book Division.

Unless otherwise noted Bible quotations are from King James Version, copyright ©1988, B. B. Kirkebride Bible Company, Inc., Indianapolis, Indiana, used by permission.
ESV *The Holy Bible, English Standard Version* ©, copyright © 2001 by Crossway Bibles, a publishing ministry of Good News Publishers. Used by permission. All rights reserved.
HCSB *The Apologetics Study Bible*, copyright © 2007 by Holman Bible Publishers, Nashville, Tennessee. All rights reserved; used by permission.
NASB *The New American Standard Bible*, copyright © 1973 by the Lockman Foundation, La Habra, California. All rights reserved; used by permission.

The author purposely used the names Abraham and Sarah throughout the discussion, except where quoting Bible verses directly.

Published by CFI Book Division
P.O. Box 159, Gordonsville, Tennessee 38563

ISBN-10: 0-9975122-9-6
ISBN-13: 978-0-9975122-9-8

Printed in the United States of America

Typeset in 11.5/13.8 Minion Pro

Note to the Reader

The material in this book is from an actual conversation that took place between the author and a newspaper editor. It was a daily dialogue via email, discussing the narrative in the Book of Genesis. The dialogue concerning Abraham is only a small part of the conversation that, as of the publication date of this book, is still on-going. The easy writing style reflects the casualness of the conversation and friendship between the author and the editor. Hope you enjoy looking over the author's shoulder as you read these daily communications, and perhaps learn something you never thought about before in Abraham's experience.

With Sir Isaac Newton, I must confess that "if I have seen further it is by standing on the shoulders of giants" who went before me, teaching me how to read and understand the Bible as God intended it to be read—a love letter to His beloved.

Contents

1. Historical Background — 11
2. Abraham's First Mistake — 19
3. Two Predicaments — 25
4. Peace-loving Abraham — 29
5. Abraham and the Land — 35
6. Lot's Predicament — 43
7. Uncle Abe to the Rescue — 49
8. Lot Returns to Sodom — 55
9. Abraham Meets Melchizedek — 59
10. Abraham's Shield — 63
11. Strange Sacrifice — 67
12. Theophany in the Night — 75
13. Nations of Canaan — 83
14. Sarah's Big Idea — 89
15. Bitter Results of Unbelief — 95
16. The God Who Hears — 99
17. Abraham's "Wild Man" — 105
18. Persistent Love — 111
19. Works of the Flesh Must Be Cut Off — 117

20. Abraham Laughed	125
21. Abraham Explains His Mistake	129
22. Visitors at Mamre	133
23. Sarah Laughed	137
24. Sarah Denies Her Denial	141
25. Abraham Teaches Us Intercession	145
26. The Man in the Gate	151
27. Another Kind of Intercessor	157
28. Night of the Dead	163
29. It's Just a Little Sin	169
30. Don't Look Back!	175
31. A Tragic Life	179
32. Abraham Does It Again	185
33. Sarah's Final Exam	191
34. What Is Faith?	195
35. Abraham's "Two Sons"	201
36. More on Faith	209
37. Still More on Faith	219
38. Justification By Faith	225
Poem: "Self Dies Hard"	233
39. Ishmael's Banishment	235
40. The Well of the Oath	241
41. "Take Your Only Son"	247

42. Bitter Deed	251
43. No Laughing Matter	255
44. Total Commitment	259
45. The Lamb of God	263

1

Historical Background

We begin our dialogue on the life of Abraham by reviewing the background for the story. All stories have inconspicuous scenery tucked in the background and that is often overlooked by the reader. Once we bring these out, the less readily noticed parts create interest and focus for the main part of the narrative, increasing the depth of our understanding of what God is trying to tell us.

In order to understand what is taking place in a Bible story, the first thing we need to look for is God's motive. The Bible should always be studied from God's point of view. It is His Word *to* us, *through* which He is trying teach us about Himself. The people in the Bible were all real persons, with real human thoughts and emotions. They had the same doubts and hopes, and experienced the same pains and joys we do. The Creator worked through those experiences to teach the people of the Bible, and through their stories, He will also teach us.

The last half of Genesis chapter 11 concerns the descendants of Shem, Noah's righteous son. We have already discussed the meaning of Peleg's name and its relation to the "shaking," or "division" events that took place over a period of a couple centuries after the Flood when the surface of the earth was still being reshaped through violent earthquakes and volcanic activity (Genesis 10:25). And we already talked about the name Eber that gave rise to the Hebrew name for the later descendants of Abraham (Genesis 11:15, 16).

Another point to glean from the history of the immediate post-Flood genealogy is the rapidly decreasing ages of the patriarchs. Noah lived 950 years, but Abraham's father, Terah died when he was 205. As a result of the world-wide Flood, the earth was changed tremendously and man's age was reduced as a consequence of those changes. It was no longer a perfect world, but was now a world scarred and transformed into a less hospitable environment with climate shifts, damaging weather patterns, and deranged and difficult landscapes.

Of the persons who survived the Flood, Abraham personally knew Noah for 48 years, and he knew Noah's son Shem, who outlived Abraham by 30 years. Abraham lived 175 years, but Shem died when he was 602 years old, 502 years after the Flood. Shem and Abraham were contemporaries. From these facts, we learn that there was no loss of knowledge concerning who the Creator was or what He did in creating this world from nothing through His spoken Word. The sad facts of the Fall of Adam and Eve were verbally transmitted to the first twelve generations post-Flood (from Shem to Jacob's twelve sons), as well as God's promise of redemption through the coming Messiah.

From the Flood to the time when Jacob's family went to sojourn in Egypt, there was no loss of the Gospel's message of salvation through faith in God's power to deliver people from their sin. The Book of Genesis is a record of God's activities as He taught people to believe in Him.

Noah and Shem both continued to teach the history of the Flood that destroyed sinners while saving those who believed Noah's message of mercy to all who would enter the refuge given to them by God. The Flood washed the face the earth clean from sin's effects, and in the transformed world, both Noah and Shem continued to preach the message of righteousness by faith in the coming Messiah. Abraham well knew these facts. God never has been without a witness in this world.

Abraham's Personal Background

Abraham lived in a city named Ur, which was in southern Babylonia. It is identified as Ur of the Chaldees in Genesis 11:28 and 31, and was the birthplace for Abraham and his brothers, Nahor and Haran. Haran died in Ur before Terah and the rest of his family moved to the city of Haran. Located in Upper Mesopotamia, Haran was in the "arch" of the "fertile crescent" where the "crescent" turned southward again along the Mediterranean Sea's eastern coastline. Terah died in Haran, and after that Abraham and his nephew Lot moved on again (Acts 7:4).

Nahor's wife, Milcah, was the daughter of his brother, Haran, making her Nahor's niece (Genesis 11:29). The father of Sarai (Sarah) is unclear, but later in the narrative Abraham would refer to his wife as his sister (Genesis 12:13; 20:2). Sarah may have been the daughter of Haran, which would make her sister to Nahor's wife and Abraham's niece, or else she was the daughter of Terah by a second wife that was not Abraham's mother. The Bible's facts on this point are limited.

Joshua 24:2 tells us that Terah was an idolater. "Thus saith the LORD God of Israel, Your fathers dwelt on the other side of the flood in old time, even Terah, the father of Abraham, and the father of Nahor: and they served other gods" (Joshua 24:2). The principle god of that region was Sin, the moon god. Sin was the father of the sun god, Shamash, by the goddess Inanna, the equivalent of the goddess Ishtar that was promoted in Nimrod's cities on the twin rivers of Euphrates and Tigris. Nimrod's cities were Babel, Erech, Accad, Calneh, all located on the Plain of Shinar through which the Euphrates and Tigris rivers flow, (Genesis 10:9, 10). Thus we have the first pagan "trinity"—father, mother and son. Satan has a counterfeit for just about everything.

The "flood" in the verse from Joshua is not the world-wide destructive Flood, but the large Euphrates River that often flooded that region. Terah and his family lived on the eastern side of the Euphrates River. The city called Ur was a large urban area with advanced amenities. God called Abraham away from all that secularism and paganism, to be a wanderer the rest of his life, never owning any land except the burial cave in Machpelah that he bought from the "children of Heth" (see Genesis 23).

Stephen, one of the first deacons of the early Christian church, said that God appeared to Abraham while he was living in Ur of the Chaldees, instructing him to get out of Babylon (Acts 7:2, 3). The call from God to Abraham was given to remove him from the religiously corrupt environment established by Nimrod in that region. Abraham was called out of Babylon, just as God's people at the end of time will be called out of spiritual Babylon and its corruption (Revelation 18:4).

"But Sarai was barren; she had no child" (Genesis 11:30). The statement that Sarai was barren sets up the theme for the next ten chapters in Genesis.

"And Terah took Abram his son, and Lot the son of Haran his son's son [Terah's grandson through Haran, who had already died in Ur], and Sarai his daughter in law, his son Abram's wife; and they went forth with them from Ur of the Chaldees, to go into the land of Canaan; and they came unto Haran, and dwelt there." (Genesis 11:31).

The city of Ur was a place of wonderful beauty. It had towers, palaces, temples, law courts, market squares, statues, religious shrines and gardens, and mosaics, friezes and bas-reliefs on the walls of buildings. The city was laid out in rectangular blocks separated by paved streets that were lined with two-story houses. The houses had running water and indoor plumbing. Ur had a man-made canal giving the city access through a seaport to the Persian Gulf and the Indian Ocean. Thus the city was open to the lucrative markets down the side of the Arabian peninsula and on the coasts of Africa and India (none of which were called by these names at that time).

From this fabulous city with its comfortable living, Abraham was called out to wander in the comparative wilderness of Canaan, living in tents, surrounded by his flocks of sheep, goats, and camels, and an increasing population of servants and herdsmen. We are not told how much wealth Abraham had while living in Ur, but while wandering through the land of Canaan, he became a very wealthy man—in material wealth—but more importantly, in spiritual wealth as he more clearly came to understand the depth of the everlasting covenant first preached to Adam.

The last verse in chapter 11 tells us of the migration of Terah and his family from "Ur of the Chaldees" to Haran, which was in the "land of the Hittites." Terah was 70 years old when he began to have his children, and he was 205 years old when he died in Haran. We are not told how many years after arriving in that city that Terah died. The original intent seems to be that the whole family was going to Canaan, but they "dwelt" in Haran until Terah died.

Since Stephen said that God spoke to Abraham concerning the move from Ur to Canaan (Acts 7:2, 3), it seems that, rather than it being Terah's idea to move, it was really Abraham who was inspired by God's Word. Terah, being the patriarch of the family, seems to get the "credit" for the idea, even though we later find out that Terah worshiped idols (Joshua 24:2).

Before leaving Ur, Nahor, Abraham's brother, married his niece (his dead brother's orphaned daughter). Nahor and his wife Milcah remained behind in the city of Haran when Abraham moved on toward Canaan, as God instructed him to do while he was still living in Ur. These facts are given to us because later in the story of Abraham we will read that when Abraham sent his servant to find a wife for Isaac, he sent the man back to Haran in hopes of making a marriage alliance with a relative who was a spiritually like-minded young woman (Genesis 22:20; 24:1-9).

Background of the City of Haran

The city of Haran was on a trade route running from the east to the west, from Babylon to Canaan, and then on to Egypt. It made a northward arch around the desert area between Babylon and Canaan, now called the Arabian Desert. From Ur, Terah and his family would have traveled north along the west bank of the Euphrates to the city of Babylon, then crossed the river to the east side, to avoid the desert on the western edge of the Euphrates. The trade route went north to Nineveh, crossed the Tigris River, turned back to the west, and then went on to Haran. Continuing to loop southward, the trade route came to Damascus, and then finally arrived at the land of Canaan.

It was about 700 miles from Ur to Haran, and another 700 miles down to Canaan from Haran, making a 1400 mile pilgrimage for Abraham, Sarai and Lot. Walking on foot or riding a camel in a caravan would have allowed them to travel about 10 or 12 miles a day. Taking the lowest mileage, to accommodate the age of Terah and his possible frailness at the age they left Ur, it would have taken more than two months to travel the 700 miles from Ur to Haran.

In Haran, which was situated just below the Taurus Mountains, the local people worshiped the nature "gods" of the mountains. Pagan idol worship was still in the land when Abraham's grandson, Jacob, exiled himself to Haran to avoid the anger of his brother, Esau (Genesis 28:10; 29:1). Jacob lived with his uncle Laban, who was descended from Nahor and Milcah, and married Laban's two daughters, Leah and Rachel. When Jacob decided to go back to Canaan after being 20 years away from home, Rachel revealed her pagan superstitions by stealing her father's idols to take them with her to their new home (Genesis 31:30-35).

When Jacob and his family arrived back in Canaan at the sacred place called Bethel, where the LORD had appeared to him (Genesis 28:10-19), Jacob took all the pagan idols and jewelry from his wives and buried them under a tree (Genesis 35:1-4). The idols were called *teraphim* and were used for consulting pagan gods to divine the future or access power, an act that is incompatible with the worship of the God who created heaven and earth and all that is in them. As it is today, in the days of Abraham paganism was very deeply entrenched in the world, even among people who knew about the one true God. Confusion comes when we compromise truth that has been revealed to us, and think that we can safely incorporate "small amounts" of paganism into our worship of the one true God. But even a small amount of arsenic poisons the entire pot of tea.

Genesis 12:1-3

When Terah died, God spoke again to Abraham, saying, "Get thee out of thy country [that now being Haran], and from thy kindred [his brother Nahor], and from thy father's house [the other relatives of Nahor and perhaps other children of their brother Haran who moved from Ur with him], unto a land that I will shew thee: and I will make of thee a great nation, and I will bless thee, and make thy name great; and thou shalt be a blessing: and I will bless them that bless thee, and curse him that curseth thee: and in thee shall all families of the earth be blessed." (Genesis 12:1-3).

God made seven promises in these verses. He asked Abraham to promise nothing in return. All God wanted was for Abraham to believe His promises to him and act on them, which he did. Abraham packed up his belongings and family, and took off down the trade route to Canaan.

"So Abram departed, as the LORD had spoken unto him; and Lot went with him: and Abram was seventy and five years old when he departed out of Haran. And Abram took Sarai his wife, and Lot his brother's son, and all their substance that they had gathered, and the souls that they had gotten in Haran; and they went forth to go into the land of Canaan; and into the land of Canaan they came." (Genesis 12:4, 5).

Those seven promises are: (1) I will show you were I want to you to go; (2) I will make you a great nation; (3) I will bless you and make your name great; (4) through My power, you will be a blessing to others; (5) I will bless those who are good to you; (6) I will defend you from those who fight against you; and (7) through your descendant (the promised Messiah) all the world will be blessed.

God only said one time that He would bless Abraham, but three times God repeated that through Abraham He would bless others, including the entire world (Genesis 12:3). The promises of God to Abraham in Genesis 12:1-3 concern the greater blessing that would come through the Messiah who would be born as a direct descendant of Abraham. God was going to establish a nation that He intended to be His missionaries to the world, to carry to the world the everlasting covenant message of a coming Messiah who would fulfill the promise given to Adam when he fell (Genesis 3:15).

The apostle Paul explains this in his letter to the Jewish Christians in Galatia who had become confused about the promise. He wrote, "Now to Abraham and his Seed were the promises made. He [God] saith not, And to *seeds* [plural], as of many; but as of one, And to thy *Seed*, which is Christ" (Galatians 3:16). The promise made to Abraham in Genesis 12:1-3 dealt with the "nation" God was going to establish, only becasue through that nation Christ would be born into the world. In Ephesians 3:3-6, Paul wrote that the "revelation that was made known to him" was "that the Gentiles should be fellowheirs and partakers of [God's] promise in Christ through the Gospel." The promise of blessing in Genesis 12:1-3 was not limited to the Israelite nation in the past or present. The promise was to have a worldwide impact as the message of righteousness by faith in Christ is carried to "every nation, and kindred, and tongue, and people (Revelation 14:6).

These promises from God would accomplish for Abraham and his faithful descendants what the men building the tower of Babel thought they were going to accomplish for themselves. Nimrod and his followers sought to be eternally established in the world by building a great city and a tower that would reach up to God's throne—which, by the way, was exactly what Lucifer thought he was going to accomplish in his challenge to God's government in heaven. Lucifer dreamed and conspired to "sit on the mount of God's assembly ... I will make myself like the Most High" (Isaiah 14:13, 14, HCSB).

Through the fame of Nimrod's delirious dream, all the world would "wonder after" the people living on the Plain of Shinar, and would come to Babel to gain access to heaven by climbing the tower. The descendants of Nimrod wanted to make a "name" for themselves, to become "men of renown" like those before the Flood (Genesis 11:4, cf. 6:4). But without God, they could achieve nothing lasting.

2

Abraham's First Mistake

Genesis 12:10-6

After arriving in Canaan, Abraham soon begins to get himself into trouble concerning his faith in God's promises stated in Genesis 12:1-3. God promised Abraham that He would take care of him and protect him from any enemies. But most importantly, God said that He would bless the whole world through Abraham.

How was this going to be accomplished? Abraham had to have children though which that part of the promise would be fulfilled. Without a son born to Abraham, no Messiah could be born any time in the future through Abraham's descendants. When they left Ur, and then Haran, Abraham had no children; Sarah was barren, incapable of having children. They had been married long enough to prove this sad fact (Genesis 11:30; 25:21; 30:1).

Sarah's barrenness notwithstanding, God made the promise that "in thee" or "through you" all the nations of the earth would be blessed. That promise included the birth of a son to Abraham and Sarah. But that was something that Abraham knew was impossible, especially since Sarah not only was barren, but she was well past normal childbearing age. She was 65 years old when the promise was made to Abraham, who was 75 at that time.

But the promise was not just made to Abraham. Husband and wife are one (Genesis 2:24), and that means that the promise made to Abraham *included* Sarah. As unable as she was to conceive, God intended that the promise would be fulfilled through her as well as

Abraham. The matter of fixing that problem belonged to God alone. Since He had made the promise to do something that man was absolutely incapable of doing, it was only through the intervention of divine power that the promise could be fulfilled.

And herein lay the problem of faith.

"And there was a famine in the land: and Abram went down into Egypt to sojourn there; for the famine was grievous in the land." (Genesis 12:10). Famine was not uncommon in Canaan. There were plagues of locusts, seasonal droughts, and wars that destroyed crops. Interestingly, locusts have two phases, one is solitary and the second is called "gregarious." In the first phase, they are just innocuous grasshoppers living here and there, not doing much damage at all. The gregarious phase follows a time of dryness in the land. After a drought the locusts band together by the millions forming massive swarms, and invade any area that has vegetation they can voraciously consume. Locust plagues are still common in the Middle East and eastern Africa.

The area of the Negev where Abraham last found himself would have been more harshly effected by either drought or locusts, since it was a dry desert region to begin with. Also, Abraham with his large flocks and herds would have been particularly unwelcomed by the Canaanite tribes living there during the devastating, "grievous" time of a drought and locust plague. Abraham was, after all, an encroacher in their territories, using up their precious natural resources.

With this situation, Abraham made the logical choice to travel on to Egypt where there was pasturage for his livestock and food for his families (his personal kin and his servant's). However, it was a choice Abraham made independently. He did not receive any "word from the LORD" concerning this move. God called him to Canaan, and in Canaan he should have stayed until God told him to do otherwise. Abraham quickly forgot God's promise that He would bless him and take care of him, no matter what circumstances developed in the land.

"And it came to pass, when he was come near to enter into Egypt, that he said unto Sarai his wife, Behold now, I know that thou art a fair woman to look upon: therefore it shall come to pass, when the Egyptians shall see thee, that they shall say, This is his wife: and they will kill me, but they will save thee alive. Say, I pray thee, thou art my sister: that it may be well with me for thy sake; and my soul shall live because of thee." (Genesis 12:11-13).

This is the Bible's first mention of Egypt as a nation. The Egyptians were descendants of Ham's son, Mizraim (see Genesis 10:6). In the narrative of chapter 12 we are introduced to the Canaanites and the Egyptians, both of whom will figure prominently in the rest of the story recorded in the Pentateuch. Here in the story of Abraham, Egypt provides a place of refuge from the famine. But it also was a dangerous place for Abraham's faith in God.

Things to note from these verses:—

(1) Sarah, even though she is more than 60 years old, was still a very beautiful woman, and obviously quite sexually attractive; men would kill to get her—an amazing statement about that society and that society's opinion of a woman's worth!

(2) Sarah *was technically* Abraham's "sister" being the daughter of his father through a second wife, or else she was a cousin.

(3) Abraham had no compunction about telling his wife to lie.

(4) Abraham obviously forgot or did not believe God's promise to protect and provide for him.

(5) Abraham did not fully accept God's promise that Sarah would be the mother of his children, and that therefore she must remain his wife exclusively—which naturally precludes selling her off to protect his own skin.

And of course, if you're going to look at this story from the feminist position, Sarah is presented as nothing more than a possession of her husband, or any other man who wanted her. It was her outward appearance that made her attractive to men, who obviously never assessed her qualities as an intelligent person, worth more than just what her body could provide to a man and his ego. Her voice went unheard. She simply had to obey her husband; she had no choice in the matter.

Worst of all, Abraham was quite willing to let his beloved wife be taken from him in order to save his own skin. A very selfish attitude, to say the least. Maybe she wasn't so "beloved" after all? Can you imagine how a wife would feel to find out that her husband didn't care enough about her to defend her in a situation, as Abraham described they would find upon arriving in Egypt? He was willing to just let her go into the hands of heathen strangers rather than boldly state that she was his wife and precious to him. Makes you just shake your head in disbelief of a professed loving husband's decision to sacrifice his wife in order to save himself. What a coward her husband was proving himself to be. After this, how could a wife trust such a husband?

But on the other side of the picture, Abraham was a little more than 75 years old, and probably didn't think he could defend himself or his wife against the strong young men of pharaoh's household that were apparently always on the lookout for an attractive woman to add to the king's harem.

Pharaoh and the young princes of the land must have had quite a reputation for violence for Abraham to have had such a fear of them. Even if he had employed his many male servants in Sarah's defense, it would have been a war that he didn't want, and would have meant that they had no place to live to survive the famine back in Canaan. The Egyptians would have driven them away, back into the desert and the famine they were trying to escape. Taking these perspectives into view, Abraham's decision maybe seems a little less heartless.

"And it came to pass, that, when Abram was come into Egypt, the Egyptians beheld the woman that she was very fair. The princes also of Pharaoh saw her, and commended her before Pharaoh: and the woman was taken into Pharaoh's house." (Genesis 12:14, 15).

As Abraham, Sarai and his tribe came into the main populated region of Egypt, the common man on the street admired Sarah as she rode though town on her camel. These common men were unable to steal her from Abraham, but the "princes of Egypt" had both authority and the power to do so. As soon as Abraham and his caravan arrived in town, these princes brought Sarah's beauty to pharaoh's attention, and "commended her" to pharaoh, knowing full well that he would take her from Abraham. The king owned the best of everything, including the most beautiful women in the land.

From the narrative, we don't know what Abraham had to say about who Sarah was to him, whether it was he who told pharaoh's princes that Sarah was his sister, or whether he left the telling of that lie up to Sarah. But he evidently was quite willing to strike a good bargain for letting her go, and ended up well rewarded. "And [pharaoh] entreated Abram well for her sake: and he had sheep, and oxen, and he donkeys, and menservants, and maidservants, and she donkeys, and camels" given to him in exchange for his "sister." (Genesis 12:16).

As a result of the lie concerning Sarah, Abraham ended up with a huge reward for turning his wife over the king's harem. In effect, through the exchange of wealth, Sarah was purchased from her husband (aka "brother"), because pharaoh gave Abraham much additional livestock, and servants, who in actuality were themselves slaves, people bought and traded without any input from them about how they felt about the situation—just like Sarah. We have a picture of exploitation on every side.

Pharaoh must have thought a lot of the new acquisition to his household to have paid such a handsome price for her. The narrative conveys the idea that for pharaoh, obtaining Sarah was equivalent to buying an exquisite Arabian horse to add to his stables. A discerning eye, a flip of the hand, and it's done.

Without saying a word about anything, apparently not even that she was Abraham's sister or wife, Sarah was taken from her family and put in the king's palace. Opulence of her new home notwithstanding, to be treated so unfeelingly by her husband must have deeply pained Sarah as she entered into a far different world than she had ever known. As she was hustled away, there was no promise from anyone, not even a whispered, "I'll get you back, some how" from her husband. We can only imagine her fear as she entered that unknown world of pharaoh's harem.

How would this event have effected the minds of all those in Abraham's clan who looked up to him as their leader, and had followed him for more than a thousand miles from Haran to Canaan, and now down to Egypt? The people of Abraham's tribe, over the many years of living under his care, had learned to trust his judgment on everything. And now, without a fight, he handed over his wife to heathens! If he was willing to trade away his wife, what would he do to *them*? Could they continue to trust this man? What spiritual message would this have sent to all his extended family? Was Abraham acting any differently than the pagan chiefs of Canaan and Egypt?

This whole event presented a serious blight upon the character of the God that Abraham claimed to worship. If the LORD's "faithful" behaved just like the rest of the world, then why worship Him? When it came right down to it, it now appeared that Abraham's God was just as impotent and uncaring as all the pagan gods in the world.

3

Two Predicaments

Genesis 12:17-20

A note about locusts before we move on in our discussion. Locusts congregate in huge hordes to migrate to places where there is food. They move en masse from the drought blighted area to another place where food is more readily available. Doing this, they increase the problem for people in the new area by eating what grain crops are available to sustain them though the famine period, thus extending the famine problem.

Getting a Grip on the Bible

When we begin to understand the Bible, we realize that it "was written for our admonition upon whom the ends of the world have come" (1 Corinthians 13:11). The people of the Old Testament, and even the New, were just the same as we are today. They faced the same issues in their daily lives, and wondered if God was "there" for them. They wondered if God was a real person who cared enough to interact with them and actually direct their lives into "paths of righteousness" (Psalm 23:3). Or was He some kind of phantom deity who could not interact with the material world. In each story in the Bible we can find ourselves, if we look carefully. Maybe just in bits and pieces scattered here and there, but like Solomon wrote, there is nothing new under the sun (Ecclesiastes 1:9).

By recognizing ourselves in the various predicaments that the people of the Bible stories got themselves into, and seeing how God handled their situations, we can learn how God works with us in guiding us off the path of rebellion and into the way of righteousness. This is God's purpose in providing us with the Bible, His more sure Word, as opposed to man's traditions that are nothing more than "good advice" that cannot solve our sin problem. The Bible assures that God "never changes." "For I am the LORD, I change not" (Malachi 3:6). "God is not a man, that He should lie; neither the son of man, that He should repent: has He said, and shall He not do it? Or has He spoken, and will He not make it good?" (Numbers 23:19).

If God was able to solve Abraham's and Isaac's and Jacob's unbelief issues, then He can and will do the same for us, if we let Him. That's *powerful good news!*

Sarah's Predicament

It would have taken some little bit of time for all the flocks to be gathered and brought to where Abraham was staying, plenty of time for Abraham to rethink what he was doing in selling his wife. But as the negotiations were completed and Abraham was paid by pharaoh's men, we are given no clue about whether Abraham had any doubts about giving up is wife to the pagan king.

Sarah was swiftly carted off to pharaoh's palace were the first thing that would have happened to her was a bath. The ancient Egyptians were very meticulous about body cleanliness. A woman or a man, for that matter, could not approach the pharaoh without being physically cleansed and clean-shaven. The pharaoh was, after all, the chief god of the realm. To come into the presence of the "god," persons had to be ritually clean.

In general, the Egyptians considered themselves a "pure" people and would not associate with dirty, smelly herdsmen or nomadic Canaanite peoples. This fact is played out later in our Genesis narrative when Joseph faced his shepherd brothers. The "unclean" shepherds had to be separated from the lord of the realm, and could only stand at Joseph's door to speak to him (Genesis 43:19).

And so Sarah was stripped of her smelly woolen clothing that she had probably worn for many months, if not years, and was washed, perfumed, and dressed in a clean, white, sheer and finely woven linen or cotton chemise that barely veiled her body from view. Then she was presented to her new husband, the pharaoh.

Pharaoh's Predicament

"And the LORD plagued Pharaoh and his house with great plagues because of Sarai Abram's wife." (Genesis 12:17). We have no indication of what these "plagues" were but they were serious and probably happened very soon after Sarah entered the palace. God would not allow Sarah to be spiritually or physically contaminated through an illicit physical relationship with anyone, especially an Egyptian king. God had much bigger plans for her.

The plague that God poured out on pharaoh's household could have been disease, death of something or someone who had contact with Sarah, or another equally disastrous calamity that brought to pharaoh's attention that Sarah was someone special. His superstitious religious beliefs would have caused him to think that she must be protected by a powerful god that he did not know, and this strange god brought the plague upon him and his household.

Whatever happened, when pharaoh inquired into the matter it became evident that Abraham had lied by omission in not telling him that Sarah was his wife. Perhaps, fearing what about to happen to her, Sarah herself confessed the truth to pharaoh when she was called before him. Or perhaps the discovery was made when pharaoh called in his soothsayers to determine the cause of the plague. Or, maybe God revealed the truth to him in a dream, as He did later with Abimelech (Genesis 20:6).

However it happened, pharaoh called in Abraham—probably without a bath since the interview was undertaken hastily to halt the plague!—and brought him to task for his lie. "And Pharaoh called Abram, and said, What is this that you have done unto me? why did you not tell me that she was your wife? Why did you say, She is my sister? so I might have taken her to me to wife: now therefore behold *your wife*, take her, and go your way. And Pharaoh commanded his men concerning him: and they sent him away, and his wife, and all that he had." (Genesis 12:18-20).

Pharaoh was not without some moral scruples. He would commit fornication with multiple women in his harem, but not adultery with another man's wife. Definitely a very fine line in defining what constitutes sexual sin. Yes, it was the king's prerogative and right to take into his harem any unmarried woman he wanted, and that meant that they were his possession for him to do as he wished with them. The father, uncle, or brother who had control of the woman might have deplored the removal of their family member as a serious tragedy, but the ancient royal right was never resisted nor questioned.

Taking a woman into his harem was a sign of the king's power and sovereignty over his nation. David later would take wives for just this reason, and when David was exiled from Jerusalem by the insurrection of his son, in an attempt to prove his claim to the crown, Absalom raped the concubines David left behind (2 Samuel 16:20-22).

The outrage of pharaoh is understandable, and just. In the first place, Abraham had no reason to be deceptive or afraid. Was not God in charge? Abraham's lie to Pharaoh—by omitting to state the fact Sarah was his wife—permitted this woman to be pawned off into his harem at a high trade value. Evidently the "she is my sister" excuse didn't come into the explanation when Abraham was confronted with his lying. Sarah technically *was* Abraham's sister but, more importantly, she was also his wife, that's where the deception fell.

So Abraham and his clan were sent packing back to Canaan. And what he might have hoped to avoid by his deception, ended up taking place anyway. They were cast out of Egypt. Even though the time frame in the narrative seems short, Abraham and his family must have been in Egypt long enough for the Canaanite famine to come to an end because nothing more is said about it.

Thus closes the first segment of the testing of Abraham's faith in God's promises. But Abraham didn't have a correct concept yet of what he was being tested on. He didn't grasp the fact that what he did in lying about Sarah was being unfaithful, not only to his wife, but also to God. We know this because Abraham repeated the exact same thing later in the narrative. Abraham had yet to comprehend the breadth and height of God's everlasting covenant.

4

Peace-loving Abraham

Genesis 13:1-13

"And Abram went up out of Egypt, he, and his wife, and all that he had, and Lot with him, into the south." (Genesis 13:1). Moses makes it clear that when Abraham was sent away by pharaoh, he was not diminished in any way. Everything that Abraham had when he entered Egypt went away with him, including his wife and Lot. And "all that he had" included all the livestock that pharaoh had given him to purchase Sarah. "Into the south" does not mean compass direction; it does not mean that Abraham continued his journey going farther south and deeper into Egypt, or down the coast of the Sinai Peninsula. "South" means back to the "south end" of the Canaanite region, which was the Negev desert area that he left when the entered into Egypt.

The Egyptians were very superstitious people, which is why they worshiped everything. They were pantheistic polytheists. They didn't want to incur the wrath of any god, so they worshiped everything that could possibly be thought of as a god, or that appeared to possess some kind of magical power.

They worshiped the Nile River because it flooded and brought fertility to the land through its slit deposits. They worshiped the frogs the river contained, the flies that occasionally plagued the land, the sun and moon, bulls, snakes, birds, and various gods they manufactured from their imaginations that they gave a semi-human form, such as Isis and Osiris, and their child Horus. All these were among the vast sacred pantheon of Egypt.

Osiris was the god of the dead and the underworld. Isis was the mother goddess of magic who protected the sick and all children. Horus was the god of the heavenly realm and of war and therefore, was the protector of pharaoh. Here we have a pantheistic pagan trinity—a male and a female god, and their son.

Pharaoh was not being magnanimous in letting Abraham get away unscathed. He was pushing Abraham out the door in haste because he was afraid of whatever god it was that Abraham brought with him into Egypt—a god that was more powerful than even pharaoh himself. Pharaoh didn't want any more trouble, and he didn't want to give this new god of Abraham's any more chances to make him look impotent.

And so, "Abram was very rich in cattle, in silver, and in gold" when he left Egypt. Pharaoh had enriched Abraham not only with cattle, but with precious metals. The possession of precious metals by nomadic people was a very important buffer against times of trouble. Since nomads by their lifestyle did not stay long enough in one place to grow food crops, they had to purchase grains from the settled tribes around them. Having metal to trade with meant that they could enter into commerce, as we find later when the Midianites bought Joseph from his brothers.

"And he went on his journeys from the south even to Bethel, unto the place where his tent had been at the beginning, between Bethel and Hai; unto the place of the altar, which he had made there at the first: and there Abram called on the name of the LORD." (Genesis 13:3, 4).

"From the south" again means that Abraham was moving from the Negev desert in the southern end of Canaan, traveling northward, where he found himself once again at Beth-el, the "house of God." The altar that he built years before was still standing there. Repeating verse 12:8, Abraham "called on the name of the LORD" and made a whole burnt offering on the altar. In doing so, he renewed his spiritual connection with the promise of God.

"And Lot also, which went with Abram, had flocks, and herds, and tents." By this time, not only had Abraham's herds and flocks multiplied, but Lot was also increased in wealth. Following the example of his uncle, Lot had gathered around him large numbers of servants and herdsmen to handle the increasing flocks.

To give some perspective on the situation, sheep and goats can reproduce twice a year (but they don't always), and they usually have twins, so flocks can increase at a rapid rate. Poorly vegetated land can only support about half a dozen goats or sheep per acre, and that only for about a month before the land becomes overgrazed. Keeping the animals on good pasturage meant being constantly on the move from one area to another. A very unsettled lifestyle, to be sure.

That there had accumulated such a large number of animals and people among both Abraham and Lot's clans, gives us a clue about the length of time the story encompasses. Years have passed since their journey in Egypt.

It was not immediately upon re-entering the Beth-el district that there was trouble between Abraham and Lot's servants. It probably took several years from their leaving Egypt to get to this part of the story in Genesis chapter 13. But eventually, "the land was not able to bear them, that they might dwell together: for their substance was great, so that they could not dwell together." It became necessary for them to separate into different districts so each of their flocks and herds would have sufficient grazing land and water.

"And there was a strife between the herdmen of Abram's cattle and the herdmen of Lot's cattle: and the Canaanite and the Perizzite dwelled then in the land." Perizzite means villager. The Perizzites were not a nomadic people, like Abraham and his clan. In a broader sense, the word Canaanite as used here, means merchants. The term was originally associated with the "sea people" who settled in the area along the eastern Mediterranean coast, who later became known as the Philistines.

There is a great deal of archeological evidence that indicates that the early Canaanites in the area did not build houses, but lived in caves and burned their dead, unlike the Semites who lived in tents and buried their dead out of respect for the body that was created in the image of God. The use of these two names for the people who dwelt in the land at that time tells us that there were villagers, and people who did not live in villages. Some people were settled and some were rural, even if not nomadic.

"And Abram said unto Lot, Let there be no strife, I pray thee, between me and thee, and between my herdmen and thy herdmen; for we be brethren." (Genesis 13:6-8). This verse reveals much to us about Abraham's tender heart. He was a peace-seeking man, wanting no strife or conflict around him.

"Is not the whole land before thee? separate thyself, I pray thee, from me: if thou wilt take the left hand, then I will go to the right; or if thou depart to the right hand, then I will go to the left." (Genesis 13:8, 9). Here Abraham displays his noble, peace-loving character. He is the older man and by that right as the head of the clan, he should have had the first choice of where to live. But Abraham turned that choice over to Lot, saying "take what you want, what you think is best for you; I will not dictate to you concerning it."

"And Lot lifted up his eyes, and beheld all the plain of Jordan, that it was well watered every where, before the LORD destroyed Sodom and Gomorrah, even as the garden of the LORD, like the land of Egypt, as thou comest unto Zoar."

We haven't had any Scriptures that revealed Lot's character, until now. In this narrative we see Lot's mind coming more clearly into focus. In his assessment of Sodom, he can't tell the difference between that wicked, depraved city and the Garden of Eden! In Lot's mind, they both looked the same from outward appearances—"well watered," and much like pagan Egypt with its Nile River. The Garden of Eden had four rivers flowing from it watering the whole land (Genesis 2:10-14). In Lot's mind, Sodom and Eden were places equally beautiful and desirable, and were perceived as much the same kind of place. The sinful character of the cities in the valley of Siddim at the southern end of the Dead Sea, and the danger to his spiritual health, were not evident to Lot's poorly developed spiritual discernment.

And neither are Lot's family sensibilities and obligations evident in this narrative. He should have turned around to his elderly uncle, and said, "Nay, but you make the first and best choice, Uncle, and I will take whatever you do not want." But he didn't, thus indicating his youthful selfishness. "Then Lot chose him all the plain of Jordan; and Lot journeyed east: and they separated themselves the one from the other" (Genesis 13:11).

The way this section of Scripture is worded, brings to our attention that Abraham, and thus Lot as his possible heir, seemed to be of the persuasion that the land was theirs by right. "Lot chose for himself all the land of the plain," as though it didn't belong to anyone else; as though it was up for grabs to anyone who wanted it. To Lot, it was perfectly acceptable for a new person, who in reality was a squatter, to just move in and take over. However, the cities on the plain had existed for some time and were well established as belonging to the people of Sodom, Gomorrah, and Zoar.

"Abram dwelled in the land of Canaan, and Lot dwelled in the cities of the plain, and pitched his tent toward Sodom. But the men of Sodom were wicked and sinners before the LORD exceedingly." (Genesis 13:11, 12). Lot "dwelt in the cities of the plain" in contrast to the "land of Canaan." These were two distinct territories and occupied by very different peoples.

At first, Lot only moved close by ("toward") Sodom and Gomorrah, and he continued to live in his tents. Keeping a little apart from those wicked cities on the plain, he continued his nomadic lifestyle, tended his flocks, and minded his own business. By doing so, he thought he was safe from trouble. Not so. Trouble invariably comes looking for us, and the closer proximity we have to it, the faster it nabs us.

We are not told, but since there is no mention of a wife for Lot until after he lives in Sodom, it is probably true that Lot married a woman from that city on the plain. That social connection certainly would have helped him make the decision to enter the city and dwell there.

Oh, how this speaks to us! At first we keep our distance from sin, knowing that wickedness is something we need to run from as fast as possible. But after constant exposure to it, even watching it from afar, sooner or later, we become inured to evil and sin doesn't appear quite so terrible as we at first thought. Through lack of discernment, we develop friendships with wicked and ungodly people, and by associating with them we decide that they don't have such bad characters after all. By no means do we want to be thought judgmental of another's lifestyle choices! Through such compromising, we diminish the real problem of sin, and come to accept that wicked people are mostly just like we are—"eating and drinking, marrying and giving in marriage"—just living ordinary lives. What's wrong with that?

And who are we to judge anyone? We want to get along with everyone and be accepted by those we come into contact with. Such reasoning causes us to weaken our convictions about right and wrong. Then Satan has his gaff in our jaw, reeling us in, and before long, Lot found himself living *inside* the city of Sodom, and thoroughly unable to tell righteousness from wickedness.

5

Abraham and the Land

Genesis 13:14-19

Lot moved down into the valley south of the Dead Sea, no doubt originally intending to only occupy the fertile grasslands with his flocks and herds. The first part of his story concerning that decision comes in the next chapter. Now we return to the narrative concerning Abraham.

"And the LORD said unto Abram, after that Lot was separated from him, Lift up now thine eyes, and look from the place where thou art northward, and southward, and eastward, and westward: for all the land which thou seest, to thee will I give it, and to thy seed for ever (Genesis 13:14, 15).

Abraham is now separated from all of his family except Sarah. Father and mother are dead, cousins and uncles were left in Haran 700 miles to the north, or in Ur 1400 miles away. And he has no children. He does, however, have many shepherds and other servants, and their wives and children, so he is not alone. As he migrates around the territory seeking pasturage for his livestock, it's like moving a village that lives in tents. They stay in one place until the grass is gone and then move to the next place where grass and water are abundant.

But before Abraham moved on from the place where he and Lot separated, God spoke to him again and told him to take a visual survey of the land around him, looking in the direct of all four points of the compass. We are not told which hill Abraham was standing on when God spoke to him, but he was somewhere on the south end of the ridge of hills that run along the western edge of the Jordan River, and then along the Dead Sea, from the Jezreel valley in the north to the Negev desert in the south. It was from this vantage point that Lot could see the plain spreading out around Sodom and Gomorrah on the southern edge of the Dead Sea.

The hills in the south are about 2000 feet above sea level. At that height, Abraham would have been able to see approximately fifty-five miles in either direction, provided there where no hills taller than where he was standing. Looking in all four directions of the compass would mean Abraham could view about fifty-five square miles, which calculates out to about thirty-five thousand acres. Not really a very large area, when all things are considered.

My point is that God said, "For all the land that you *see*, to you will I give it, and to your children forever." People who say that God made an irrevocable promise to Abraham and his descendants down to the present day, take these verses in a most literal fashion, claiming that these verses actually promise the entire land of Canaan, from Syria to Egypt, to the Jewish descendants of Abraham. If you take the broader view of a *literal* interpretation, then the promise includes the entire region of the present Middle East west of the Jordan River, from Mount Hermon to the Negev desert. However, if God promised him that his descendants would inherit all that he could *literally see*, it would be quite a limited area near the south end of the Dead Sea bordering on the Negev desert.

But there is an overlooked conundrum in this position. People who take the literal view conveniently limit the promise to the Jewish people, while excluding Abraham's other descendants through Ishmael, and his five sons born to him through Keturah (Genesis 25:1-4). Scripture does tell us that Abraham "gave all that he had to Isaac," but it also tells us that his other sons were given gifts and sent away "to the east," or across the Jordan River and Dead Sea, an area that would have been visible to him as he stood on that mountaintop surveying the land.

At the time the promise of land was made, Abraham had no children, so all his children, yet unborn, logically should have been included in the promise to possess the land. God is not a respecter of persons; all are equal in His eyes.

If one is going to be literal about the situation, then it is only logical to carry that literalness all the way to include all the literal descendants of Abraham, even those born through Ishmael and Keturah. And, if literalness is the rule, then the land would be limited to that small thirty-five thousand acre tract at the south end of the Dead Sea. It must either *literally* be the fact that only that small portion was meant as the gift of land, or else it must *literally* be true that all of Abraham's sons where included in the promise. You can't have it both ways; you can't stand on one point and ignore the other.

A Broader Consideration

With these issues before us, let's consider that maybe God had something else in mind when He made that promise to Abraham. Maybe what Abraham could "see" was not of this world, because the promise concerned a spiritual inheritance, not a literal one. To confirm the answer we have to look at the New Testament, specifically the whole Book of Galatians, and Hebrews 11:8-10, 13, 39, 40.

The Book of Hebrews says that Abraham obeyed and went out to the place that he would afterward inherit, not knowing where he was going. Farther down in the verses it says that Abraham, Sarah, Isaac, and Jacob were all strangers in the land of Canaan, never owning any property, living in tents, looking for a *city* built by God Himself—*that* place was going to be their inheritance, that *eternal land* is what they were "seeing" by faith. Then verse 13 says, "these all died in the faith *not having received the promise*." The promise was for an *eternal inheritance* in the earth made new, and they knew it, and looked forward to it by faith. They had "seen" the promise from "afar off," and "confessed that they were strangers and pilgrims on the earth" (Hebrews 11:13).

All of the verses that follow describe people who lived by faith in God's promise of a better world that is yet to come. Paul's list eventually comes to King David, who ushered in a time of relative peace among the nations. After David the verses describe Daniel and his three faithful friends during their captivity in Babylon (vss. 33, 34), Isaiah who was sawn in half by Manasseh (vs. 37), and many others who lived by faith in God's *eternal* promise. They all lived in the land of Canaan. But the entire chapter is summarized by this statement: "And these all, having obtained a good report through faith, *received not the promise*: God having provided some better thing for us, that they without us should not be made perfect" (Hebrews 11:39, 40). All of Abraham's descendants, from Isaac to Jesus, did not "receive the promise." The fulfillment awaits the second coming of Christ.

The final word in Hebrews 11:40 in the Greek is *teleioo*, meaning to be brought to full completion, to consummate. The distribution of God's "living trust" made with Adam and then renewed with Abraham must include all the people that the promise included. Galatians tells us who those "all" people are. All God's people—faithful ancient Israelites who are listed in Hebrews 11, Gentile Christians in Paul's day, and modern believers from all over the world—are to be made "perfect" together at the consummation of the everlasting covenant promise when Christ comes again. We are all to be gathered at once to receive the inheritance. No one precedes anyone else in the distribution of the eternal inheritance.

From the beginning when the promise was stated to Adam in Genesis 3:15, there were conditions for receiving the inheritance: faith in Christ, and possession of His righteousness in the life, called Christ's "robe of righteousness," (see the parable of the wedding garment in Matthew 22:1-14).

From creation, Adam was given the whole earth as his dominion on the condition that he would believe God's Word. He failed and lost the right of ownership. Through unbelief, he sold his birthright possession to Satan, making Satan the "prince of this world." To restore what was lost, Adam's inheritance had to be redeemed by humanity's nearest of kin, who is Christ, the Last Adam, our Kinsman Redeemer (the "type" of which was Boaz in the story of Ruth).

This is why the human nature which Christ assumed in His incarnation is so important for us to understand correctly. Jesus had to assume the nature that which He came to redeem, or else He was not truly our "nearest of kin," but was some "foreigner" who could not relate to us at all, could not understand what we had to deal with in our everyday lives. The apostle Paul wrote "For we have not an high priest which cannot be touched with the feeling of our infirmities; but was in all points tempted like as we are, yet without sin." (Hebrews 4:15).

And Paul also declared to us, "Forasmuch then as the children are partakers of flesh and blood, He also Himself likewise took part of the same; that through death He might destroy him that had the power of death, that is, the devil; and deliver them who through fear of death were all their lifetime subject to bondage. For verily He took not on him the nature of angels; but He took on Him the seed of Abraham." (Hebrews 2:14-16). The Greek word translated "seed" is "sperm," the sexual cell that contains the genetic material needed to reproduce another human being with the same characteristics as the parent. Through His mother who was of the tribe of Judah, Christ Jesus was the literal genetic descendant of Abraham (see Matthew 1:1). And in this way, Jesus is humanity's "nearest of kin" and therefore qualified to be our Kinsman Redeemer.

All the people described in Hebrews chapter 11 lived by faith, and where counted righteous, and only the faithful righteous can inherit the eternal promised land. Righteousness comes only through Christ, and only those who have His faith actively motivating them are counted worthy of the inheritance.[1]

Since the obvious truth is that the promise to Abraham had not been fulfilled when Paul wrote the letter to the Hebrews, it shows that the promise cannot be fulfilled until all those in Paul's list are made "perfect," until those who are embraced in the term "us"—which embraces all Christians in the current age—are "made perfect." So the fulfillment of the Abrahamic promise must, of necessity, look forward to the second coming of Christ.

Who Are the Children of Abraham?

In the above discussion we have identified three things: (1) only righteousness can inherit the promise, (2) the necessary righteousness comes only from Christ, and (3) no one has yet obtained the promise.

The bigger questions are: Who are the "children of Abraham," and What is the "land" which they will inherit?

"Know ye therefore that they which are of faith, the same are the children of Abraham. And the Scripture, foreseeing that God would justify the heathen through faith, preached before the gospel unto Abraham [Abraham heard the same Gospel given to us], saying, In

---

1. "Knowing that a man is not justified by the works of the law, but by the faith of Jesus ... I am crucified with Christ: nevertheless I live; yet not I, but Christ liveth in me: and the life which I now live in the flesh I live by the faith of the Son of God, who loved me, and gave Himself for me." (Galatians 2:16, 20 KJV). "For Christ's love compels us, since we have reached this conclusion: If One died for all, then all died. And He died for all so that those who live should no longer live for themselves, but for the One who died for them and was raised." (2 Corinthians 5:14, 15 HCSB).

thee shall all nations be blessed [the whole world, and especially the faithful who will be heirs of the promise]. So then they which be of faith are blessed with faithful Abraham" (Galatians 3:7-9). That promise to Abraham embraces Christ as the true Seed. "He saith not, And to seeds, as of many; but as of one, and to thy *Seed*, which is Christ." (Galatians 3:16). Christ is the "Seed" (true descendant) to whom the promise of Genesis 12:1-3 pointed. Only through Christ can the promise be fulfilled to "bless all the families of the earth." Abraham, nor any of his descendants until or since Christ, possessed any capacity to fulfill this promise to "bless the world."

All the faithful will be "blessed with faithful Abraham" when *he* receives the promised inheritance; we all will receive it *together*. Since Abraham didn't receive it during his lifetime, then the fulfillment of the promise of necessity must yet be future. Therefore, they who have the righteousness of God, which is by the faith of Christ, are ever "looking for that blessed hope, and the glorious appearing of the great God and our Saviour Jesus Christ" (Titus 2:13).

The land promised is the *whole earth* made new after sin has been destroyed. That is the kingdom which God prepared for His people "from the foundation of the world." (Matthew 25:34; Genesis 1:26, 28). To the meek it is promised that they shall inherit the earth (Matthew 5:5). They "shall inherit the earth; and shall delight themselves in the abundance of peace" (Psalm 37:11). The "earth" is not some small territory in the Middle East. It is the world made new, forever free from sin and death. But this cannot be done while the wicked remain in the world, for "there is no peace, saith the Lord, unto the wicked."

Therefore, before the righteous can delight themselves in "the abundance of peace," the wicked must be removed from the earth. And so when, in prophetic vision, John saw the kingdoms of this world become "the kingdoms of our Lord and of His Christ," he heard the elders around the throne in heaven say: "We give Thee thanks, O Lord God Almighty, which are, and were, and are to come; because Thou hast taken to Thee Thy great power, and have reigned. And the nations were angry, and Thy wrath is come, and the time of the dead that they should be judged, and that Thou should give reward unto Thy servants the prophets, and to the saints, and them that fear Thy name, small and great; and should destroy them that corrupt the earth" (Revelation 11:17, 18). "The nations are angry"—that time is just before the second coming when Christ comes to claim His kingdom and His heirs who are scattered among the wicked.

And that time is upon us now.

Christ Himself said that when He should come, it would be to "reward every man according to his works." (Matthew (16:27). So then, Christ's second coming means the salvation of the righteous, and the destruction of the wicked who shall be "destroyed with the brightness of His coming" (2 Thessalonians 2:8-12; cf. Revelation 6:14-17).

Abraham's Second Walk

"And I will make thy seed as the dust of the earth: so that if a man can number the dust of the earth, then shall thy seed also be numbered. Arise, walk through the land in the length of it and in the breadth of it; for I will give it unto thee. Then Abram removed his tent, and came and dwelt in the plain of Mamre, which is in Hebron, and built there an altar unto the LORD" (Genesis 13:18).

This sounds as though Abraham went on another exploratory hike though the land of Canaan, but he didn't. He moved his tent town to the plain of Mamre, which is in Hebron, just a short distance from where he scoped out the land from the mountaintop overlooking Sodom. And this is where he stayed throughout the rest of the narrative concerning him. We find him in Mamre in Genesis 14:13, in Genesis 18:1, and it was in Mamre where Abraham bought the cave to bury Sarah in, and his sons buried him in the same cave (Genesis 23:17; 25:9).

Okay, let's wrap up this seemingly confusing discussion. You are probably scratching your head about all this rambling excursion about the land. But the "land" is tied to the "promise" and it is important that we know what "land" the promise is speaking about. If we misinterpret what the word "land" is referring to, then we can easily be deceived into believing the error of futurism's view of modern Israel and the Jewish nation.

The promise God made first to Adam, then to Noah after the Flood, and then to Abraham, included land which was to be conveyed to the heirs of God on condition of righteousness. Only the righteous will dwell in the land, so the promise must be talking about the new earth, not any literal territory in this wicked world. "For the promise, that he should be the heir of the world, was not to Abraham, or to his seed, through the law, but through the righteousness of faith" (Romans 4:13). Note it: Paul said, "world" not just the land of Canaan. The promise of God concerned something that is much bigger than any territory that Abraham could see standing on that hilltop.

No man-made law and no attempts to obtain righteousness through a legalistic "works" approach to "faith" can ever give title to the promise made by God to His heirs. Only by the faith of Christ can it be received. Righteousness and the inheritance are gifts included in the promise made first to Adam, and then to Abraham. "If ye be Christ's, then are ye Abraham's seed, and heirs according to the promise." (Galatians 3:29).

The everlasting covenant is a much, much bigger concept than which people group should possess the rocky little nation of modern Israel. God's covenant has always been about making a people fit to live in the new earth, and that "making fit" can only be done through Christ and His righteousness.

6

Lot's Predicament

Genesis 14:1-12

Today's study concerns a topic we looked at earlier, called a suzerain covenant. This ancient form of covenant was a political tool used by a powerful king who ruled over a group of weaker kings, who were forced to serve him as vassals. Under the terms of the covenant treaty, the vassals were required to do several things, such as support the suzerain if he went to war by providing the suzerain with armed forces. Additionally, they had to pay taxes into the suzerain's treasury, and they were required to appear before the suzerain every year to renew their pledges of allegiance to him. That is the background for the story that took place in Genesis 14. The kings of Sodom and Gomorrah had not paid their taxes and the suzerain came to collect his due, bringing with him other vassals who were doing their part in providing an army.

About five years have passed since Lot took off on his own to live in the valley around Sodom and Gomorrah. And then he found himself on a battle field.

"And it came to pass in the days of Amraphel king of Shinar, Arioch king of Ellasar, Chedorlaomer king of Elam, and Tidal king of nations; that these made war with Bera king of Sodom, and with Birsha king of Gomorrah, Shinab king of Admah, and Shemeber king of Zeboiim, and the king of Bela, which is Zoar. All these were joined together in the vale of Siddim, which is the salt sea. Twelve years they served Chedorlaomer, and in the thirteenth year they rebelled." (Genesis 14:1-4).

Names Define Character

Amraphel means "the mouth of god has spoken." His home location is given as Shinar, which is the same plain where Nimrod began to build his empire on the Euphrates River. Arioch has been identified with various kings from the Babylonian area, but none have panned out through successive archeological evidence. No one has been able to positively identify the name's meaning. His home city of Ellasar was mentioned in Hittite documents, and is thought to have been near Haran in northen Mesopotamia, where Abraham and his family made their home for a while. Haran was on the main trade route between Egypt and Babylon.

A lot more archeological evidence is available concerning who Chedorlaomer was. From the narrative itself we see that he is the strongest king of the bunch, and just by his name, the status comes with good reason. His name means "servant of the goddess Laqamar." The goddess's name means "she who has no mercy as judge." If he was named for his character, then we are given a glimpse of his unmerciful attitude toward his erring vassals who failed to pay him tribute.

Chedorlaomer's kingdom was Elam which was located in western Persia, in the shadow of the Zagros Mountains. The Elamites were descendants of Shem who obviously, like so many tribes after the Flood, had turned to the worship of pagan gods. Long before this story takes place, the Elamites were a powerful kingdom that occasionally dominated the Mesopotamian region.

The meaning of Tidal's name and the explanation of his kingdom are interestingly the same thing—"king of nations," the Hebrew word for nation is *goyim*. The title literally means "king of a gang" or group of people of mixed ethnicity who were most likely nomads living in Tidal's region of northern Canaan. How he managed to be king over them is a mystery. A later king of the same designation is mentioned in the Book of Joshua along with more information about where this area was located. "The king of Dor in the coast of Dor, one; the king of the nations of Gilgal, one" (Joshua 12:23). Dor was located in the area of Mount Carmel. The "king of nations" was from Gilgal, which was the royal city for the region of Dor. If these two uses of the same title, "king of nations" can be put together, then Tidal would have lived in the north end of Canaan.

The Suzerain Takes His Revenge

From this gathering of information, we discover that these kings were stretched over a very wide area, more than 1400 miles. By some means they maintained a confederation that allowed Chedorlaomer to keep his vassals in Canaan under control, because he was the farthest removed from Sodom and Gomorrah. His reputation must have been fierce for him to control people from that far away. For twelve years the kings of Sodom and Gomorrah submitted to his suzerain treaty with them, but in the thirteenth year, they failed to make their tax payment.

"Bera king of Sodom, and with Birsha king of Gomorrah, Shinab king of Admah, and Shemeber king of Zeboiim, and the king of Bela, which is Zoar. All these were joined together in the vale of Siddim, which is the salt sea."

Sodom and Gomorrah were located at the southern end of the Dead Sea. The cities of Admah and Zeboiim were lost in the same catastrophe that later rained down on Sodom (Genesis 19:23-25), so they are also buried under the southern end of the Dead Sea. Zoar is the only city of the plain that was not destroyed in that event.

"And in the fourteenth year came Chedorlaomer, and the kings that were with him, and smote the Rephaims in Ashteroth Karnaim, and the Zuzims in Ham, and the Emims in Shaveh Kiriathaim, and the Horites in their mount Seir, unto Elparan, which is by the wilderness. And they returned, and came to Enmishpat, which is Kadesh, and smote all the country of the Amalekites, and also the Amorites, that dwelt in Hazezontamar." (Genesis 14:5-7). Evidently, there were quite a few tribes that had not paid their taxes.

Here again we encounter the people called "Rephaims" or giants. It's the same name used in Genesis 6:4, though not the same people. The Rephaims of chapter 6 were destroyed in the Flood. This group occupied the territory of Canaan on the east side of the Jordan River. Some Rephaims are mentioned by name, such as Og, king of Bashan. Og's bedstead of iron was 9 cubits long, and 4 cubits wide (Deuteronomy 3:11). A cubit is approximately 18 inches in length, which would make Og's bed 13 feet long and 6 feet wide. He was one big boy! And it is no wonder that his bed was made of iron.

It seems that all these peoples, even though not associated with kings or tribal leaders, must have also been vassals of Chedorlaomer.

If not, then he must have just decided to clean house as he was passing through their areas on his way to his target of the cities on the plain of Siddim. The Rephaims were later replaced by the Ammonites, and the Zuzims were replaced by the Moabites. The Ammonites and Moabites were brother tribes, descendants of Lot's two sons born to his daughters after the destruction of Sodom and Gomorrah.

Approaching Doom

It took a year for Chedorlaomer to make his complete sweep through his territories, from the thirteenth year when the kings of Sodom and Gomorrah failed to pay their taxes, until the forteenth year when Chedorlaomer descended upon them with his armies.

As Chedorlaomer was sweeping south toward his rebellious vassal cities, word of his devastation along the way reached the kings on the Plain of Siddim. Word travels fast, even if it comes by caravan on camels. When the vassal kings of the plain heard about Chedorlaomer's advance in their direction, they banded together for the fight.

"And there went out the king of Sodom, and the king of Gomorrah, and the king of Admah, and the king of Zeboiim, and the king of Bela (the same is Zoar;) and they joined battle with them in the vale of Siddim; with Chedorlaomer the king of Elam, and with Tidal king of nations, and Amraphel king of Shinar, and Arioch king of Ellasar; four kings with five." (Genesis 14:8, 9).

Siddim valley was located at the southern end of the Dead Sea, with the cities of the plain being clustered in that area. The valley was also identified by the asphalt, or bitumen, found there. Asphalt is a semi-solid form of petroleum, while "tar" is derived from coal. Natural asphalt is a black, sticky substance that bubbled up to the surface of the land in that place. It is the only place in the Middle East where this type of natural asphalt is found.

"And the vale of Siddim was full of slimepits; and the kings of Sodom and Gomorrah fled, and fell there; and they that remained fled to the mountain. And they [Chedorlaomer's armies] took all the goods of Sodom and Gomorrah, and all their victuals, and went their way. And they took Lot, Abram's brother's son, who dwelt in Sodom, and his goods, and departed." (Genesis 14:10-12).

No discrimination. If you were living in Sodom, then you must have been a Sodomite, and as such you were subject to the suzerain and the conditions of his contract. Therefore, despite his arguments to the contrary, Lot was captured along with the rest of the citizens of that wicked city. He was taken, along with his wealth, as payment for the taxes demanded by the suzerain, Chedorlaomer. Lot was declared guilty by association, and shown no mercy by the man who worshiped the goddess known for having "no mercy as judge."

The area where the battle took place was not very conducive for warfare, being full of those slimepits of asphalt. It would be like trying to fight in a swamp riddled with quicksand, only the tarry substance would have been more difficult to slog through. Whether everyone who fell in the pits were killed by Chedorlaomer, or died because they could not free themselves from the tar and suffered asphyxiation, or perhaps died from exposure to the elements they were mired in, we are not told. But Scripture says they died there in the asphalt pits.

In this, we find a perfect illustration of how sin brings destruction. We are mired in sin, lost in the "sticky" and unrelenting grip of Satan's power as he plays our weaknesses to his advantage, bring reproach upon God who claims us as His own. King David felt this grip of sin when he wrote Psalm 40. And David knew that only the Kinsman Redeemer could pull him up from the pit into which he was sunk.

"I waited patiently for the LORD; and He inclined unto me, and heard my cry. He brought me up also out of an horrible pit, out of the miry clay, and set my feet upon a Rock [Christ Jesus], and established my goings [in paths of righteousness]. And put a new song in my mouth, even praise unto our God: many shall see it, and fear, and shall trust in the LORD." (Psalm 40:1-3).

What a powerful witness we are able to give when we let God save us from our pit of sin! It proves to everyone who knows us, that God is more powerful than Satan. God is able to save to the uttermost anyone who will believe He is able to do as He promised.

Temporary Escape from Judgment

But some of the city dwellers and army fled into the mountains around the plain and survived. The king of Sodom must have been one of them because we see him again later in the narrative.

It was a thorough rout for the people of the plain. Other than the ones who were not killed but hid in the mountains, few escaped death or capture, which meant they became slaves to their conquerors. One who was captured was Lot. Foolish Lot, who thought that the plain of Siddim was as beautiful as the Garden of Eden. Now he is tramping north along with other citizens of Sodom, headed back along the route he had taken with his uncle when they moved from Haran to Canaan. Because he made a wrong choice in moving to those wicked cities, he now was no longer a free and wealthy man, but was destined to an abject existence as a slave.

One has to wonder about what Lot's thoughts must have been. He didn't enter into the war, but was taken captive and assumed to be just as guilty as any other resident of Sodom. Chedorlaomer didn't bother to ask Lot if he was really a native of Sodom or just a visitor. He didn't care. Lot was living there, and that made Lot guilty of the same sins against the suzerain lord.

Did Lot's conscience condemn him for his foolish move to those wicked cities? All of his wealth, all of his easy living, evaporated in that battle on the plain, and now he was headed for a life of misery. Did he see his error and repent, or just rue his fate, as one who is sorry he got caught, but not sorry for what he did? (see 2 Corinthians 7:9, 10). Did he now realize the ingratitude and insult he showed toward his uncle Abraham, and even toward God Himself who had given him his wealth, when he withdrew from his righteous uncle to live among the wicked?

Whatever he might have been thinking, one thing he was not thinking was that there was some way of escaping from his predicament. He knew of none. He was bound to be a slave without any mercy being shown to him by his captors.

Whenever we go out of the path of duty, we put ourselves away from God's protection, and cannot expect that the choice we make will be for our lasting good, or that God will prevent the consequences of our choice from befalling us. If we choose not to serve Him, He will let us go in our chosen path to destruction. But He is ever ready to hear our cry of remorse and repentance and will rush in to save us from the miry pit we have gotten ourself into.

7

Uncle Abe to the Rescue

Genesis 14:12-24

They took Lot, Abram's brother's son, who dwelt in Sodom, and his goods, and departed." (Genesis 14:12). Lot was taken captive and destined to be a slave to Chedorlaomer or one of his confederates who attacked Sodom and the other cities on the plain. Lot had no real idea where he was headed because he didn't know who it was that swooped down on the city where he was living. He was just taken as part of the spoils of war. There was no one to help him get out of this situation. If he had any faith left in the God of heaven, perhaps he was exercising it now, "calling on the name of the LORD."

"And there came one that had escaped, and told Abram the Hebrew; for he dwelt in the plain of Mamre the Amorite, brother of Eshcol, and brother of Aner: and these were confederate with Abram" (verse 13). Abraham is identified here as the "Hebrew" and this is first time the designation appears in the Bible. The word Hebrew was expanded from the name Eber, a grandson of Noah, who was a direct ancestor of Abraham (Genesis 11:16ff.). Even though called a "confederate" with the tribes he lived near, but unlike Lot living among the people of Sodom, Abraham is clearly distinguished from those among whom he was dwelling on the plain of Mamre.

Earlier the plain of Mamre was said to be where Hebron was located (Genesis 13:18). There must have been a sizable spring or deep well there for all of these tribes to be content to dwell together in the same place without squabbling over water rights.

Mamre was the man's name, but his name was given to the area where all these peoples were living, in the "plain of Mamre." The three brothers named here, Mamre, Eshcol and Aner, were apparently the aristocrats of the land. Mamre (the man) is identified as an Amorite, a tribe that are later revealed to be a people who lived totally contrary to God. They were a group of people who were to be utterly destroyed in the future (see the prophecy of Genesis 15:16). However, at this point in time the tribes of Canaanites seem to be friendly and accepting of Abraham's presence among them. Mamre's two brothers are not mentioned anywhere else in the Bible or in history.

"And there came one that had escaped, and told Abram" about all that had taken place in Sodom. This little snippet "and there was one that escaped" reminds us of the "one that escaped" from Satan's terror poured out upon Job's family (Job 1:15, 17, 19). The tragedy was so awful that only "one" escaped. But this one man from Sodom must have known Lot well enough to know that Lot had an uncle living near Hebron, and was a trustworthy enough friend to run to Abraham to tell him about what had happened.

Hebron was at least 50 miles northeast of where Sodom was located on the plain south of the Dead Sea. It is certain that eventually, those living in Hebron would have heard about the war with the kings of the plain as the trade caravans brought their tales to them. But they had not yet heard the news, until this "one who escaped" came to tell them of the tragedy.

"And when Abram heard that his brother was taken captive, he armed his trained servants, born in his own house, three hundred and eighteen, and pursued them unto Dan" (verse 14). "Armed his trained servants"—really? Did Abraham have an armory sequestered somewhere? No. Peaceful Abraham had no reason to have armed men in his tribe. Probably he purchased weapons from the Amorites he was living with. He had plenty of wealth to make the purchase, having gold and silver that was given to him by the pharaoh when he left Egypt after the debacle over Sarah being his "sister."

Another amazing fact is that Abraham's clan must have been huge. He had 318 men he could readily pull away from the rest, and go racing off after Lot, without any fear that his flocks and herds, or women and children would not be adequately provided for and protected while he was gone. These 318 men had wives that were left behind, too. If we assume that at least a couple children per family were are also part of the clan, it would mean that Abraham's group was approaching about a 1000 people, or more. Incredible! And they all looked up to Abraham as their father figure, and obeyed him without question.

The tribes that Abraham was living among were related to those living in Sodom and the surrounding plain, and suddenly, Abraham's battle was also their battle. They confederated with Abraham and swelled the size of the army mustered to rescue Lot.

It would have taken a couple of days for the messenger who escaped from Sodom to get to Abraham. A well conditioned horse can be ridden no more than 30 miles without exhausting him. A donkey won't go that far before they balk. Donkeys have a mind of their own and if they're tired, they quit. A camel can walk about 30 or 40 miles a day, so if the man was on a camel, he could get from Sodom to Hebron in a day and a half, or less, if he could make the camel hurry.

Chedorlaomer was marching up the east road, called the "king's highway" because it was the main trade and caravan route from Egypt, running eastward, skirting across the northern edge of the Arabian desert, then turning north until they arrived at Damascus. From there the road curved following the fertile crescent trade route and headed south to Babylon. The east road ran the ridge and was easier traveling than the road on the west side of the Jordan River, where the rugged territory was filled with hills and deep wadis. Abraham was camped on the west side of the Dead Sea. The roads through those two areas, east and west of the Dead Sea and the Jordan River, ran more or less parallel northward, but the road on the side where Abraham was, was rough and hilly, making travel slow until they could descend to the river valley on the north end of the Dead Sea.

Abraham had a couple of advantages. The first was that he received notice of Lot's capture very quickly through Lot's friend. Second, Chedorlaomer was traveling home burdened with goods that he pilfered from Sodom and the other cities of the plain, plus keeping all the prisoners corralled would naturally slow things down. To keep the captives from running away, they were probably hobbled, making their walking difficult and slow.

And last, Chedorlaomer had just won a big battle. He originally believed that he was the chiefest of the chiefs, the baddest of the bad, the top dog that no one dared to mess with. After beating everyone as soundly as he did on the Plain of Siddim, he was in no fear or hurry to get home. He had stolen all the food they could find in Sodom, which meant that the army was well provisioned for the slower trek home.

At this point in the narrative we are introduced to Abraham the warrior. Our previous information concerning Abraham's character has revealed him to be a calm, gentle man who does not want conflict from any corner of his life. Yet here he goes running after a powerful king with five armies! How unlike the Abraham we have been reading about so far in the narrative. Now he's like a mad hen running to protect her chicks from the fox!

Hastening north, Abraham stops for nothing until he is within striking distance of his enemy. One has to wonder where Abraham got his skills at tactical maneuvering. Never before had he been involved in warfare, yet he knew exactly what he had to do without any prior military experience.

He correctly calculated the enemy's northward march. Travelers they encountered on their journey would have provided reconnaissance for him, revealing the location of the massive army on the other side of the river. And perhaps he kept abreast of Chedorlaomer's position by occasionally sending a scout over the river to do some reconnoitering. A few questions at a village would be sufficient to know what progress Chedorlaomer was making, the condition of his men, and how many captives where with him.

When Abraham caught up with Chedorlaomer's army at Dan, he still had the advantage. Chedorlaomer was not expecting to be attacked at all, by anyone. He had marched 150 miles without knowing anyone was pursuing him. The town of Dan was in the far north of Canaan, just a few miles from Mount Hermon.

In those days armies did not normally fight or travel after sundown. Chedorlaomer's army was settled in for the night when Abraham caught up with them. "And he divided himself against them, he and his servants, by night, and smote them, and pursued them unto Hobah, which is on the left hand of Damascus" (the "left hand"meaning to the west of Damascus).

By dividing his men, Abraham was able to surround Chedorlaomer's entire army. The surprise attack in the dead of night would have put Chedorlaomer at a serious disadvantage. Before his men could shake themselves awake and reach for their weapons, they were being slaughtered by Abraham and his confederates who overran the tents, slashing and stabbing every man they came upon. In the ensuing confusion, the captives would have had to identity themselves as not being part of the enemy's army to avoid being killed with the enemy. Perhaps their native language helped to identify and distinguish them from the enemy who spoke different language.

Chedorlaomer roused and ran toward Damascus ahead of Abraham's onslaught. Before he got there, they reached a place called Hobah. There the battle came to an end. How many of the enemy were killed we are not told. Whether they surrendered and negotiated to give up the captives in order to save their own lives, we also are not told. Obviously, when they fled, in their haste they did not pick up the spoil they took from Sodom. And so, Abraham "brought back all the goods, and also brought again his brother Lot, and his goods, and the women also, and the people." And they returned to Sodom.

This narrative began as a recitation of a political situation concerning a suzerain and his wayward vassals living at the south end of the Dead Sea. The suzerain was powerful enough and prideful enough that he thought nothing of calling his armies together and marching 1400 miles just to inflict punishment upon the ones who withstood him by not paying their taxes. By taking this action against the rebels, Chedorlaomer proved that it was dangerous to rebel and not pay your taxes on time. It proved that vengeance was certain to be inflicted upon the rebellious vassal who violated the stipulations of the suzerain's contract.

However, Chedorlaomer made a critical error in capturing Lot. Except for Lot's part in the story, this political ruckus would not have been included in the Bible. It probably would have made the historical record of the king's affairs, but not everything that happened in the history of the world is recorded in the Bible. We only have history as it effected God's people recorded for us in the Bible. But histories from other sources give us greater background for the Biblical narrative, putting the Bible's story into a vivid and valid context.

If he had left Lot and his family alone, Chedorlaomer could have returned to Persia with his booty, and his renewed status as a king with a great power to be reckoned with left intact. Sodom would have been vanquished and the remnant still living there would have known they could not afford to defy their suzerain lord.

Instead, Chedorlaomer went home with the certain reality that he had been beaten by a gang of sheep herders who were led into battle by an old man intent on rescuing his foolish nephew.

When we move forward in faith, we go with the power of God to certain victory over our Enemy—Satan and sin—and our weaknesses are made strong. We find that we "can do all things" in Christ, who gives us His strength (Philippians 4:13).

8

Lot Returns to Sodom

Genesis 14:16-24

Abraham made his way back south, traveling along the King's Highway, the easy route. "And he brought back all the goods, and also brought again his brother Lot, and his goods, and the women also, and the people." Abraham didn't just rescue Lot (his "brother"), but also everyone else who had been captured by Chedorlaomer and his confederated armies. All the material goods that were taken as war spoils were gathered up and toted back to Sodom and the cities on the plain.

Word travels fast down the king's highway. The remnants of the cities on the plain had already heard what Abraham and his band of shepherds had accomplished in the north. When Abraham and his tribe of shepherd-warriors came within shouting distance of Sodom, "the king of Sodom went out to meet him after his return from the slaughter of Chedorlaomer, and of the kings that were with him, at the valley of Shaveh, which is the king's dale." (Genesis 14:17).

From this part of the narrative, we discover that some of the kings named in verse 2 managed to escape Chedorlaomer's attack by fleeing into the mountains (vs. 10), so that this "kings that were with him" were not among the people that Abraham was bringing back with him from the battle at Dan and Hobah. The kings of the cities that were killed in the attack by Chedorlaomer were from Sodom and Gomorrah—Bera and Birsha where their names (14:2, 10). The king who came up from the plain of Siddim to meet Abraham and welcome his citizens home, must have been either a newly elected king or Bera's heir. To elect a new king in the short time that Abraham was off fighting the battle, would have been a rapid campaign and election! The fact that by the time he returned, they already had a new king, indicates that these people were politically minded, and felt a strong need to have someone to rule over them.

The "king's dale" described here as the valley of Shaveh, has been identified with the Kidron Valley which runs just east of the ridge upon which the ancient city of Salem was located. The east side of the valley is called the Mount of Olives in the New Testament. This valley runs the entire length of the Dead Sea, from Sodom to the Jordan River's inflow into the sea on the northern end. The "king's dale" is also mentioned in 2 Samuel 18:18, where Absalom erected a pillar and named it after himself. Absalom had no sons to keep remembrance of him alive, so before he was killed by Joab, he had built a memorial to himself.

The king of Sodom and his friends brought nothing with them when they came to meet Abraham and their rescued friends and family members. They had been impoverished by Chedorlaomer's attack upon their cities. Now Abraham had all their material goods and former belongings, and by the rights of war, had won them fairly. All those goods were now Abraham's property. The king of Sodom came to the meeting empty handed, hoping to find mercy in Abraham's heart so he could regain his wealth from him without a fight.

In the manner of the East, the king of Sodom began his bargaining by not asking for what he really wanted. Trying to sound very kind and generous, he said to Abraham (who is still recognized as the general of this returning army), "Give me the persons, and take the goods to thyself." (Genesis 14:21). He was telling Abraham that he could keep what by right of war, was already his and in his possession! The king of Sodom already knew that Abraham didn't keep slaves and had no need of all those many people who had been taken from the cities, so he asked only for them, instead of his material goods.

Speaking in the falsely magnanimous way of a true power hungry person who thinks he has great control over the situation, he said, "Just keep the goods, Abraham, I don't need them; you take them!" as though they were in his possession to give. Saying this saved his wounded ego. He knew he was completely at the mercy of this man who had expended great energy in rescuing his own nephew and destroying five kings and their armies. If it required a fight to get his goods back from Abraham, he knew he was not equal to the task.

"And Abram said to the king of Sodom, I have lift up mine hand unto the LORD, the most high God, the possessor of heaven and earth, that I will not take from a thread even to a shoelatchet, and that I will not take any thing that is yours, lest you should say, I have made Abram rich" (Genesis 14:22, 23).

Before undertaking this endeavor, Abraham had already promised God—lifted up his hand—that he would not take anything that did not belong to him. He went forth to that battle and rescue effort completely relying on the power of "the most high God, the possessor of heaven and earth," knowing that it was only through Him that he could hope to succeed. And now, here stands this wimp of a man, thinking that he is a mighty king from Sodom, the city of corruption and evil, where everyone were "exceedingly wicked sinners before the LORD" (Genesis 13:13). This audacious man thinks he is going to give Abraham anything when in reality, he possess no wealth worth having, neither material nor spiritual.

Abraham's reply is both humble and cutting at the same time. Nothing you possess is worth anything to me, thou mighty king of Sodom. And if it would give anyone the opportunity to think that you had enriched me, even by giving me a thread or a shoelace, I would refuse to take it. What a rebuke Abraham laid at the feet of this wickedly arrogant man!

Abraham had not gone to war for the people of Sodom, but because one of his family members had been taken captive and was in grave danger. If Lot had not been living in that city, and had not been taken captive by Chedorlaomer, Abraham would never have interfered in the affairs taking place on the Plain of Siddim.

However, as the weary citizens of Sodom and Abraham's army traveled home, they had eaten the foods taken by Chedorlaomer from the cities, and so Abraham said, "Save only that which the young men have eaten." But not wanting to deny that the Canaanite tribes who went with him might be expecting to take their share of the recovered spoils, he added, "The portion of the men which went with me, Aner, Eshcol, and Mamre; let them take their portion" of the spoils.

And things were there divided among the princes of the Hebron Valley, but Abraham took nothing.

9

Abraham Meets Melchizedek

Genesis 14:18-20

Another king also came along to this reunion party that we're studying about in Genesis 14:17-24. The second one is quite mysterious. He just appears from nowhere, except that the Bible identifies him as "Melchizedek, king of Salem." Genesis chapter 14 and a reference in Psalm 110:4 tell us all that we know from the Old Testament concerning this man called Melchizedek. But Paul repeats the history and expands it in Hebrews chapter 7. Paul tells us that he was the "King of righteousness, and after that also [was called] King of Salem, which is, King of peace." Salem means peace.

But Paul adds a mysterious description concerning the man, saying that he was "without father, without mother, without descent, having neither beginning of days, nor end of life." Melchizedek had no known history. No mother, father, family members, or descendants. A key point is that he had no beginning and no end of days. This man "was made like unto the Son of God" and was a "priest forever." (Hebrews 7:3).

The next thing we learn from the Genesis narrative is that this king "brought forth bread and wine: and he was the priest of the most high God." The king of Sodom came empty handed, with nothing to give Abraham but his good will and thanks for bringing his people home safe from the battle. The King of Salem brought refreshment for Abraham. The Scripture is not clear as to whether the bread and wine was only enough to give to Abraham, or whether there was enough to serve the whole troop that was with Abraham, which would have been hundreds of men. Most likely, the bread and "wine" were symbolic of the message brought by Melchizedek, and were meant only for Abraham, as the remaining interaction is only between the two men. Symbolism is the focus of this short section of Scripture.

When Christ instituted the New Testament rite of Communion which symbolizes His death for our sin, He used unleavened bread and fresh grape juice—both made without fermentation because fermentation is a symbol for corruption and sin (Leviticus 10:8-10; Isaiah 28:7). Jesus and Paul both used leaven—yeast and its fermentation properties—to illustrate how sin has a multiplying effect. One sin or false doctrine will compound into another sin or false idea until the "whole loaf" is permeated with sin and false doctrines (Matthew 16:6; 1 Corinthians 5:6–8).[1]

As Jesus handed the unleavened bread and fresh grape juice around the table to His disciples, He said, "This is My body," and "this is My blood." Here in Genesis in the interaction between Melchizedek and Abraham, it may accurately be stated that the bread and wine were only for the refreshment of Abraham and his followers. Certainly that may be correct, but that does not in the least detract from the significance of the fact that it is the very same symbolism we find in the New Testament Communion rite, especially since the apostle Paul ties Melchizedek with Christ in his letter to the Hebrews. This fact points us forward to Christ's work in our behalf, and is therefore a connecting link between Melchizedek and Christ.

Melchizedek came out of his city of "peace" to meet Abraham in his capacity of king and priest, and apparently without knowing the man before this event, Abraham recognized who He was. As in the upper room the evening of the final Passover meal before Christ died for our sins on the cross, so here in Genesis 14 we read that the bread and wine were administered by "the priest of the most high God" who was the "priest of righteousness" and the "King of peace," to those standing in His presence.

---

1. "Know ye not that a little leaven leaveneth the whole lump?" (1 Corinthians 5:6). "Then Jesus said unto them, Take heed and beware of the leaven of the Pharisees and of the Sadducees. ... Then understood they how that He bade them not beware of the leaven of [ordinary] bread, but of the doctrine of the Pharisees and of the Sadducees." (Matthew 16:6, 12).

It is evident that the bread and wine which Melchizedek brought to Abraham possessed special significance, just by the fact that the One who brought it was the priest of the Most High God. Jesus told the Pharisees that "Abraham rejoiced to see My day: and He saw it and was glad" (John 8:56). The Jews scoffed at the statement. They could see no evidence of the fact, and thought that Jesus was crazy for making such an assertion. When Jesus pressed the point home by stating that He was the I AM who had existed even before Abraham knew Him, the Pharisees took up stones to kill Him (vs. 58).

But if, as Paul does in Hebrews, we connect the symbols of the bread and wine, and the type of priesthood —"Thou art a priest for ever after the order of Melchisedec" (Hebrews 5:6)—which would have no other meaning in the Genesis story, if not pointing forward to the symbols used in Communion—unfermented bread and fresh grape juice that point us to the Saviour who knew no sin, then why did God give us this story? Can we see in this transaction between Melchizedek and Abraham, evidence that the Holy Spirit enlightened Abraham's mind, and in the symbolism he "saw [Christ's] day," which is the day of salvation from sin? (Abraham will have this symbolism presented to him again in chapter 22.)

The priesthood spoken of here in Genesis 14:18 was the same then as now, since Christ is our High Priest "after the order of Melchizedek." Therefore, not only are we the children of Abraham if we live a righteous life through the faith of Christ (Galatians 2:16, 20), who is our great High Priest that is passed into the heavens (Hebrews 4:14), and is by the oath of God, our High Priest for ever "after the order of Melchizedek" (Hebrews 7:21), but also in these verses we find a confirmation that "if ye be Christ's, then are ye Abraham's seed, and heirs according to the promise" (Galatians 3:29). These truths are connected through the symbols.

"And [Melchizedek] blessed [Abraham], and said, Blessed be Abram of the most high God, possessor of heaven and earth: and blessed be the most high God, which hath delivered thine enemies into thy hand." We learn from this verse that Melchizedek was a greater man than Abraham, because, "without all contradiction the less is blessed of the better" (Hebrews 7:7).

Because Abraham realized how significant a figure this man was, he "gave Him tithes [tenth part] of all" (Genesis 14:2; Hebrews 7:2).

In Hebrews chapter 7 we are referred to the case of Abraham and Melchizedek for proof that the paying of tithes is not a Levitical, or "old covenant" ordinance. Long before Levi was born, Abraham paid tithes to his God through the priest of the Most High God, Melchizedek. The Scripture also tells us that Levi "paid tithes in Abraham" (Hebrews 7:9). And he paid them to Melchizedek, whose priesthood is the symbol of Christ's own priesthood. Therefore those who are Christ's and thus children of Abraham, will also return "tithes of all."

From this story we learn: (1) that Abraham tithed all that he captured from the kings, giving the tithe to the Lord's representative; and (2) that he did not recognize the goods as belonging to the king of Sodom at all. For he was not taking anything *from* the king of Sodom in paying tithe on the property that he rightfully gained as spoils of the war. When the king of Sodom's property came into the hands of Abraham, it belonged to him by right of capture. It was "increase" in his wealth, and Abraham had every right to return to the LORD that which belonged to Him (all things belong to God), and then give the remainder to the original owner. We learn, in short, that one is duty-bound to tithe the whole of his income—all that comes into his hand that can be called his own.

And the final point to glean from this narrative is that at the very least this man called Melchizedek, if not an actual pre-incarnate appearance of Christ, he was a *type* of Christ in that he was both king and priest, and was described as the king of both righteousness and peace, just as the Bible says of Christ (Jeremiah 23:6; Isaiah 9:6).[2]

But the greater truth may be that this "man" was in reality Christ in a pre-incarnate appearance who came to bless His faithful servant, Abraham. It would not be the last time Abraham came face to face with the LORD in a pre-incarnate state.

---

2. "This is His name whereby He shall be called, THE LORD OUR RIGHTEOUSNESS." (Jeremiah 23:6). "For unto us a Child is born, unto us a Son is given: and the government shall be upon His shoulder: and His name shall be called Wonderful, Counsellor, The mighty God, The everlasting Father, The Prince of Peace." (Isaiah 9:6).

10

Abraham's Shield

Genesis 15:1-6

After these things the word of the LORD came unto Abram in a vision, saying, Fear not, Abram: I am thy shield, and thy exceeding great reward." (Genesis 15:1).

"After these things" points us back to the previous chapter and the events that took place there. "The word of the LORD came to Abraham in a vision." It was not an audible voice that spoke to Abraham, but a voice in a vision or a dream. It was night, and Abraham was in his tent sleeping when he had this vision of the LORD speaking to him.

Abraham had just beaten five enemy armies, recovered all that was taken from Sodom and the surrounding towns, and returned in safety. After that battle he had been blessed by the Son of God speaking through Melchizedek, the high priest of his eternal God and the king of peace. Quite an exciting set of events had taken place in the previous few weeks.

Abraham put his life on the line taking off on that adventure to rescue Lot. Now, as he lies in his tent, thinking and dreaming, he is wondering about what would have happened if he had not been victorious over Chedorlaomer. He could well have been killed up there near Damascus. Sarah would have been left alone at an advancing age without a son to take over her care, protecting and providing for her. The only person Abraham felt he could rely on to manage things after he died was his servant and estate manager, Eliezer. This man had lived with him for many years and had proven himself trustworthy.

There was no one to whom he could leave the estate that Abraham had amassed over the years. Lot had proven himself uninterested by returning to his former home in Sodom. Even after the narrow escape from slavery that was his destiny under Chedorlaomer's hand, Lot willingly chose to return to the city blatantly sunk in vile sin. If not for Abraham's rescue, Lot was bound to a life of misery. When they got back to the south, not discerning the lesson God was giving him through that violent experience, Lot returned to his city as though nothing had happened. He was not a worthy prospect as heir to Abraham's estate, morally or spiritually. He did not have a proper sense of family obligations, but put materialism and comfort foremost in his life.

In Abraham's thinking as he lay there on his bed, there was so much that was unsettled. If anything happened to him, who would manage the herdsmen and the flocks, and feel concern for all the families—hundreds of people—that had grown up under Abraham's loving care? It was more than enough to cause an old man nightmares.

And then he heard, "Fear not, Abram: I am thy shield, and thy exceeding great reward." The first thing that the LORD said to Abraham was "fear not!" This is a powerful promise from God. Three more times in Genesis we read "fear not" in the context of God's promise to be with the person He spoke to. "Go forward in faith, and fear not, for I am there to protect you from all harm." God Himself was Abraham's shield. A shield is held before, or in front, of the body as the soldier advances toward the enemy. If you turn around and run from the enemy, you're as good as dead with your back exposed. "Fear not" to go forward in the LORD's power and protection.

Subtly included in this statement was God telling Abraham that he had not won that battle against Chedorlaomer by his own cunning and strength. It was Christ, the Commander of the LORD's army that had gone before him, preparing the way for Abraham's victory in the dead of night. The great "I AM" was his Shield and Protector.

In that vision God communicated to Abraham that since that is what He is—our shield and protector—then, Abraham, you need to remember that I am also the one who is going to reward you by fulfilling My promise to you. Until My promise is fulfilled, you will come to no harm, Abraham. Fear not those things that you cannot explain.

But as Abraham lay there contemplating his childless condition, his natural response was "O Lord GOD, what wilt thou give me, seeing

I go childless?" What good is anything that you have already given to me, or will give to me, if I don't have a son to inherit it all? Possessions are worth nothing if there is no one to receive them when you are laid in your grave. Abraham wondered, what's the point of it all?

As he drifted in and out of sleep, Abraham thought, Maybe the solution to the problem is Eliezer? Even though of Damascus parentage, he was born in my house, and has been the "steward of my house" many years. Eliezer has been as faithful to me as any son could have been, if I had one. He could run the estate, he knows how to manage the young men who shepherd my flocks, can keep account of my goods, and would care for my dear wife after I'm dead. "Yes, that must be the solution!" was the conclusion Abraham came to that night.

We have only a limited amount of information concerning Eliezer from the Word of God. He was Abraham's "eldest servant of his house, that ruled over all that he had" (Genesis 24:2). The man had proven himself reliable and capable, so it was natural that Abraham would consider Eliezer as his heir in lieu of a natural-born son that, so far, seemed impossible to bring into the world.

And this is what Abraham proposed to God as the remedy for his childlessness. "And Abram said, Behold, to me Thou hast given no seed: and, lo, one born in my house is mine heir." Ah, now the problem is thrown back into God's lap! "*You* have not given me a son! You promised me a son, and I have not had a son, and therefore *You* are the one who has been neglectful in providing me with an heir. So I nominate my faithful servant, Eliezer, as my heir."

But man's ways are not God's ways. And so, the response to Abraham's proposition was: "And, behold, the word of the LORD came unto him, saying, This *shall not* be thine heir; but he that shall come forth out of thine own bowels shall be thine heir." (Genesis 15:3, 4).

You can almost feel the frustration Abraham must have experienced when he heard this definite statement from God concerning an heir. The promise had been given nearly ten years before, and Sarah was as barren now as she had always been. Viviparity seemed to have passed her by completely. How in the world were two old people going to produce a child? It was impossible! And yet, God kept insisting that it would happen "naturally" from his own body.

Then God "brought him forth abroad, and said, Look now toward heaven, and tell the stars, if thou be able to number them: and He said unto him, So shall thy seed be." Abraham arose, went out of the tent and looked at the vast sky spread out above his head. Tens upon tens of thousands of stars were brightly shining in the clear night sky. If Abram had sighed and shaken his head, we cannot blame him. So many from nothing certainly appeared an impossibility to him. Countless descendants from two old people who were essentially dead as far as their ability to have children?[1] But we are told that "he believed in the LORD; and He counted it to him for righteousness."[2]

Abraham, in his weariness, may have questioned the promise of God to him concerning an heir, but still he "believed in the LORD" and knew in his heart that God would do what He said He would do. How God would accomplish it, he did not know. It was still a mystery to him, but he was willing to leave it in God's hands. If God was able to scatter all those stars above his head, and keep them hanging up there, each one running in its own course and appearing night after night in the same place, then somehow He must be able to produce a child from Sarah's dead womb.

Abraham believed the Word only, and that is what constitutes true faith. We find another man who "believed that the Word only" had power to do what that Word said, and Jesus commended him above all Israel for his faith (Luke 7:1-9). If we could learn to believe that the Word of God that will heal us from sin, is the same Word that spoke the universe into existence, then we too would have that faith that could move mountains. "Lord, I believe, help Thou my unbelief!" (Mark 9:24).

---

1. "Through faith also Sarah herself received strength to conceive seed, and was delivered of a child when she was past age, because she judged Him faithful who had promised. Therefore sprang there even of one, and him as good as dead, so many as the stars of the sky in multitude, and as the sand which is by the sea shore innumerable." (Hebrews 11:11, 12).

2. "For what saith the Scripture? Abraham believed God, and it was counted unto him for righteousness." (Romans 4:3). "(As it is written, I have made thee a father of many nations,) before Him whom he believed, even God, who quickeneth the dead, and calleth those things which be not as though they were. Who against hope believed in hope, that he might become the father of many nations, according to that which was spoken, So shall thy seed be. And being not weak in faith, he considered not his own body now dead, when he was about an hundred years old, neither yet the deadness of Sarah's womb: he staggered not at the promise of God through unbelief; but was strong in faith, giving glory to God; and being fully persuaded that, what He had promised, He was able also to perform. And therefore it was imputed to him for righteousness. (Romans 4:17-22).

11

Strange Sacrifice

Genesis 15:7-18

Regarding the word *viviparity*. Yes, it is a weird word. Many years ago when I kept lots of aquariums, both fresh and salt water, I learned that some fish are viviparous, meaning they bear live young instead of laying eggs. The word came to mind when I was considering Sarah's continual barren state. She had no natural capacity for bearing live young.

Yes, you're right. Faith is a choice. It must be, because God has given us free will. We chose to love Him and obey Him; He will not force us to do either. Forced love is not love at all. Forced obedience is slavery. Paganism is slavery to an angry, unloving, unmerciful deity who must be appeased through sacrifice. And the one who worships such a god never knows if he has done enough to pacify the deity's wrath against him. But the God of heaven and earth is not such a god. The true God of heaven is Love, and that Love seeks the lost to win us back into His fold.[1]

But, more importantly, faith is a gift according to Romans 12:3.[2] Faith is not something that we can generate of ourselves. All people

---

1. "He that loveth not knoweth not God; *for God is love*. ... Herein is love, not that we loved God, but that He loved us, and sent His Son to be the propitiation for our sins. (1 John 4:8, 10, emphasis supplied). "For the Son of man is come to seek and to save that which was lost." (Luke 19:10).

2. "According as God hath dealt to every man *the* measure of faith." (Romans 12:3, emphasis supplied). Christ is not divided, but the whole of His faith is given to every person. (1 Corinthians 1:13).

have been given "*the* measure of faith." That "measure" is the *fullness* of the faith of Christ—*His faith*—by which we are to live and overcome "even as He also overcame."[3] The apostle Paul understood this, saying, "... and the life which I now live in the flesh I live *by the faith of Jesus*, Who loved me and gave Himself for me" (Galatians 2:20, emphasis supplied).

That tiny preposition "of" is very significant. The original Greek word is in the genitive case, in the possessive form. The word faith in this verse literally means the faith that *belongs to* Jesus Christ, it is His own faith that He gives to us for us to exercise according to His will for us. And Christ has given us "the *full* measure" of His faith; it is not a division or fragment of His faith, but the whole measure of it.

Galatians 2:16 tells us that we are justified *by* or *through* the faith of Jesus Christ—His personal faith in His Father's power to deliver Him from sin (see John 5:19, 30; 8:28).[4] We are not justified by our own works, or our own "faith in" Him. We have no faith except that which has been given to us from God. The *faith of Jesus* is given in the life of Jesus Himself, that was given to every person, and Christ can not be divided. Therefore, to every person has been given all of Christ who died for our sins, and all of His faith has been given to us for the transformation of our characters. It is only through and by His tested and proven faith that we can ever hope to overcome sin.

Faith "in" something is altogether different. Faith "in" is really a work, something we feel compelled to do, and like you observed, "some choices are hard to stick to." That's because we have made those choices from a wrong motivation. You fell in love with your wife, and it has not been hard for you to stick to that choice all these years,

---

3. "To him that overcometh will I grant to sit with Me in my throne, even as I also overcame, and am set down with My Father in His throne." (Revelation 3:21). "He that hath an ear, let him hear what the Spirit saith unto the churches; to him that overcometh will I give to eat of the tree of life, which is in the midst of the paradise of God." (Revelation 7:7).

4. "Then answered Jesus and said unto them, Verily, verily, I say unto you, The Son can do nothing of Himself, but what He seeth the Father do: for what things soever He doeth, these also doeth the Son likewise." (John 5:19). "I can of Mine own self do nothing: as I hear, I judge: and My judgment is just; because I seek not Mine own will, but the will of the Father which hath sent Me." (John 5:30). "Then said Jesus unto them, When ye have lifted up the Son of man, then shall ye know that I am He, and that I do nothing of Myself; but as My Father hath taught Me, I speak these things." (John 8:28).

because the motivation is right. When we truly fall in love with Christ our Saviour, it will not be hard to follow Him wherever He leads us,[5] no matter how difficult it may seem at the time.

The apostle Paul grasped this amazing concept when he wrote, "For the love of Christ constrains us [motivates us]; because we thus judge, that if One died for all, then were all dead: and that He died for all, that they which live [eternally] should not henceforth live unto themselves [in this world], but unto Him who died for them, and rose again." (2 Corinthians 5:14, 15).

A true heart appreciation of the gift of the Son of God to save us from sin,[6] will wring the heart of the most hardened sinner, and transformation of that character will follow as naturally as day follows night. All it takes is a right motivation and a love response to the gift of the Son of God, who came to same us from sin (Matthew 1:21).

But back to Abraham and his confusion as he stood there in the middle of that starry night gazing heavenward. Abraham believed *mentally* in God. He accepted the intellectual truth that there was only one true God, Who created and controlled everything. He had to have believed in that truth or he would never have walked out of Ur in the first place. But a *mental assent* to a fact is not a *saving faith*. That mental assent is like the choice you mentioned in your reply, that is hard to stick to by your own efforts. So many distractions come to lure us away. We lose our grip and are snatched back by Satan.

The agonizing father who approached Jesus to heal his son was prompted to say, "I believe, Lord help my unbelief," because he knew his mental assent to who Jesus was had done nothing to help his sick child (see Matthew 9:17-24). Saving faith involves a heart transformation. Saving faith is making the choice to allow Christ to live His life though us.

And this is what God was trying to teach to both Abraham and Sarah. Their story is exciting to study because we can see just how

---

5. "These are they which follow the Lamb whithersoever He goeth. These were redeemed from among men, being the firstfruits unto God and to the Lamb." (Revelation 14:4).

6. "And she shall bring forth a son, and thou shalt call His name JESUS: for He shall save His people from their sins." (Matthew 1:21). "And there is no God else besides Me; a just God and a Saviour; there is none besides Me. Look unto Me, and be ye saved, all the ends of the earth: for I am God, and there is none else." (Isaiah 45:21, 22).

patient and loving God is as He works to draw us to Himself and away from the slimy pit of sin, and teach us what faith really is all about.

"And [pre-incarnate Christ] said unto him [while Abraham was still experiencing his vision], I am the LORD that brought thee out of Ur of the Chaldees, to give thee this land to inherit it" (Genesis 15:7). God always begins His blessing by reminding us of what He has already done for us. He tells us to *remember*, and if we remember and *appreciate* all He has already done for us, and *thank* Him for all those blessings we *have already been given*, then we are ready to receive His increased blessing.

God was in essence telling Abraham, Remember, you're only here in this foreign land because I brought you here; you are here as a fulfillment of My eternal purpose, that through you I will bless all nations and all people everywhere through the Messiah who will be your descendant (Genesis 12:3).[7]

In essence, God was telling Abraham, I had to bring you out of your comfort zone in Babylon (Ur of the Chaldees), to this comparative wilderness so that you would learn to depend completely on Me for all your needs.

God said that He would "give" the land, and that Abraham would "inherit" it. These are two different concepts. God gives us all things in Christ, both temporal and eternal, and that gift we can keep and cherish, or throw away—it is our choice. Even inanimate things are said to "give" to us, such as a tree or the land "giving" or "yielding" to us its fruit. All we can do is receive that gift, or throw it away by letting the gift from heaven rot on the ground.

However, to *inherit* means to take possession of something that has been given. We are told in Scripture, and have already looked at the Biblical fact that Abraham never possessed anything in the land of Canaan except the burial cave he purchased with money. There he placed Sarah when she died, and there his sons put him when he died.

---

7. "Know ye therefore that they which are of faith, the same are the children of Abraham. ... There is neither Jew nor Greek, there is neither bond nor free, there is neither male nor female: for ye are all one in Christ Jesus. And if ye be Christ's, then are ye Abraham's seed, and heirs according to the promise." (Galatians 3:7, 28, 29). God is no respecter of persons; no nation or people group is more acceptable to God than any other people. "Then Peter began to speak: 'Now I really understand that God doesn't show favoritism, but in every nation the person who fears Him and does righteousness is acceptable to Him.'" (Acts 10:34, 35, HCSB).

That was all the land that Abraham owned and all that he could pass on to his sons through the legal process of inheritance.

The "inheritance" of the land God spoke of has a much broader and eternal meaning. The inheritance given "in Christ" is forever, but this world full of sin will not last forever. This world is not our home, and like Abraham, we are strangers and pilgrims here, looking for that "better land" of the earth made new (Hebrews 11:13; Revelation 21:1). That land is the "inheritance of the saints" (Matthew 25:34).

"And [Abraham] said, Lord GOD, whereby shall I know that I shall inherit it?" Good question. All that had been said that night between Abraham and God pointed forward to some things that Abraham could not fathom: the birth of a son through a barren woman, and the inheritance of a land already populated by heathen sinners who had possessed that land for centuries.

Now, this next section of Scripture baffled me for many years as I studied Genesis. I could not find any source that adequately explained this strange event concerning the splitting of the animals and laying them out on the ground. For two and a half years, I searched and read and searched some more to come to an understanding of the mystery of these few verses.

Finally, one day I was reading Alfred Edersheim's *History of the Old Testament* on this section of Scripture, and there it was! An explanation that made perfect sense because it was not based on speculation or men's ideas, but on an historical and archeological fact. After I discovered what Edersheim wrote, I found confirmation in other sources because I then knew what to look for.

"And [God] said unto [Abraham], Take Me an heifer of three years old, and a she goat of three years old, and a ram of three years old, and a turtledove, and a young pigeon." That's all God said. He did not instruct Abraham what to do with them. He just said, "take them to Me."

My questions for those two and a half years had been, What is this all about? and How did Abraham know what to do with these animals?

God only instructed Abraham to "take them to Me" and then named out the kinds of animals He wanted. By the way, all those kinds of animals would later be designated as "clean" animals fit for use in the various sanctuary offerings when God gave Moses instruction for building the earthly tabernacle at Sinai. The animals would later be given greater definition in the sanctuary service as "types" because they were used to point to Christ's sacrifice for mankind that was demonstrated in the various sanctuary rituals.

But what Abraham was supposed to do with these animals seemingly was left wide open. No instructions from God on that point. And what Abraham did do with them was not like any sacrificial offering that had been recorded before this time in the Bible. Sacrificial animals had always been burned up completely on an altar of stones, not split down the middle and laid out side-by-side on the ground.

Somehow Abraham already knew what to do with those animals, and so, "he took unto him all these, and divided them in the midst, and laid each piece one against another: but the birds divided he not" because they were small. That's why there were two, one for each side of the path that was created between the animal halves.

It was the morning following his midnight conference with God that Abraham went among his flocks and herds and selected out these animals: a heifer, a female goat, and a ram, all three years old. Then he had to catch the turtledove and pigeon. Selecting the perfect animals, as well as catching the birds would have taken him some time. When Abraham had finished this part of the project, it was afternoon. He still had to take the animals some distance away from the tents where the women and children lived, and kill the animals, dress them and cut them in half. A three year old heifer weighs more than half a ton. It would have been a major slaughtering task to kill and dress these three fully-grown animals, and would have required assistance from his household servants.

When they had finished their work, Abraham sent his servants away, and sat down beside the carcasses to see what would happen next. He had done what God told him to do—now what? While he was waiting, vultures and carrion eating crows descended to feast on the carcasses. "And when the fowls came down upon the carcasses, Abram drove them away."

"And when the sun was going down, a deep sleep fell upon Abram; and, lo, an horror of great darkness fell upon him." Abraham had been working all day, and sitting there patiently watching and waiting for hours, his eyelids drooped heavily. As dusk was gathering upon the land, things began to grow silent. Birds went to roost, the flocks and herds lay down for their evening rest, and became quiet. Abraham's shepherds and herdsmen returned to their tents for the evening meal, and a general calm settled upon the camp.

And still, nothing was happening where Abraham was sitting next to those carcasses. The approaching darkness brought with it a profound and eerie silence.

As Abraham waited in the deepening gloom, a terrible dread and fear descended upon his mind and heart. What was going to take place there in the dark? He did not know what to anticipate. This type of sacrifice that he was familiar with, was not happening according to any he had witnessed before this time. Where was the other party with whom he was supposed to make this covenant? Lack of knowledge about coming events always brings a certain amount of fear and dread, and when experienced in darkness, it can be an awful experience. What Abraham did know was that this plot was not following any script he had previously seen among the Canaanites.

Sitting there in the deepening night chill, he had never experienced such a dread, and a "great horror of darkness fell on him." The sun's last glow in the western sky faded away, and the stars failed to appear before his troubled eyes. The darkness was so great to Abraham, that he could see nothing except blackness all around him. Silence and blackness, that was all he could perceive. It was like being in a deep cave, blinded by the darkness, and in such a situation we feel very vulnerable and alone. What we cannot see or hear causes a deep fear in the human heart.

Suddenly, from out of that darkness a voice that he recognized spoke to him, "Know of a surety that thy seed shall be a stranger in a land that is not theirs, and shall serve them; and they shall afflict them four hundred years; and also that nation, whom they shall serve, will I judge: and afterward shall they come out with great substance. And thou shalt go to thy fathers in peace; thou shalt be buried in a good old age. But in the fourth generation they shall come hither again: for the iniquity of the Amorites is not yet full."

God's prophecy of what would happen to Abraham's descendants covered four hundred years, a series of events, and involved a nation that was unidentified except by saying that the nation would be powerful enough to enslave Abraham's people for a period of time. But then God would judge them. With the proclamation concerning enslavement, also came the greater promise of divine deliverance.

God's desire that no one should be lost (2 Peter 3:9) included a promise to the Amorites. He was giving them four hundred years of additional probation during which they could turn from their wicked ways and serve the one true God, and in Him find salvation. Or certain destruction awaited them when their "cup of iniquity" overflowed. The Amorites were not "predestined to be lost"; it was their choice to believe or disbelieve God's word concerning them.

God's call to the Amorites was the same as He gave to the Israelites before they entered the promised land: "I call heaven and earth to record this day against you, that I have set before you life and death, blessing and cursing: therefore choose life, that both thou and thy seed may live" (Deuteronomy 30:19).

While Abraham has pondering this deep revelation, "it came to pass, that, when the sun went down, and it was dark, behold a smoking furnace, and a burning lamp passed between those pieces" of the animals. Whoa! Out of the blinding darkness now comes an even more blinding brightness! A blazing furnace and a burning lamp appeared from nowhere, and passing in the midst of those animal carcasses, consumed them all up into smoke. God waited until it was so dark that nothing could be detected before He presented Himself as the Consuming Fire.[8] What a mind-blowing theophany that was!

Abraham was left speechless by the experience. But God had one more thing to say to His faithful servant: and "In the same day the LORD made a covenant with Abram, saying, Unto thy seed have I given this land, from the river of Egypt unto the great river, the river Euphrates."

---

8. "For the LORD thy God is a consuming fire, even a jealous God." (Deuteronomy 4:24). "For our God is a consuming fire." (Hebrews 12:29).

12

Theophany in the Night

Genesis 15:9-18

Now for the rest of the story. I just laid out the scene, but not the meaning, in the previous discussion. Something may be "deeply mysterious" at the beginning, but when we get all the information, the riddle is easily solved.

The reason that God did not tell Abraham what to do with the animals was because Abraham already *knew* what to do. Having lived among the Canaanites for a few years, he had become familiar with the form of covenant-making God was indicating, because it was commonly used among the Canaanite people to settle disputes and make peace among tribes.

Abraham asked for assurance of God's promise to him: "How shall I know that what You told me is really going to happen?" God replied by telling him to gather the animals. That's all Abraham needed to be told. He knew it was in preparation for a covenant-making ritual, but he remained unsure how this covenant was going to be carried out. Abraham knew it took two parties as well as the animal parts laid out on the ground. He might have thought he was one half of the bargaining party, but who and where was the representative for the other covenanting party? The mystery was, who was God going to send to be the other participant in this ritual?

This covenantal form was well-known among the Canaanites and Hittites that lived in that part of the Middle East during the second millennium BC. It is called a "parity covenant" because it involved two parties of *equal stature* who entered into a *mutual* agreement. In the Canaanite ritual the two parties were "on par," or equal to each other socially and politically, whether they were kings, chieftains, or common men.

In a previous discussion we looked at the suzerain covenant when studying Chedorloamer and his confederates who attacked the cities in the Valley of Siddim. The covenant type that Chedorlaomer used to control his conquered states was made between two *unequal* parties: the powerful suzerain and his weaker vassal who was forced to be subservient or face severe punishments. The suzerain covenant required the vassal to promise to obey a list of nine stipulations, which included, among other things, his promise to pay an annual tribute (tax) to the suzerain, to raise an army to help the suzerain fight a war against his rebel vassals (as in the narrative concerning the kings of Sodom and Gomorrah), and appear once a year in the suzerain's court to reaffirm his commitment to his promises, pledges and vows of perpetual obedience.[1] The suzerain covenant was between a conqueror and his vassals, and by its very nature was a covenant that expressed the *unequalness* of the parties involved.

The parity type of covenant had no connection to the suzerain covenant. It was of a much different type, but carried just as serious and weighty consequences for failure of execution by either party. In the ancient Near Eastern culture, a covenant of parity was a covenant of promise between equals to do or to refrain from doing something that was mutually beneficial to both of the promising parties. In many instances, it brought an end to strife concerning water rights, property disputes, and war.

The parity covenant was usually sealed by the promising parties walking together between the halves of a sacrificial animal, such as a bullock or a ram. In essence, the parties were giving witness to each other, and those standing by, that if either of them should break his promise, or fail to uphold his side of the covenant bargain, then what had happened to the animal should befall him also (i.e., death).

---

1. We can read an example of this annual get-together of vassals before their suzerain lord in Esther chapter 1, where Ahasuerus gathered his vassals from all the territories over which he ruled, from India to Ethiopia. "In the third year of his reign, he made a feast unto all his princes and servants; the power of Persia and Media, the nobles and princes of the provinces, being before him." (Esther 1:3).

The idea behind this covenant form was that if either party failed to uphold his end of the bargain—if he broke his promise—then he was willing to lay down his life, just as the sacrificial animal had done. He was agreeing that if he failed on his part of the arrangement, then he could be "drawn and quartered."

Other instances of parity covenants in the Bible are found between Abraham and Abimelech in Genesis 21:22-32; and between Isaac and Abimelech in Genesis 26:17-31. In both of these cases the parties "made (cut) a covenant" to end strife concerning water wells. The literal translation of the Hebrew word "made" is "to cut," signifying that the covenants Abraham and Isaac formed with the two men named Abimelech were of a type similar to the one that we read about in Genesis chapter 15, being the common form of covenant in that culture between two equal parties or tribal leaders. In both of the cases with Abimelech it was a covenant of promise to refrain from war over the denial of certain property rights (the wells of water).

Not all covenants of parity involved the cutting of a sacrifice, but this type of covenant was always made between two equal parties and was for the purpose of settling a dispute and creating a binding peace between the two parties. Other examples of covenants of parity are found in 1 Kings 5:1-12, 15:16-20; and 20:31-34. In the last reference we find that king Ahab not only gave his word, but right there on the battlefield he "cut" a covenant with king Ben-hadad before sending him away in peace.

In Genesis 15, God restated the land grant covenant He gave originally to Adam, then Noah, and finally to Abraham when He called him out of Haran (Genesis 12:1-3). Formerly, God had just *stated* His promise, but now, because Abraham needed greater assurance, God *sealed* His promise using the ritual that used the sacrifice of animals. It was a physical and visual demonstration of God's promise.

Taking the heifer, female goat, ram, a turtledove and a pigeon, Abraham did what he knew to be the preparatory form of the ritual. He killed the animals, then cut each of them asunder down the length of the spine, and laid out the halves of their bodies, with space enough for two people to walk between the pieces—two halves each of the heifer, goat, and ram, and two whole birds, laid parallel to each other making a walkway between them. And then Abraham sat down to wait, unsure of what would follow.

Evidently, because it required two parties to perform this Canaanite form of the covenant, Abraham anticipated his participation in the covenant ritual when the second party eventually showed up on the scene. However, "it came to pass, that, when the sun went down, and it was dark, behold a smoking furnace, and a burning lamp passed between those pieces." When the "second party" finally did show up, Abraham was left sitting on the sideline with his mouth gaping open, totally awestruck by what he witnessed blazing out of the deep blackness of that night.

God purposely chose the parity form of covenant when sealing His promise to Abraham. By doing so, God was saying to Abraham, "Let what happened to these animals happen to Me if I do not keep My promise to you to give you an inheritance of children and land." God was laying His eternal existence on the line in promising Abraham that He would give him an *everlasting inheritance* and the righteousness to obtain it. In this instance, the covenant was made between two members of the Godhead (Father and Son) who appeared as a red-hot smoking furnace and blazing torch that passed between the parts, invoking the curse upon Themselves if They failed to do as They promised.

The Scripture tells us that there were two entities that passed between the animal parts, "a smoking furnace *and* a burning lamp." The Godhead was present that evening on the hills in Hebron. The glorious theophany that blazed through those animal parts was a demonstration of the everlasting covenant between the Father and the Son that *They* would restore humanity's eternal inheritance of the earth, should sin cause mankind to forfeit it (which it did when Adam sinned in Eden). Both the Father and the Son passed between the pieces of those animals that evening, giving visible evidence of the

---

2. "And I will put enmity between thee and the woman, and between thy seed and her seed; He shall bruise thy head, and thou shalt bruise His heel." (Genesis 3:15). Here the promise sets in motion the plan of salvation from sin. God promises to put hatred (enmity) in our hearts that will turn us from sin. The declaration of doom against Satan and his plot to destroy God's creation includes the promise that even though Satan would attempt to kill Jesus through the crucifixion, the resurrection would prove that in reality, Christ's death "crushed" Satan's head, bringing an end to his power—"that through death He might destroy him that had the power of death, that is the devil" (Hebrews 2:14). The everlasting covenant included the promise to restore Adam's lost dominion, which will take place when Christ comes as King of kings and LORD of lords (Revelation 19:16). "The kingdoms of this world are become the kingdoms of our LORD and of His Christ: and He shall reign for ever and ever" (Revelation 11:15).

everlasting covenant made from the foundation of the world[2] (Genesis 3:15; Revelation 13:8; Titus 1:2; 1 Peter 1:19, 20). Present also as the eternal Witness was the Holy Spirit who would testify of the truth of the everlasting covenant (John 15:26). The covenant of parity could not be made between God and Abraham, because no claim could be made that God and Abraham were equals.

Knowing that the ritual form required two equal parties to complete it, Abraham would not have taken it upon himself to pass between those pieces of carcasses alone. That would have been a violation of the ritual method, and he knew it. He knew it took two parties, and so when he had laid out the carcasses, he sat down and waited for the second party to show up, though he didn't have a clue how that was going to work.

Additionally, since Abraham was seeking affirmation *from God* concerning God's promise to him, why would Abraham think *he* should pass through the animals and make a promise to God about anything? He was asking God for an answer to the question concerning his lack of an heir. He was not in a situation to promise God anything concerning *that* problem. It doesn't make sense at all that Abraham would perform half of the ritual by walking by himself through the animals, when he had no promise to make to God concerning the problem of an heir. And so, after slaughtering the animals and laying them out on the ground according to the common ritual form, Abraham naturally would have sat down, waiting for the "other party," not really understanding how it was going to be carried out. And after waiting several hours, the "other party" showed up in brilliant, mind-boggling style!

This particular covenant of parity could only be made between members of the Godhead who were eternally equal. There was nothing greater that God could swear by except Himself.[3] The apostle Paul helps us understand the covenant made with Abraham by describing the usual manner in which two men of equal stature swore to one another, "an oath for confirmation [which was] to them an end of all strife" (Hebrews 6:16; cf. Genesis 21:22-32).

---

3. "For when God made promise to Abraham, because He could swear by no greater, He sware by Himself, saying, surely blessing I will bless thee, and multiplying I will multiply thee." (Hebrews 6:13).

As we have previously detailed, through the making of the covenant of parity two men swore to one another that all strife between them would be at an end. While there was no "strife" between the Father and the Son, since the Fall of Adam there *was* a conflict (enmity) between mankind and God (see Romans 8:7).[4] The only solution for an end to this conflict was that which the Godhead took upon Themselves in order to bring about the remedy.[5]

Think of the enormity of this situation! God pledged Himself and His own existence for our salvation through the redemptive work of Jesus Christ. He put His entire universe on the balance scale, indicating by this covenant with Abraham, that if He was unable to perform the promise He made, then He didn't deserve to be King of the universe, or God—exactly what Satan had been trying to prove since his rebellion in heaven—God didn't deserve to be God. Lucifer wanted to take His place on the throne.

Two thousand years later, the universe witnessed just how serious the Godhead was in making this pledge to save mankind, when Christ Himself laid down His own life "for His friends" [6]

The apostle Paul stated, "For when God made promise to Abraham, because He could swear by no greater, He sware by Himself, saying, surely blessing I will bless thee, and multiplying I will multiply thee. And so, after he had patiently endured, he obtained the promise. For men verily swear by the greater: and an oath for confirmation is to

---

4. "Because the carnal mind *is enmity* against God: for it is not subject to the law of God, neither indeed can be." (Romans 8:7, emphasis supplied). "But the natural man receives not the things of the Spirit of God: for they are foolishness unto him: neither can he know them, because they are spiritually discerned." (1 Corinthians 2:14).

5. "For all have sinned, and come short of the glory of God; being justified freely by His grace through the redemption that is in Christ Jesus: Whom God hath set forth to be a propitiation through faith in His blood, to declare His righteousness for the remission of sins that are past, through the forbearance of God." (Romans 3:23-25). Also see footnote page 76.

6. "Greater love hath no man than this, that a Man lay down His life for His friends." (John 15:13). "I am the Good Shepherd: the good shepherd giveth His life for the sheep." (John 10:11). "For when we were yet without strength, in due time Christ died for the ungodly. ... But God commends His love toward us, in that, while we were yet sinners, Christ died for us. ... For if, when we were [His] enemies, we were reconciled to God by the death of His Son, much more, being reconciled, we shall be saved by His life." (Romans 5:6, 8, 10). "Now the God of peace, that brought again from the dead our Lord Jesus, that Great Shepherd of the sheep, through the blood of the everlasting covenant." (Hebrews 13:20).

them an end of all strife. Wherein God, willing more abundantly to shew unto the heirs of the promise the immutability of His counsel, confirmed it by an oath: that by two immutable things [God's *promise* and His *confirming oath*], in which it was impossible for God to lie, we might have a strong consolation, who have fled for refuge to lay hold upon the hope set before us." (Hebrews 6:13-18).

God could find no one greater than Himself to sware by when demonstrating His everlasting covenant to Abraham, so He made the oath "between" Himself. Christ confirms that He and His Father are co-participants and co-witnesses in the plan of salvation. "And yet if I judge, My judgment is true: for I am not alone, but I and the Father that sent Me. It is also written in your law, that the testimony of two men is true. I am one that bear witness of Myself, and the Father that sent Me beareth witness of Me." (John 8:16-18).

The "two immutable things" Paul mentions are first, the promise of God to give the land as an everlasting inheritance, which in itself should have been sufficient for Abraham's faith (Genesis 15:6). God also gives us the righteousness that is required to be able receive the everlasting inheritance of the earth made new. The restoration of the land (this world as our eternal home) will take place after the second coming of Christ and the annihilation of the wicked in the lake of fire (see Revelation 20:12-15; 21:1-5).[7]

But Abraham needed more assurance than just a "word" and so he asked, "*How* shall I know?"—*prove* it to me. Therefore, the oath God made to Abraham in taking the curse upon Himself by "walking between the pieces," constituted a more certain pledge of God's commitment to fulfill His promise. God's promise and His oath are both immutable, unchangeable, enduring forever, and unamendable. He will restore this lost world to Adam and all his righteous descendants as their eternal abode. And sin nor its results shall be seen no more.[8]

---

7. "And I saw a new heaven and a new earth: for the first heaven and the first earth were passed away; and there was no more sea. And I John saw the holy city, new Jerusalem, coming down from God out of heaven, prepared as a bride adorned for her Husband ... and He that sat upon the throne said, Behold, I make all things new, and He said unto me, Write: for these words are true and faithful."

8. The Scriptures reveal to us that God promised that "He will make an utter end: affliction [sin and its results] shall not rise up the second time" (Nahum 1:9). The righteous redeemed and all the unfallen angels will know and appreciate the cost of sin—the death of God's dear Son—and it will place enmity between them and any desire to ever rebel against their Creator and Redeemer.

Thus the covenant in Genesis 15 is seen in its uniqueness as the embodiment of the everlasting covenant; a fully legal and immutable promise to Abraham who is the father of all the faithful, Gentile and Jew. The covenant includes all who will believe God's promise to deliver them from sin—faithful Jews who accept the Messiah as their Saviour, and believing Gentiles who turn from their paganism to believe in the one true God.[9]

The theophany Abraham witnessed that dark night on the hill in Hebron, was a revelation of God's plan of redemption, enveloping in the singular effect of this one demonstration, the entire scope of God's redemptive covenant to save lost humanity from their sin, and restore to them their everlasting possession—this earth when it has been made new after sin and sinners are destroyed in the lake of fire.[10]

The redemptive blessing to mankind, which includes the power to overcome all sin and thereby recieve the righesouensss of Christ as both our title (justification) and fitness (sanctification) to inherit the earth made new, is the ultimate promise of God to humanity. In this parity covenant made between the Father and Son, all this is guaranteed as the gift of the King of the universe to every person who will believe His promise, and allow Him to work out His plan of salvation in our daily lives. God takes full responsibility upon Himself to perform the stipulations of the everlasting covenant.

---

9. "For ye are all the children of God by faith in Christ Jesus. For as many of you as have been baptized into Christ have put on Christ. There is neither Jew nor Greek, there is neither bond nor free, there is neither male nor female: for ye are all one in Christ Jesus. And if ye be Christ's, then are ye Abraham's seed, and heirs according to the promise." (Galatians 3:26-29).

10. "And I saw the dead, small and great, stand before God; and the books were opened: and another book was opened, which is the book of life: and the dead were judged out of those things which were written in the books, according to their works. And the sea gave up the dead which were in it; and death and hell delivered up the dead which were in them: and they were judged every man according to their works. And death and hell were cast into the lake of fire. This is the second death. And whosoever was not found written in the book of life was cast into the lake of fire. And I saw a new heaven and a new earth: for the first heaven and the first earth were passed away; and there was no more sea. ... He that overcometh shall inherit all things; and I will be his God, and he shall be My son." (Revelation 20:12-15; 21:1, 7).

13

Nations of Canaan

Genesis 15:18-21

In the same day the LORD made a covenant with Abram, saying, Unto thy seed have I given this land, from the river of Egypt unto the great river, the river Euphrates: the Kenites, and the Kenizzites, and the Kadmonites, and the Hittites, and the Perizzites, and the Rephaims, and the Amorites, and the Canaanites, and the Girgashites, and the Jebusites." (Genesis 15:18-21). The prophecy does not say that these nations were going to be utterly destroyed so the children of Abraham could move in. In this promise, there is no implication that there would not be a cohabitation of the various nations in Canaan.

The designated territory extended from the Nile River to the Euphrates River. The ten nations of people who populated that area between the two "great rivers" were named by tribes in this prophecy. All these tribes were descendants of Canaan, the son of Ham (Genesis 10:6). The first were Kenites who were nomads, always mentioned in association with various other peoples. They are first mentioned in this text along with the Kadmonites and Kenizzites as being among the peoples whose land was promised to Abraham (Genesis 15:19).

The false prophet Balaam, when standing on the hill in Moab overlooking the encampment of the children of Israel, could see the Kenites in the distance. He made a joke of their name by calling them a "nest" of people, and said though they build their nest in a rock, they would still be destroyed (Numbers 24:21, 22).

They never were.

The Kenites were often connected in history with the Midianites, which is the tribe that Jethro, Moses' father in law, came from (see Exodus 3:1, 18:1; cf. Judges 1:16). The Midianites were descended from Abraham through his second wife, Keturah (Genesis 25:1-4). The Midianites were the same people who bought Joseph from his brothers (Genesis 37:28). Kenites were still in the land at the time of King Saul, when he went to war against the Amalekites (1 Samuel 15:6). From the verse in 1 Samuel 15:6, it seems that the Kenites were not troublesome to the Israelites because Saul had no quarrel with them and didn't want to fight them. The ancient Israelites did not war with the Kenites or destroy them. They co-existed in the land peaceably for centuries.

Kenizzites were the clan that Jephunneh, the father of Caleb came from (Numbers 32:12; Joshua 14:6, 14). When Jacob and his family emigrated to Egypt about 1875 BC, the Kenizzites evidently had been previously absorbed into the tribe of Judah. In Egypt, they become identified with Judah's family while living there.

When David was exiled among the Philistines, we read that the nations of the Gezrites, Geshurites, and Amalekites lived in southern Canaan,[1] "for those nations were of old the inhabitants of the land, as you go to Shur, even unto the land of Egypt" (1 Samuel 27:8). During his political exile and while fighting for the Philistines, young David carried the battle into the "south of Judah" and reported to Achish, the prince of Gath, that he and his army had fought against the Kenites who were dwelling in the southern section of Judah (1 Samuel 27:10).

In 1 Chronicles we find that a Kenite was the father of the Rechabites (1 Chronicles 2:55). When David took the throne, he married Maacah, daughter of Talmai, king of Geshur, who became the mother of Absalom and Tamar (2 Samuel 3:3). Even down to the Babylonian captivity, Kenites then known as Rechabites, continued as nomadic people in Canaan (Jeremiah 35:1-11). Six centuries later

---

1. The name "Palestine" does not appear in any written records until the fifth century BC. In his *The Histories*, an accounting of the origins of the Greco-Persian Wars, the Persian historian Herodotus, coined the term that is now almost universally applied to the entire region west of the Jordan River, a region that was formerly known in history as the "Land of Canaan." The word Palestine occurs only one time in the KJV Bible, and is found in Joel 3:4, where the prophet coupled the word with the two coastal cities of Sidon and Tyre. The Hebrew word translated "Palestine" in this verse literally means "to roll" or to be migratory.

when Jesus walked the earth, remnants of the Girgashites continued to live in western Canaan along the Mediterranean coast.

The Kadmonites were known as "easterners" which tells us that they lived on the east side of the Jordan River in the land of Edom, and are doubtless the same as "the children of the east," whose wisdom was widely known and appreciated (1 Kings 4:30). They, too, seem to be a peaceable group of people with whom ancient Israel had no quarrel, and among whom they lived for an extended period.

The Hittites appear to have been non-Semites. In later times the "land of the Hittites" (Joshua 1:4; Judges 1:26) was located in Syria, and near the headwaters of the Euphrates River. Not all Hittites were enemies because we read of Uriah the Hittite (2 Samuel 11) who lived in Jerusalem and served King David—a faithful and loyal servant and yet David betrayed him to be murdered and stole his wife!! Abimelech the Hittite also followed David (1 Samuel 26:6). In the time of Solomon the "kings of the Hittites" are mentioned with the "kings of Syria" (1 Kings 10:29), and were still powerful a century later (2 Kings 7:6). Solomon himself married Hittite wives (1 Kings 11:1), and a few Hittites seem still to have been left in the south after the Babylonian captivity (Ezra 9:1; Nehemiah 9:8).

Perizzites were not included among the sons of Canaan in Genesis chapter 10, but are coupled with the Canaanites in Genesis 13:7; Genesis 34:30; Judges 1:4. The Perizzites were associated with villages or small towns, and in Deuteronomy 3:5 and 1 Samuel 6:18, the literal translation of the Hebrew is "cities of the Perizzite" or "villager" and "village of the Perizzite." In Joshua 17:15 and 18, where the Manassites are instructed to take possession of the forest land of Carmel, the "Perizzites and Rephaim" are given as the equivalent of "Canaanite," even though they were not descendants of the man Canaan.

The name Amorite is used in the Old Testament to denote (1) the inhabitants of Canaan in general, (2) the population living in the the hills as opposed to the plain, and (3) a specific people under a king of their own. Thus we read of them living on the western shore of the Dead Sea (Genesis 14:7), at Hebron (Genesis 14:13) and at Shechem (Genesis 48:22), in Gilead and Bashan (Deuteronomy 3:10) and near Mount Hermon (Deuteronomy 3:8; 4:48). They were a widespread people.

The Amorites were named as the inhabitants of Canaan whom the Israelites were required to exterminate upon their occupation of the land after returning from Egypt (Genesis 15:16; Deuteronomy 20:17; Judges 6:10; 1 Samuel 7:14; 1 Kings 21:26; 2 Kings 21:11). The ancient population of Judah were called Amorite in Joshua 10:5-6, in conformity with which Ezekiel (in 16:3) states that "Jerusalem" had an Amorite father and a Hittite mother. The Gibeonites are said to have been "of the remnant of the Amorites" (2 Samuel 21:2).

On the other hand, in Numbers 13:29 the Amorites are described as dwelling in the mountains like the Hittites and Jebusites of Jerusalem, while the Amalekites or Bedouins lived in the south, and the Canaanites on the seacoast and in the valley of the Jordan River. Lastly, we hear of Sihon, "king of the Amorites," who had conquered the northern half of Moab (Numbers 21:21-31; Deuteronomy 2:26-35).

The Canaanites were descended from Canaan who, according to Genesis 10:6, was a son of Ham and brother of Mizraim (father of the people who dwelt in Egypt). In Numbers 13:29 the Canaanites are described as dwelling "by the sea, and along by the side of the Jordan," that is, in the lowlands of the land of Canaan. The people seemed to be confined to the country west of the Jordan River (Numbers 33:51; Joshua 22:9). The Canaanite name was especially applied to people living in the region known as Phoenicia (Isaiah 23:11; cf. Matthew 15:22). And Sidon is called the "firstborn" of Canaan (Genesis 10:15; cf. Judges 3:3).

Girgasites were descended from Canaan and were named along with the Canaanites in the list of tribes or nationalities inhabiting that country (Genesis 15:21; Deuteronomy 7:1; Joshua 3:10; Joshua 24:11; Nehemiah 9:8). It has been supposed that the name survived in that of "the Gergesenes," or "the Gadarenes" of Matthew 8:28, who lived on the east side of the Sea of Galilee, though there is no archeological proof of the connection.

And let us not forget the Jebusites who were descended from the third son of Canaan. They were later associated with the town that became known as Jerusalem. At the time of the exodus from Egypt, Jerusalem was still known by the Babylonian name of Uru-Salim, and its king was a Hittite. When the children of Israel returned to their homeland, the Hittites had been destroyed by enemies who then moved into the city. Those enemies seem to have been the Jebusites, since it is after this period that the name "Jebus" becomes associated with the city of Uru-Salim.

And yes, we still find the "giants" in the land. You asked me about the Rephaims some time ago and I never did give an answer. Though the devilish Rephaims who lived prior to the Flood were all destroyed in that world-wide catastrophe, evidently the "giant" genes were still present in Noah's sons. Giantism was not extinguished in the Flood. We find the Rephaims living in the valley of Rephaim southwest of Jerusalem (Joshua 15:8). They are associated with other giant races, such as the Emim and Anakim (Deuteronomy 2:10-11), and the Zamzummim (Deuteronomy 2:20).

Og was king of a sixty city district that was conquered by Moses and the Israelites immediately after Sihon, king of the Amorites was destroyed (Numbers 21:33-35; Deuteronomy 3:1-12). Og is described as the last of the Rephaim, or giant-race of that region. His giant stature is indicated in Deuteronomy 3:11 by the dimensions of his "bedstead of iron" which is said to have been 9 cubits long and 4 broad (13.5 ft. by 6 ft.). His bed had to be made from iron to support his massive size, which, judging from his height and necessary size of his bed, if he had been a lean muscular man he would have topped 600 or more pounds, even more than that if he was obese.

And of course that most famous of all Biblical giants, Goliath, is identified with the Philistines. Goliath was nine feet tall, and had four brothers just a big as he was. All of the giants living among the Philistines also are reported has having another physical anomaly called *polydactylism*—an excess of fingers and toes.[2]

All the giants in the Bible are known as fierce warriors. It is probable that they were all of the same genetic stock that developed into a race of people after the Flood, that dispersed across what is now the Middle East. Even though they have different names here and there in Scripture, they were related. The difference in names is probably due to who it was that came into contact with them, and what they chose to call them.

We see from this brief history of the Canaanite nations that though the children of Abraham through Isaac were promised that they would dwell in the land inhabited by all these other nations, the "land of Israel" historically has never been entirely in the hands of the descendants of Abraham through Isaac and Jacob. There always

---

2. "And yet again there was war at Gath, where was a man of great stature, whose fingers and toes were four and twenty, six on each hand, and six on each foot: and he also was the son of the giant." (1 Chronicles 20:6).

have been other nations from the list in Genesis 15:19-21, coexisting side-by-side with the "children of Israel." God's promise to Abraham in Genesis 17:4 was that he "would be the father of many nations" and indeed, he was. Abraham is the father of Ishmael and Midian, and through just those two men, sprang most of the Arab nations.

Even though the land was promised to Abraham and his descendants through Isaac, the only tribe God commanded to be completely destroyed were the Amorites, and the children of Israel never did exterminate them. After Jacob's family's four hundred year sojourn in Egypt, and their subsequent resettlement in Canaan, they existed or cohabited with all of these peoples and more—including the descendants of Lot's two sons, known as the Edomites and Moabites, and the twelve sons of Ishmael, and all the descendants of Abraham through Keturah's six sons.

The current claim that the land belongs exclusively to the modern Jewish people is fictional, with no Scriptural foundation. From the beginning of their resettlement after their exodus from Egypt, the children of Israel have always lived among people who were not "Jews"[3] (or direct descendants of Jacob), and most of the time they lived peacefully with them. The peoples who have always lived in "Palestine" are direct descendants, or relatives of, Abraham though either Hagar, Keturah, or Lot (Abraham's nephew), as well as the descendants of Jacob through his twelve sons.

---

3. The word "Jew" denotes those people originally inhabiting the region of Judah, but 2 Kings 16:6 applies the word to the two tribes of the southern kingdom at the time of the Babylonian captivity. Upon their return from captivity, the title "Jew" was applied to the entire people who were the remnant descendants of Abraham.

14

Sarah's Big Idea

Genesis 16:1-4

"Now Sarai Abram's wife bare him no children"—this is not news. We have known this problem existed since we were first introduced to Abraham and Sarah when they were still living in the Chaldean city of Ur.

But it's been ten years since they came to Canaan, when Abraham received from God Himself the promise of an heir. Now they were a decade farther past normal childbearing years. Abraham is now 85 years old and Sarah is ten years younger at 75 years old. It had been an impossibility for Sarah to have children for more than 60 years. If hope of conceiving a child for her husband ever existed in Sarah's heart, it surely is gone now.

And so, Sarah devised a scheme. "She had an handmaid, an Egyptian, whose name was Hagar." This young Egyptian woman was a present from Pharaoh during their brief sojourn in Egypt ten years before. Hagar is not an ordinary slave girl, but is Sarah's personal property. She thus had been a close companion and servant to Sarah since their time in Egypt. Hagar would have lived in Sarah's own tent with her, not in a servant's tent, so that she was at the ready whenever Sarah wanted anything. From ten years living in close quarters, they knew each other very well. (As was the custom of that time, Abraham lived in a separate tent close by.)

In the last chapter we learned about Abraham's bright idea for producing an heir—adopt his Damascus servant/steward named

Eliezer. And we learned God's response to his idea—a blazing fireworks display showing His divine power and majesty to fulfill His promise in His own way.

Eliezer was rejected, and now Sarah has a bright idea.

"And Sarai said unto Abram, Behold now, the LORD has restrained me from bearing." Abraham blamed God in 15:3—"Despite Your wonderful promise, LORD, *You* have not given me any children. So it's *Your fault* that I am childless." Here Sarah does the exact same thing. "The LORD *has restrained me* from bearing." It isn't just that she's unable because of some malfunctioning of her normal bodily processes, but she claims that God has actively "restrained" her from having children. That makes it doubly His fault. LORD, You formed me wrong, and You haven't done anything to remedy the problem.

At least at this point, she was finally admitting her own helplessness in solving the problem of her infertility.

Her big idea seems outlandish to our Western sensibilities, but it was not out of line in the cultures of the ancient Middle East at the time Sarah worked out her solution. Having pondered the idea for some time, weighed it in the balances of her mind, it ended up to her as being a viable option. It seemed the only reasonable alternative to her intractable barrenness.

How much longer would she live, anyway? If she was to be the mother of Abraham's child, something drastic needed to take place before she went to her grave. Abraham apparently had given up trying to invent a scheme for an heir, and seemed content to just wait things out. But one hot afternoon, Sarah wandered out of her tent to put the proposition to her husband: "I pray thee, go in unto my maid; it may be that I may obtain children by her."

One must immediately ask: Did Sarah discuss this proposition with Hagar? And if she did, how did she handle it? Did Sarah just command her maid to allow her husband to take her as his sex partner? What would have been the natural response from a young virgin ordered into an old man's bed? Would the Egyptian girl have been familiar with this surrogate mother thing? We wonder, but the Bible is silent on the matter from Hagar's point of view.

Even more astonishing, we read that without any apparent argument concerning the plan, Abraham agreed to Sarah's proposal. "And Abram hearkened to the voice of Sarai." Uh-oh. Not again! The husband "hearkening to the voice" of his wife is what started the whole problem of sin in the first place. When Eve brought the forbidden fruit to Adam, he hearkened to the voice of his wife and brought sin and misery upon God's perfect world. And not just misery to the human race, but pain and suffering to the Godhead, who would bear the penalty for Adam's sin so that men could be saved from their iniquity and rebellion.

Adam doubted God's love and sided with his wife instead of standing true to his Creator. Here Abraham does the exact same thing by yielding to the voice of his unbelieving wife.

Maybe Abraham has been thinking that the blazing vision in the middle of the night had only been his imagination, some kind of wild kaleidoscopic dream. Maybe he had not really stood out there looking at the myriad stars over his head and heard God speaking to him concerning a son and heir through Sarah. Maybe Sarah didn't matter.

No, he was certain of the events of those two nights. He harbored no doubt about what had happened that night, or the next. The impression was too vivid, seared into his brain. God had reassured him that He would give him a son that would be his heir, through whom the Messiah would come to bless the whole world. At that moment in time, "he believed in the LORD, and it was counted unto him for righteousness."

Cogitating on this conundrum while considering Sarah's solution, suddenly a thought came to him. Ah!—but God told him that the promised child would be a product of *his body*; nothing was said about Sarah's aging barren body. God said, the son "shall come forth out of *your own body*." These twisted interpretations of God's word lent credibility to Sarah's proposition, so when it was presented to him, his wife's novel notion seemed to confirm the word of God.

Not receiving any resistance from her husband against her plan, "Sarai, Abram's wife, took Hagar her maid the Egyptian, after Abram had dwelt ten years in the land of Canaan, and gave her to her husband Abram to be his wife." Moses' restating the names and status of the characters, makes it quite clear to the reader that there is no mistake concerning the people involved in this plot.

God wants us to see this clearly. Sarah and Abraham were married. Marriage was supposed to be between one man and one woman, as from creation it had been ordained by God. "Therefore shall a man leave his father and his mother, and shall cleave unto his wife: and they shall be one flesh" (Genesis 2:24). Jesus quoted this verse and added, "Wherefore they are no more twain, but one flesh. What therefore God hath joined together, let not man put asunder" (Matthew 19:6).

Therefore, we read the double declaration concerning who belonged to whom. Sarah belonged to her husband, and when that truth was ignored and Pharaoh took her to be his concubine, God made it very apparent to Pharaoh that he was violating God's order of things. And just the same, here in this part of the narrative, Sarah's husband also belongs to *her*, and so long as she was alive, *he* was not free to be given into the arms of another woman for any reason.

But expanding her knotty notion, Sarah came up with the idea that since Hagar belonged to her, Hagar might be considered an extension of herself. Using her imagination, "corporate" representation meant that Hagar, as Sarah's personal property, was expected to carry out Sarah's wishes without argument. When Hagar went on an errand for Sarah around the camp, she spoke with the authority of her mistress, as though she *were* Sarah. So far the scheme seemed unassailable in Sarah's mind.

But Hagar had to be Abraham's "wife" in order to "legally" have sexual relations with him (instead of committing adultery if they were not legally married). That was easily remedied. Sarah herself performed the "marriage" ceremony by taking Hagar to Abraham's tent and handing her property over to her husband. Her property was therefore considered as an extension of herself, and Abraham accepted Hagar as such, without objection.

After ten years living in the land of Canaan, the customs of the land were known to all of them. A surrogate mother was not a daring thought. The Canaanites and the Egyptians for some centuries had been practicing it as a means of dealing with a wife's infertility. They had even developed a "birthing stool" to carry out the fiction, making it seem real.

When the surrogate mother was ready to deliver the baby, the wife would sit on a low stool and the surrogate mother sat on the wife's lap. When the child was delivered by the midwife, the substitute moved out of the way and the baby was handed to the "real" wife. It was her child, received into her arms as soon as it was born. The surrogate mother became the child's wet-nurse, since the "mother" was incapable of suckling the infant. Through these fictions an infertile woman became a "mother."

"And he went in unto Hagar, and she conceived." Amazingly quick work! Just had to have the right, that is, a properly functioning piece of equipment. Nothing to it. Why hadn't they thought of this years ago? Surely now they had done all they could do on their part to produce the "promised" child. They were on their way to receiving all the blessings God had promised them.

Everyone seemed happy enough, except that when Hagar "saw that she had conceived, her mistress was despised in her eyes." Pride always comes creeping into the picture. Hagar now believed that she was ever so much better than her mistress, who could not have children, and in fact had spent all of her life trying and continually failed. But the Egyptian slave girl excelled where the honored mistress had failed, and even though she was a slave, her Egyptian pride swelled. She was pregnant with the master's heir and could lord the fact over her mistress.

Before this, Abraham paid very little attention to this young woman who lived in his wife's tent. But now that Hagar was pregnant with the master's child, she had status, she was noticed. She was no longer just a shadow slaving in the background, unseen and uncared about. Abraham treated her with kindness, and gave her proper attention due to the mother of his child. Hagar was assured of a special place in the family. No longer was she just a piece of property to her mistress. She was the mother of the heir of Abraham's vast wealthy estate! She was special and she would never be cast away. Hagar assumed that nothing but great things would ever happen to her.

15

Bitter Results of Unbelief

Genesis 16:4, 5

Yes, the birthing stool was a real obstetric tool. Archeologists have found many among Egyptian and Middle Eastern artifacts, and the process is well illustrated in Egyptian hieroglyphics.

Sarah was not the first, nor last, to use a surrogate mother. The idea of handing a servant girl to your husband occurs again later in the Genesis narrative. Jacob's two wives used their maids to control the affections of their husband. Barren Rachel gave her servant girl to Jacob saying, "Behold my maid Bilhah, go in unto her; and she shall bear upon my knees [using the birthing stool], that I may also have children by her" (Genesis 30:3). "Bear upon my knees" is referring to the method I described about the birthing stool.

I wholeheartedly agree with you. Why didn't Abraham ask the LORD what he should do concerning Hagar—*before* he got into it any deeper? It seems like falling to his knees in prayer would be the logical (and faithful) thing to do. Why accept Sarah's plan without even a whimper of an argument? It shows a weakness in Abraham.

Abraham could have said, Well now, dear, let us seek an answer from God before we rush into this thing with your servant girl. Let us get on our knees and pray about this first. It didn't have to be a nerve-racking experience, like the night of the fiery theophany. A simple prayer sent up in earnestness, would have surely brought an answer from the LORD, since this idea with Hagar was totally contrary to His plan for Abraham and Sarah as man and wife.

Abraham's actions indicate that he had abdicated his position as leader of the family. He surrendered his God-given male headship role to Sarah's opinion and argument. Instead of standing up to her as the husband, head of household, and priest of the family, and reminding her that the conception of a son was *God's* promise, and they needed to keep waiting on the LORD to fulfill His promise, Abraham just groveled in the dust and let Sarah have her way without any objection. Where was the man's faith? Where was his confidence in the God who made heaven and earth and all things in them, and as the Creator of all things, He was perfectly capable of producing a son from the reproductively dead body of Sarah.

But maybe there was a reason he kept silent. Maybe Abraham's grip on the headship role had been slipping for some time. Maybe Sarah was not such a sweet person as we tend to think. If we read a little farther in the narrative concerning Hagar's uppity attitude toward Sarah after she conceived, I think we can glean some insights into both Sarah's and Hagar's less-than-pleasant characters.

There is no more history on Hagar's background than what we find here in these chapters. Genesis 25:12 tells us definitely that she was an Egyptian. When Sarah was in Pharaoh's harem, he gave Sarah a young girl to be her maid, and when Abraham and Sarah were expelled after Abraham's lie was discovered, everything they had received from Pharaoh went with them back to Canaan, including this young girl as Sarah's servant (see Genesis 12:16). Except were Paul refers to Hagar in Galatians chapter 4, we only find her mentioned in the Genesis narrative in connection with Ishmael.

But it does seem a bit much to comprehend, that it was expected of a young woman to submit so totally to her mistress's demands as to allow her husband to impregnate her! How demeaning that would be. You were nothing by an unfeeling piece of flesh to be used any way your owners demanded. You, as an individual, had no say in the matter. When she knew she was pregnant, Hagar became insolent and perhaps even brazen toward her mistress. That would have been her way of retaliating. After all, what could Sarah do to her? Hagar was by fiat of her mistress, now Abraham's legal concubine, a real "second wife." She was the mother of the heir of the estate, and that fact gave her a high status and a certain amount of protection.

Or so she assumed.

But from the story we can see that Hagar's character was less than rosy sweetness. She submitted to Sarah's whim because she was a slave, but her attitude was not truly submissive. She had arrogance and bitterness in her nature.

Being an Egyptian, Hagar may have always harbored a resentful attitude of racial superiority over her mistress. Egyptians considered all sheep herders and nomads as lower class humans. The Egyptians had an advanced civilization long before Abraham's time, and considered themselves on an elevated plane intellectually and socially above all other peoples. The Egyptians were very clean people, bathing often, using perfume to disguise body odors, and wearing finely woven garments instead of woolen wraps like the shepherds. They had developed advanced weaving of the finest linen threads, to produce beautiful gossamer, lightweight clothing. Their homes were adobe brick, their furniture made from wood. They made paper from papyrus, had a written language, and compiled documents into books. Their kings' tombs were decorated with magnificent artworks. Their primary diet consisted of breads made from wheat and barley, vegetables, legumes, and eggs. Animal flesh made up a smaller portion of their daily intake. In all these things the Egyptians felt superior.

Everything about the Egyptian culture was contrary to the nomadic way of life. The nomads rarely bathed, wore heavier woolen clothing made from the fibers of their sheep and goats. Because they were an unsettled people, grains were a smaller part of their diet, which consisted mostly of legumes and small domestic animals. The rural Canaanites and other Bedouin people lived in leather tents and slept on the ground on piles of skins and woolen blankets. The smells of unwashed people and the constant musky scent of animals was an affront to the Egyptian's more refined sensibilities.

When Abraham lived, the Egyptians were in their twelfth dynasty. The great pyramid at Giza had been standing for more than five centuries by the time Abraham wandered down to Egypt to avoid the famine in Canaan. The Karnak temple complex at Luxor was already under construction at this time. There was much for Hagar to be haughty and bitter about as an Egyptian woman being forced to serve nomadic people that smelled constantly of their livestock!

If Abraham had shared with his immediate family group what God told him the night of the flaming theophany, then Hagar would have known that God prophesied that there would come a time when a powerful nation would enslave Abraham's descendants. It is not outlandish to consider that the implied nation was Egypt, which at that time was the largest, longest established, and most powerful nation in existence. What a turnabout! The Egyptian slave girl who is pregnant with the heir would be vindicated by her own native people enslaving those who had abused her. Is that poetic justice, or what?

"And when [Hagar] saw that she had conceived, her mistress was despised in her eyes." Perhaps Hagar showed her contempt through her uppity speech, or by insolently telling her mistress that she did not have to do what Sarah told her to do anymore; she was now Abraham's wife, too. However it was expressed, Sarah felt keenly the contempt shown to her by her pregnant handmaid.

And her attitude and complaint to her husband tells us much about Sarah's character. In angry tones she confronted poor Abraham about the problem *she* had caused herself, laying the blame at *his* feet. "My wrong be on thee: I have given my maid into thy bosom; and when she saw that she had conceived, I was despised in her eyes."

She said, "my wrong be on me," but she was not going to exonerate her husband from guilt. When she released Hagar into Abraham's tent, she also released control over her, so now Sarah could blame Abraham for Hagar's irreverent behavior toward her. Abraham had accepted the scheme without complaint or counsel concerning what might be the end result of this plan. He should have known better, and refused to participate, but he didn't, which made him equally complicit in the sin.

We can easily see that Sarah had a temper and maybe even a mean streak, if Hagar's response to it is any indication of the harshness of the mistreatment that was heaped on her head. The abuse must have been both psychological and physical. How Sarah treated Hagar doubtless had a corporal element to it; it had to have been much more severe than name-calling and yelling at her that caused pregnant Hagar to run off alone into the desert in order to escape the abuse.

16

The God Who Hears

Genesis 16:6-14

Sarai said unto Abram, My wrong be upon thee: I have given my maid into thy bosom; and when she saw that she had conceived, I was despised in her eyes: the LORD judge between me and thee."

As I mentioned yesterday, Sarah now blamed her husband for this problem of Hagar's insolence toward her mistress. While Sarah admitted that the original plan for Hagar to become the mother of Abraham's child was her idea, she is now making the complaint that the trouble in the family unit was Abraham's problem because he didn't adequately control Hagar's words and actions toward his lawful wife. Even though it was her big idea in the first place to bring a second woman into the marriage, Sarah now felt that she had lost her place as the supreme female in the clan, and that was intolerable to her.

"But Abram said unto Sarai, Behold, thy maid is in thy hand; do to her as it pleaseth thee." Abraham was not going to accept the blame for this problem, nor was he going to provide a remedy. He threw the problem back in Sarah's lap. You can just see him throwing up his hands at this point. What does this woman of mine want from me? I did what she asked me to do; I got the girl pregnant. And now I have to bear the curse of the problem caused by that? No! It is Sarah's problem; let her do what she wants about it.

"And Sarai dealt hardly [harshly] with her." The girl was now aggressively abused by Sarah, perhaps beaten for small infractions of acceptable behavior, and certainly verbally maligned. She had no rest from the maltreatment, as Sarah's anger and hatred toward her flared continually. Searing looks , sharp words, blows, all with Hagar as the target. Confined to Sarah's dwelling tent, there was no escape. Hagar was forced to continually serve her mistress's daily needs, and suffer abuse as well. No wonder that, "she fled from [Sarah's] face."

When Hagar ran, she went south following a road through the Negeb wilderness toward Egypt (Negeb means "the south"), the only place besides Hebron that Hagar was familiar with. She stopped at a spring between Kadesh and Bered. Kadesh was the same place where, 400 years later, the children of Israel were camped when the twelve spies returned from scoping out the Promised Land. It was here that Israel rebelled again against God, by rejecting the encouraging message of Caleb and Joshua that they "were well able" to take the land. Instead, the people believed the ten unfaithful spies who denied God's power to drive the native peoples from the land. From Kadesh, the children would wander for forty years, until every unbelieving Israelite over the age of 20 was dead and buried in the desert.

"And the Angel of the LORD found her by a fountain of water in the wilderness, by the fountain in the way to Shur." Shur means "wall" and this barrier was on the road to Egypt, so this definitely tells us that she was headed back to Egypt, to sanity and safety, as far as she was concerned. After about 8 or 10 hours walking from where Abraham had been camped at Mamre, she came to a natural spring ("fountain of water"). There she wearily sat down in the shade to rest. We know from her arrogance toward her mistress, that she was a self-willed and strong-headed young woman. She also had grit and determination to survive, or she never would have struck out on her own to return to Egypt.

In those days, a woman alone did not possess much chance for safety. The road was well-traveled by merchants taking their wares between the cities of the east and Egypt. She could have been captured by some of them and enslaved again, or worse. The area was not without wild predatory animals, like lions and bears, and she had no weapons or other means of protecting herself. If she thought that she had been vulnerable while living in Sarah's tent, out here in the wilderness she was completely insecure and friendless.

As she sat there, the day drew to a close. Perhaps she was pondering what the next few days would be like. Where would she get food? How many days would she have to walk before she got to Egyptian civilization? Should she hide if she saw a caravan coming? So many things she had not fully considered before she ran away.

Apparently, Abraham did not attempt to go after her personally, nor did he send any servant to find her. If someone had been sent to bring her back, they would have been riding a donkey and would quickly have overtaken her. But Abraham had handed off Hagar to Sarah to do with her as she would, and what Sarah did to her servant drove the girl away. So be it. That would bring an end to the household conflict.

And also an end to the "promised son." One wonders what Abraham thought about the loss of this son they had worked so hard to produce, and now he is gone before he is born.

As she sat there pondering her predicament, suddenly Hagar was confronted by the Angel of the LORD—pre-incarnate Christ again shows up in our narrative, interacting in a personal way with a lost and confused person. He came looking for this abused and discouraged young woman to bring her encouragement and hope.

Even then, Christ was the Good Shepherd who comes looking for His lost sheep, wherever she may have wandered. And He did not let her get too far down the road before He confronted her. If God had not intervened, Hagar probably would have made it all the way back to her homeland, and Abraham's first son would have been born illegitimately and into slavery, and as an Egyptian.

Hagar had been in an intimate relationship with Sarah for ten years. She would have heard Sarah and Abraham talking as they sat outside their tent in the cool of the day. She would have overheard many conversations that took place between her mistress and Abraham, which would have included discussions about God's plans for them; and included Abraham's stories about God's protection and guidance over the many years Abraham had been following Him. From these conversations between her mistress and Abraham, Hagar learned about the Living God who personally interacts with His people. She knew about the theophany in which God promised Abraham that He would give him land and a son to inherit it.

Thus, she was prepared by this knowledge to accept this Angel's appearance before her. She had learned that Abraham's God did things like this, it was nothing to be frightened about. Awestruck, but not frightened. Abraham's God was a beneficent and compassionate God.

"And [Christ] said, Hagar, Sarai's maid, where have you come from and where are you going?" Christ called her by her personal name, but He carried it further when He identified her specifically as Sarah's maid. By thus identifying her, though she had never seen Him before, Hagar was assured that the Angel knew exactly who He was talking to. He was personally acquainted with her. He was not a stranger come to harm her. And He was reminding her of her obligations toward her mistress—you are Sarah's maid, and you have run away from your responsibilities toward her.

Even though He already knew the answers, His questions about her intentions—where have you come from and where are you going—gave Hagar opportunity to speak for herself, to explain her actions and her plans for her future. By giving voice to her situation, she had to mentally assess its validity. By questioning her in this manner He was telling her, "Come, let us reason together" about the problem. Together we will find the answer. God wants to do the same for each of us in solving our problems.

"And she said, I flee from the face of my mistress Sarai." And she had nothing more to say about herself and her reasons for leaving. That was it ... I'm running away; that's all I can say about my situation. Interestingly, Hagar did not give the reason why she was running away from Sarah. No mention of the abuse she had received under Sarah's hand. Perhaps since this Angel stranger already knew her name and who she belonged to, He didn't need any explanation about why she left. But if He knew about Sarah's abuse, He would also know about her own bad attitude toward her mistress. Maybe it was best to just not mention any of that at all, and thereby avoid condemnation for *her* behavior that precipitated Sarah's attitude change toward her.

And Hagar didn't include an answer about what she contemplated for her future. In her haste to flee the abuse, she had made no plans. She could only state that she was running away from her mistress. So uncertain was her future, that she did not voice any plans, even for tomorrow. She just wanted to escape the abusive situation.

Like a small child who got spanked, making him mad enough to want leave the security of his home, he grabs his favorite toy and runs down the road as fast as he can. But it doesn't take a child long before he realizes that his decision to run didn't include any real idea about what life would be like on the street by himself. His loneliness quickly births doubt about his decision to run, which then begins to diminish the memory of the punishment he fled from. But how to return is a conundrum. Will he be in even more trouble if he returns home? Since he ran away from them, will his mother and father even want him anymore, or do they think "good riddance"? Depression easily follows in the tracks of loneliness.

"And the Angel of the LORD said unto her, Return to thy mistress, and submit thyself under her hands." Submission was something that had been hard for Hagar. She had served in Sarah's tent for ten years, and probably had not murmured or complained. She was young, probably barely a teenager when she had been given by Pharaoh as a servant to Sarah. She didn't really know much else than service. Stepping and fetching, yes ma'aming and no ma'aming was her way of life. But when given an opportunity to elevate her status as a concubine to the master of the estate, her natural pride came bursting forth. And that created problems for her. Submission was not in her plans.

But now comes a promise just like the one God gave to Abraham. "And the Angel of the LORD said unto her, I will multiply thy seed exceedingly, that it shall not be numbered for multitude." This was something Hagar had heard Abraham speak about concerning his own relationship with God. He had been promised, "I will make thy seed as the dust of the earth: so that if a man can number the dust of the earth, then shall thy seed be numbered" (Genesis 13:16). Since the promise was the same, Hagar thought that surely this meant that the son that had been promised to Abraham was the very one that she was pregnant with! She was indeed the mother of the promised heir!

Confirming her thought, "the Angel of the LORD said unto her, Behold, thou art with child, and shall bear a son, and shall call his name Ishmael; because the LORD has heard your affliction." The name God gave to this son of Abraham means "God hears."

"And she called the name of the LORD that spake unto her, 'You God, see me': for she said, Have I also here looked after Him that sees me? Wherefore the well was called Beer-lahai-roi"—literally, "the spring of the One who sees me."

From this last bit of information we learn that as Hagar sat there by the spring, she must have been praying for help from the God of Abraham. She "looked after Him" or sought Him. She did not know what to do, except that she could no longer take the abuse from Sarah.

She knew she was pregnant, but how to live as a single mother in an uncertain world, she did not have any answers to that. Evidently, in her heart, she must have called upon the name of the LORD, and He answered her by appearing before her with His instructions.

What an awesome God we worship! Hagar's pregnancy was not according to His divine plan for Abraham. What Sarah did in giving her maid to her husband for him to impregnate was a sin. Abraham's acceptance of Sarah's plan was also a sin. The poor girl caught in the middle was at first a victim, but she soon showed her sinful nature through her haughtiness and self-righteous attitude toward Sarah.

God did not condone any of these sins, but He did present a solution for the immediate problem. Go home, Hagar, back to your mistress, and submit yourself under her hand, even if it is not a pleasant relationship. By sending her back, God was promising to take care of her and protect her. The son would be born and she was to call his name "God hears." God hears and He answers our earnest prayers, even if we do not fully know Him. He is the God who is near to us, loving us and wanting to save us for His eternal kingdom.

17

Abraham's "Wild Man"

Genesis 16:11, 12

"He will be a wild man; his hand will be against every man, and every man's hand against him; and he shall dwell in the presence of all his brethren." (Genesis 16:12). As you already noted, Ishmael and all of his descendants would forever remain fiercely independent and running wild in the desert places. The Arab Bedouins are Ishmael's children, and their untamable nature is his legacy. Until the last hundred years, they had no interest in building cities or developing a civilization, but the wealth of oil has changed them—not psychologically or socially, but materially.

We read later (jumping ahead of our story here) that after Hagar and her son were banished forever from Abraham's family, "God was with the lad; and he grew, and dwelt in the wilderness, and became an archer." (Genesis 21:20). The "wilderness" is the Negev desert area toward Egypt. They "dwelt in the wilderness of Paran: and his mother took him a wife out of the land of Egypt." (Genesis 21:21). That Hagar was wealthy enough to get Ishmael a wife from Egypt, means that Abraham must have sent them away with sufficient property to be able to take good care of themselves. Abraham was generous with them even as they were exiled from his home. He probably even continued to know their whereabouts and how they were succeeding, because caravans would have brought him such information.

When Ishmael died, he was living in the area of south Canaan from "Shur down to Havilah," (Genesis 25:18) which is the name for the upper Arabian Peninsula. Why they never went all the way back to Egypt is not stated. But Hagar and Ishmael must have kept some type of association with their Egyptian side of the family for her to be able to find her son an Egyptian wife.

That Ishmael married an Egyptian woman means that all of his sons were three-quarter Egyptian. Another interesting point concerning Ishmael and his descendants is that they are mentioned right through the Genesis narrative where we find them called both Ishmaelites and Midianites, being merchants between the cities of the East and Egypt. Esau married Ishmael's daughters (Genesis 28:9; 36:3), which tied Ishmael back to Abraham through the tribe known as the Edomites, making them Abraham's great-grandchildren.

It is significant that the Bible tells us that "Abram was fourscore and six years old, when Hagar bare Ishmael to Abram." (Genesis 16:16). This means that Hagar's son was born within the year after the promise of God in chapter 15.

Three times God promised Abraham that He would do a great thing for him, and that promise included, or more properly, necessitated Abraham having a son. When nothing had happened for ten years after the promise was first given, both Abraham and Sarah decided that it must mean that the problem was left up to them to solve. Without inquiring of God if their plan was permissible, they proceeded, and it caused a disaster.

Actually, it is a "disaster" that has continued to unfold for four millennia. A great deal of history hinges on this wrong choice made by Abraham and Sarah to "help" God fulfill His promise to them. Without Ishmael there would have been no Islam. Without Islam, the world's history would have unfolded in an entirely different manner. There are both positives and negatives brought into the world through Ishmael's children.

What we most often do not realize is that without Islam there are numerous things that would not be, including stylized calligraphy and illuminated book pages, algebra, trigonometry and our Arabic numerals. Advances in astronomy, and other physical sciences can be attributed to Muslims. Without their mathematics, we'd still be using Roman numerals, and an Akkadian abacus for our accounting.

Islam is responsible for many medical and surgical advances made during the Dark Ages, a time when the Roman Catholic Church suppressed any learning that was not affirmed by Rome. The Catholic heathcare system was based on superstition and a type of magic to treat diseases. However, from the seventh to the twelfth centuries, the Muslims became advanced in their scientific healthcare methods and taught them in their colleges in Spain, where these methods had a strong influence in the rest of Europe.

Except for Islam's presence in Spain with its emphasis on higher learning through Islamic Madrashas where literature, science, and the arts were taught, the European Renaissance would never have gotten its start. Without the Renaissance, there would be no Michelangelo's Pieta or statue of David, nor da Vinci's Mona Lisa. The Dark Ages would have continued for many more years if Islam's higher education centers had not existed in Spain through which their advanced learning was spread to the rest of Europe.

Neither would we have had those beautiful domed and round-arched buildings in Spain covered in mosaics, or today's hang gliders (created by a Muslim inventor in the ninth century), the game of chess, petroleum and alcohol distillation (learned from the Chinese and brought to Europe by the Muslims).

Neither would there have been any crusades to rescue Jerusalem from the "infidels," nor the Iranian Revolution, nor "9-11" (which we certainly could have done without!), nor the never-ending war in Afghanistan, etc., etc. History would be entirely different if Ishmael had never been born.

We have examined the social and psychological issues in these chapters, but we have not talked about the most important aspect of the narrative: the spiritual meaning of what took place in Genesis chapter sixteen.

Man's Efforts to Fulfill God's Promise is the "Old Covenant"

When Abraham allowed Sarah's plan to overrule his faith in God, Abraham and Sarah both succumbed to an old covenant idea about God. There is a lot of confusion about what the "old covenant" really means—but it *does not* mean "Old Testament." The "old covenant" idea is simple to understand because, in reality, it is any thing that man thinks he can dream up to augment or help to fulfill the promise that God gave first to Adam, then to Noah, and to Abraham. The often heard adage, "God helps those who help themselves" is a prime example of the pervasiveness of the old covenant attitude.

However, Genesis 15 made it perfectly clear that God and God alone will fulfill the everlasting covenant. All Abraham (and anyone else) had to do was believe the word of God, and patiently wait for Him to do what He promised He would. Abraham and Sarah's impatience perhaps is understandable after the promise went so long a time unfulfilled. Nevertheless, their impatience was the result of a lack of faith in God's word, and that slip in faith led them to commit sin, all the while thinking they were doing God's will in fulfilling the promise by producing an heir through Hagar.

We find a clear discussion of this in Paul's letter to the Galatians. Paul stated that "these two woman *are the two covenants*" (Galatians 4:24, emphasis supplied).[1] Hagar "gendered to bondage" that is, gives birth to spiritual slavery, the bondage of sin. While Sarah points us to freedom from bondage and the New Jerusalem, where the faithful will dwell for eternity.

In Paul's analogy, Hagar symbolizes unbelief and the old covenant, and in contrast, (eventually, after twenty-five years of unbelief) Sarah represents how to live by faith in God. When Sarah's faith education was finally complete, it resulted in the promised son, through whom the real Promised Son—God's Lamb foreordained from the foundation of the world—who would come "in the fullness of time" to bless the world through His sacrifice for the sins of the whole human race.[2]

The fact of the matter in the narrative of Genesis 16 is that Abraham and Sarah rashly undertook for themselves the work of fulfilling the

---

1. "For it is written that Abraham had two sons, one by a slave and the other by a free woman. But the one by the slave was born according to the impulse of the flesh, while the one by the free woman was born as the result of a promise. These things are illustrations, for the women represent the two covenants. One is from Mount Sinai and bears children into slavery—this is Hagar. Now Hagar is Mount Sinai in Arabia and corresponds to the present [earthly] Jerusalem, for she is in [spiritual] slavery with her children. But the Jerusalem above [the heavenly] is free, and she is our mother." (Galatians 4:22-26, HCSB).

2. "But when the fulness of the time was come, God sent forth His Son, made of a woman, made under the law, to redeem them that were under the law, that we might receive the adoption of sons." (Galatians 4:4, 5). "The next day John saw Jesus coming unto him, and said, 'Behold the Lamb of God, who takes away the sin of the world.'" (John 1:29). "Who verily was foreordained before the foundation of the world, but was manifest in these last times for you" (1 Peter 1:20; cf. Hebrews 4:3; Revelation 13:8).

promise, using their own ingenuity and self-sufficiency. By thinking that they could, of *themselves*, work out a plan that would satisfy God's promise, they left God out of the picture. They assumed that *they had power within themselves*, or available to them though Hagar, and didn't need God's strength to overcome their seventy years of sexual impotence. They could use man's methods and overcome the problem through a surrogate mother.

When they did this, they entered into the sin of unbelief and fell into an old covenant plan to accomplish God's promise all by themselves. The next chapter tells us what God thought of that plan.

18

Persistent Love

Genesis 17:1-6

With you, we cannot condone the widely held American attitude toward "all things Muslim." I have friends who harbor the same feelings toward a Muslim that they assume all Muslims hold against Americans—kill them first, "they don't deserve to live!" All Muslims are jihadists!

But if our Constitutional rights mean anything, then peaceable Muslims living in this country, born in this great nation of ours, who want to practice their religion, should be allowed to do so, *provided* that their practice does not infringe upon anyone *else's* freedom to worship as they please, or violate any individual's personal freedom to choose how they will live in our society. Muslims must be accorded the same First Amendment rights as the Baptists, Methodists, Lutherans, Pentecostals, Catholics, Jews, Jehovah's Witnesses, Mormons, and any other religion.

As a national or state government, if we deny *any* religion, church, or faith their Constitutional freedoms, then we are building a precedent under which *anyone* can have their rights denied at the stroke of a pen. And that is a very dangerous precedent that will play itself out in the fulfillment of Revelation 13. Oppression will be the sure result of such an action taken on the part of our government.

There are certain organizations in America that are seeking to establish our nation as a government supported "Christian nation." While they are concerned about the rapid expansion of paganism, and legislation promoting immorality that is being passed in some states, their methods will eventually destroy the First Amendment that prohibits the "establishment" of any one particular faith.

Genesis 17:1-6

"And Abram was ninety years old and nine" (Genesis 17:1). Thirteen years have passed since the birth of Ishmael. Evidently, striving to anticipate God's promises through human ingenuity, retarded instead of accelerated the divine purpose. Abraham and Sarah are no closer than before to the fulfillment of the promise. Sarah remains as barren as ever, and is now eighty-nine years old. Hagar has probably been removed to her own tent with her child, and a new maid brought in for Sarah's comfort in her old age.

Since no other place has been named in the continuing narrative, it seems that Abraham has remained in the same area of Hebron, near Mamre, for about 15 years. Though still dwelling in leather tents, they are no longer living the nomadic lifestyle. Everyone living in the area knows Abraham and his tribe as a quiet and peaceable group of people. Let us not forget—there are many hundreds people of all ages living in Abraham's extended family, that includes servants, shepherds and herdsmen, and their wives and children.

Our Persistent and Loving God

"And the LORD appeared to Abram, and said unto him, I am the Almighty God; walk before Me, and be thou perfect." I have never had God talk to me face to face, but I have had Him talk to me through His written Word. And He told me the same thing—"Walk before Me and be perfect." God's Gospel has not changed from Adam's day, through Noah, Abraham, and all the way down to our day. His desire is that His people will heed His call to "walk before Me," and if we always keep in mind that God is before us, leading us in "paths of righteousness," then how can we find it difficult to follow the "Lamb whithersoever He goeth"? (Psalm 23:3; Revelation 14:4).

Enoch "walked with God" in a world that was more wicked than our present world. It was shortly afterward destroyed by the worldwide Flood. Therefore, Enoch gave us the example of God's power to preserve His people amid prevailing sin, and to translate us out of the world controlled by sin, which is soon to take place at His second coming. Jesus' commandment "be ye perfect" [1] is not an impossibility. Our loving God would never ask us to do something that He did not also give us the power to accomplish.

God promised us, "I will instruct thee and teach thee in the way which thou shalt go: I will guide thee with Mine eye." (Psalm 32:8). "Thus saith the LORD, thy Redeemer, the Holy One of Israel; I am the LORD thy God who teaches thee to profit, who leads thee by the way that thou should go." (Isaiah 48:17).

Jesus taught us to "enter into the strait [narrow] gate, because wide is the gate and broad is the way that leads to destruction, and many go in that way" (Matthew 7:13). The way to sin is wide open, and many (most) people choose to take that path, to enjoy the "sins for a season." But it is the path to eternal destruction.

However, there is to be a distinction between those who "work evil continually" and God's people who have learned righteousness by the faith of Jesus Christ. God's people are supposed to be "peculiar" or *unlike* those around them in the world (Titus 2:14; 1 Peter 2:9). We will be thought "peculiar" only because we do not fit secular society's idea of "normal." The Bible teaches us that "whosoever is born of God does not commit sin; for His Seed remains in him: and he cannot sin, because he is born of God. ... We know that whosoever is born of God sins not; but he that is begotten of God keeps himself [through the faith *of* Christ [2]], and that wicked one touches him not." (1 John 3:9 and 5:18).

Even knowing this truth, as you commented, we often find ourselves wandering off the path into sin all the time, and wonder, "Why?" But it is not necessary for us to wander off into the wrong path. Freedom of choice doesn't mean that we have to make the *wrong* choice!

---

1. Jesus commanded us: "Be ye therefore perfect, even as your Father which is in heaven is perfect." (Matthew 5:48). "The disciple is not above his Master: but every one that is perfect shall be as his Master." (Luke 6:40). "Be perfect, be of good comfort, be of one mind, live in peace; and the God of love and peace shall be with you." (2 Corinthians 13:11).

2. "Knowing that a man is not justified by the works of the law, but *by the faith of Jesus Christ*, even we have believed in Jesus Christ, that we might be justified *by the faith of Christ*, and not by the works of the law: for by the works of the law shall no flesh be justified. ... I am crucified with Christ: nevertheless I live; yet not I, but Christ lives in me: and the life which I now live in the flesh I live *by the faith of the Son of God*, who loved me, and gave Himself for me." (Galatians 2:16, 20). It is Christ's gift of the full measure of *His faith* working in us that will perfect our characters (Romans 12:3).

In the Bible we have so many promises concerning overcoming sin through the power of God—but, like Abraham, we have to *believe* God's promise to us before He can do what He wants to do in our lives. Unbelief was Abraham and Sarah's stumblingstone, and so it is for us today. We just continually choose to *not* believe the Word of God, when in reality, it is just as easy to believe, as it is to *not* believe.

Making the choice is simple; one choice is as easy as the other for us to make. The motive behind the choice is the problem. Do we want to serve God or our own desires? That's what we really have to decide. When we choose to follow a path of sin, we are struggling all the way *against* the wooing power of God's love that is calling us to righteousness. Sinning is in reality *harder* than believing.

And so God came to Abraham yet again, and gave him the same promise: "I will make My covenant between Me and thee, and will multiply thee exceedingly." And then Abraham did the only appropriate thing: he "fell on his face" in worship of the *El Shaddai*, the LORD God Almighty, who is powerful enough to do anything—except stomp on our free will and force us to believe in Him and obey Him out of fear of eternal torment or hope of heavenly reward. Those motivations are not from the God of heaven, but are instilled by Satan into our unconverted hearts, so that he can attempt to convince us that God has an angry, violent nature. However, the true God of the Bible does not work through coercion or fear of punishment. His only *modus operandi* is everlasting love which draws the sinner to Him.

Patiently, "God talked with [Abraham], saying, As for Me, behold, My covenant is with thee, and thou shalt be a father of many nations." (Genesis 17:2-4). Listen to Me, Abraham. This is not a new thing I am telling you, but so far you have not believed My words, no matter what I have done to show you My strength. You are still bound by your own ideas concerning how you will become the "father of many nations." When you finally learn to give up on yourself, to give up your old covenant ideas, then you will be ready for Me to do My work in you. Self must die, Abraham, then I can resurrect you to new life.

To emphasize God's point once again He said, I am giving you a new name. "Neither shall thy name any more be called Abram, but thy name shall be Abraham; for a father of many nations have I made thee. And I will make thee exceeding fruitful, and I will make nations of thee, and kings shall come out of thee." (Genesis 17:5, 6).

Abram, you have been known all of your life as "the exalted *father*" even though you had no children. That name was given to you by your parents in their expectations of what you would become. You have been a good "father" to the many children born into your clan—to your servants and pasture-hands—all have looked up to you as their trusted spiritual leader, temporal provider, and protector.

But God told him, I am naming you "Abraham," that is, "the father of a multitude." A *real* multitude, more than you could ever number. I alone have the power and authority as your heavenly Father to change your name, and your new name reflects My expectation of what you will become though Me. I *"have made* thee*"*—I *have already done it,* Abraham. If you simply will believe My Word to you, then what I *have already* said will be true in your life. My promise is as good as done, except your unbelief is standing in the way of its fulfillment.

Patiently, ever so perseveringly patient, God repeated His promise. We learn here that God never gives up on us no matter how we resist His will. He just keeps knocking on our head and heart, trying to get our attention, to wake us out of our spiritual stupor caused by our love of self. When we finally learn that "self" is the roadblock to faith, then the door opens wide to God's transforming power.

Faith is not a mental consent to a set of ideas, or philosophy, or a list of rules. Faith is *believing* the Word only, that the Word will do exactly what He says He will do.[3] This faith is what made the lame walk, the blind see, the insane rational again, and the lepers to be cleansed from their destructive disease. It even raised the dead to life again. Jesus raised the daughter of the ruler of a synagogue who believed the Word would do what He said. The Word also raised the son of a widow,[4] and one of His own best friends.

When Martha and others who were mourning at Lazarus's grave complained about the stench that would be relased when Jesus told

---

3. "The centurion answered and said, Lord, I am not worthy that you should come under my roof: but *speak the word only*, and my servant shall be healed." (Matthew 8:8).

4. "Now when He came nigh to the gate of the city, behold, there was a dead man carried out, the only son of his mother, and she was a widow: and much people of the city was with her. And when the Lord saw her, He had compassion on her, and said unto her, Weep not. And He came and touched the bier: and they that bare him stood still. And He said, Young man, I say unto thee, Arise. And he that was dead sat up, and began to speak. And He delivered him to his mother." (Luke 7:12-15).

them to roll away the stone that sealed the tomb, He said to them, "Said I not unto you, that *if you would believe*, you should see the glory of God?" (John 11:40). *Unbelief* is the barrier that prevents God from doing what He wants in transforming our lives, and prevents us from seeing the manifestation of the glory of God in our own personal experience.

It is what Abraham and Sarah had not quite gotten figured out yet, and it hindered God's full and complete work in them and for them. And so God continued to work with them, patiently reaching down to them where they were mired in their unbelief, seeking to bring them up and stand them upon the Rock of faith.[5]

---

5. "He brought me up also out of an horrible pit, out of the miry clay, and set my feet upon the Rock, and established my goings. And He hath put a new song in my mouth, even praise unto our God: many shall see it, and fear, and shall trust in the LORD." (Psalm 40:2, 3).

19

Works of the Flesh Must Be Cut Off

Genesis 17:7-14

"And I will establish My covenant between Me and thee and thy seed after thee in their generations for an everlasting covenant, to be a God unto thee, and to thy seed after thee." (Genesis 17:7). The first part of God's everlasting covenant concerns worship of the Creator—"I will be your God"—meaning: you shall have no other gods before Me. I AM the true God who alone is able to take care of you and save you (Exodus 20:2, 3).

"And I will give unto thee, and to thy seed after thee, the land wherein thou art a stranger" [cf. Hebrews 11:13, 14 [1]], "and I will be their God." (Genesis 17:8). This is a repeat of the same covenant given in 13:15 and 15:7. It is not a different covenant at all, as many want to claim. The only way for this "land" to be "an everlasting possession" is if what is being spoken of here, is the *new earth* where we will live for eternity—everlasting life is necessary for "everlasting possession." The "everlasting possession" does not mean anything in this temporal world full of sin.

"And God said unto Abraham, Thou shalt keep My covenant therefore, thou, and thy seed after thee in their generations. This is My covenant, which ye shall keep, between Me and you and thy seed

---

1. "These all died in faith without having received the promises, but they saw them from a distance, greeted them, and confessed that they were foreigners and temporary residents on the earth. ... But they now desire a better place—a heavenly one. Therefore God is not ashamed to be called their God, for He has prepared a city for them." (Hebrews 11:13, 16, HCSB).

after thee; Every man child among you shall be circumcised. And ye shall circumcise the flesh of your foreskin; and it shall be a *token of the covenant* betwixt Me and you" (17:10, 11). The rite of circumcision was a "token" or symbol. It was not the covenant. Circumcision was given *after* the covenant was given to Abraham nearly 25 years before.

What then, was the reason God gave the symbol of circumcision? The Bible tells us. "He is not a Jew, which is one outwardly; neither is that circumcision, which is outward in the flesh; but he is a Jew, which is one inwardly; and *circumcision is that of the heart*, in the Spirit, and not in the letter; whose praise is not of men, but of God." (Romans 2:28, 29, emphasis supplied). True "circumcision" must be of a converted heart that is willingly submissive to God, the lusts of the flesh having been "cut off" through faith.[2]

In chapter 15 we read that Abraham "believed God and it was counted unto him for righteousness." But shortly after that, in chapter 16 we find that he listened to the voice of Sarah instead of to God. Listening to his unbelieving wife, he sought to fulfil the promise of God by the power of his own flesh. The result was a failure—a bond-servant instead of an heir (see Galatians 4:24, 25).

Then God appeared to him again after thirteen more barren years, exhorting Abraham to walk before Him with singleness of heart, and then He repeated His covenant (Genesis 17:1–8). The addition of circumcision was to forever remind Abraham and his descendants of his utter failure in striving to produce the promised heir through the "works of the flesh." Cutting off the flesh by circumcision demonstrated the fact that "the flesh profiteth nothing" (John 6:63).

Because Abraham attempted to fulfill God's promise through the "works of the flesh," God instituted a "cutting of the flesh" to show that in the flesh "dwelleth no good thing" (Romans 7:18).

Outward circumcision was never anything more than a sign of the real circumcision of the heart; when this was absent, the sign was a fraud. But when the real circumcision of the heart was present, the sign could be dispensed with. Abraham is "the father of all them that believe, though they be not circumcised" (Romans 4:11). The

---

2. "For everything that belongs to the world—the lust of the flesh, the lust of the eyes, and the pride in one's lifestyle—is not from the Father, but is from the world. And the world with its lust is passing away, but the one who does God's will remains forever. (1 John 2:16, 17, HCSB).

"false brethren" who visited the church at Antioch (see Acts 15:1, 24 ff)[3], subverting the thinking of the disciples, and those of the same class who afterwards troubled the Galatians (Galatians 2:4)[4], were perverting the Gospel of Christ by insisting on substituting the empty sign for the reality.

"Works" were for them supreme in the process of "obtaining" righteousness, "obtaining" being the operative word here. Ever seeking how to add more "good works" to their stack, the Pharisees asked Jesus, "What shall we do that *we might work the works of God*?" (John 6:28, emphasis supplied). What can *we do* to accomplish our salvation and gain heaven? Jesus' answer completely befuddled them. "And Jesus answered them, "This is *the work of God*, that ye believe on Him whom He has sent" (John 6:29).

Then Jesus explained to those cavilers that He was the Bread of Life, and the only source of salvation. Their response was, "This is a hard saying, who can hear it [or believe it]?" (John 6:60). And "from that time many of His disciples turned back, and walked no more with Him" (vs. 66). They could not accept that righteousness is the gift of Christ, freely given to all. Like the majority of humanity, they spurned this gift and threw it away through their persistent unbelief.

Salvation is not accomplished by us "playing our part" in doing the "works of the law," no matter how "good" that "work" appears to be. So many have a hard time accepting this glorious truth because they want to be a partner *with* God in their salvation, even if that "part" is a tiny percentage they refer to as "my faith."[5]

If anything we did earned merit or credit with God toward getting us into heaven, then when we got to the pearly gate, we would be able to boast of those merits, and claim that we "earned our right" to sit

---

3. "And certain men which came down from Judaea taught the brethren, and said, Except ye be circumcised after the manner of Moses, ye cannot be saved. ... Forasmuch as we have heard, that certain which went out from us have troubled you with words, subverting your souls, saying, Ye must be circumcised, and keep the law: to whom we gave no such commandment." (Acts 15:1, 24).

4. "And that because of false brethren unawares brought in, who came in privily to spy out our liberty which we have in Christ Jesus, that they might bring us into bondage" [to the "works of the flesh"—the old covenant of man seeking to do the work of God in his own power]. Galatians 2:4).

5. Even our faith is a gift from God. Romans 12:3 tells us that "God *has given* to every man *the* measure of faith"—the *full measure* of Christ's *own* faith. We are free to exercise that faith to the transformation of our characters, or we can throw it away.

down with Christ at the marriage supper of the Lamb. However, this is totally contrary to everything the Bible teaches about salvation.

In Matthew 22:1-14, Jesus presents the parable of the wedding feast of the great King. Many were bidden to come to the feast, but most refused the gift, "making light of it and going their way." To attend this wedding feast, the individual had to be wearing the garment given to them by the king. But there was one who slipped into the banquet hall without the special garment. He was brought before the king and asked why he did not have on the proper garment, and "he was speechless." That man, thinking that he should be accepted on his own merit, was "cast into outer darkness" because of his unbelief.

The apostle Paul taught everywhere he went that the promises of God can be realized only by putting off the "body" of the sins of the flesh, through the Holy Spirit's work in our lives. "Knowing this, that our old man is crucified with Him, that the body of sin might be destroyed, that henceforth we should not serve sin" (Romans 6:6). "For they that are after the flesh do mind the things of the flesh; but they that are of the Spirit, the things of the Spirit" (Romans 8:5).

"For *we are* the circumcision, which *worship God in the Spirit*, and rejoice in Christ Jesus, and have no confidence in the flesh" (Philippians 3:3, emphasis supplied). Here Paul is telling his listeners that even though he was "of the circumcision"—a Jew who had all his life followed the "letter the law"—yet he now had *no confidence* in the "works" of the flesh. When faith came into his heart, the works of the flesh were seen for what they really are: a total *lack* of faith in God's power to transform our characters and save us from sin. The "works of the flesh" are our attempts to help God "save us" by accumulating "merit" through the "good things" we do—a purely legalistic approach to "salvation." This is the very basis of all pagan religions.

The man who had circumcision in the flesh only, but did not have faith in Christ as his Saviour from sin, was reckoned by the Lord as uncircumcised, becasue there was no change of the rebellious heart. Such persons "gloried" or boasted in the "works of the flesh" and, like the Pharisees who boasted of their ability to keep the law and yet denied the cross of Christ, they "were cast off." To be saved, all must be grafted into the Vine (John 15:1-6), both Jew and "Gentile." The "vine" is not Israel or any descendant of Abraham, literal or spiritual. The Vine is Jesus Christ, and life comes only from our connection to Him.

Here are a few verses, all written concerning the fact that there is no difference between Jews and Gentiles, as far as God is concerned. These verses are addressing the "universal" application of the Gospel's message that is to be preached to the whole world with a loud voice.[6] No one is "more special" in the eyes of God; genealogy and racial or family heritage mean nothing at all to God. All stand equal before Him only when we're humbled at the foot of the cross.

"Not as though the word of God has taken none effect. For they are not all Israel, which are *of* Israel [the literal descendants of Jacob]: neither, because they are the seed of Abraham, are they all children [of God]: but, In Isaac shall thy seed be called [because Isaac was born when Abraham's faith in God's power was mature]. That is, They which are the children of the flesh [literal descendants, as well as those who rely on "works" to contribute to their salvation], these are not the children of God: but the children of the *promise* are counted for the seed." (Romans 9:6-8). The "promise" is the the promise of "faith" that Abraham finally realized. Genealogy does not save anyone. Only the faith *of* Christ working in us will save us and give us eternal life.

"What shall we say then? That the Gentiles, which followed not after righteousness, have attained to righteousness, even the righteousness which is of faith. But Israel [literal Jews as a race of people], which followed after the law of righteousness, has not attained to the law of righteousness. Wherefore? *Because they sought it not by faith*, but as it were by the works of the law. For they stumbled at that Stumblingstone; as it is written, Behold, I lay in Sion a Stumblingstone and Rock of offence: and whosoever believeth on Him shall not be ashamed." (Romans 9:30-33, emphasis supplied). In the days of Christ and the apostle Paul, "Israel" and Gentiles alike, just as they continue to do now, seek righteousness through their own works. But without believing in the faith of Jesus Christ, there is no salvation.

"Brethren, my heart's desire and prayer to God for Israel is, that they might be saved [Paul is speaking here of the Jewish race, his own ancestors]. For I bear them record that they have a zeal of God,

---

6. "And I saw another angel fly in the midst of heaven, having the everlasting gospel to preach unto them that dwell on the earth, and to every nation, and kindred, and tongue, and people, Saying with a loud voice, Fear God, and give glory to Him; for the hour of His judgment is come: and worship Him that made heaven, and earth, and the sea, and the fountains of waters." (Revelation 14:6, 7).

but not according to knowledge. For they being ignorant of God's righteousness, and going about to establish their own righteousness, have not submitted themselves unto the righteousness of God." (Romans 10:1-3). Without faith in Christ, the Jews have no special "election," but are "cut off" from the Vine and are withering away in their faithless legalism.

"Thou wilt say then, The branches were broken off, that I might be grafted in. Well, *because of unbelief they were broken off*, and thou standest by faith. Be not highminded, but fear: for if God spared not the natural branches ["natural" descendants of Abraham, the unbelieving Jews], take heed lest He also spare not thee. Behold therefore the goodness and severity of God: on them which fell, severity; but toward thee, goodness, if thou continue in His goodness: otherwise thou also shalt be cut off. And they also, if they abide not still in unbelief, *shall be grafted in*: for God is able to graft them in again." (Romans 11:19-23). Through faith in Christ as their Saviour all persons, Jew and Gentile, can be "grafted into" Jesus, who is the true Vine, and from the "sap" of that Vine all will have eternal life.

The fact is, God broke down the "partition wall" between Jews and Gentiles by the death of His Son, and He never intended that any distinction should exist after "the Seed should come to whom the promise was made." That "seed" is Christ (Galatians 3:16).[7] Christ, says the apostle Paul to the Ephesians (2:14), "is our peace, who hath made both one, [Jews and Gentiles] and hath broken down the middle wall of partition." If there is a distinction between Jew and Christian, it is a distinction made by human invention and unbelief, not by God, who is "no respecter of persons" (Acts 10:34).

Enough of this sidetrack about circumcision not being part of salvation, either for ancient Israel, the Jews of Jesus' day, or the modern political/social Israel. We have seen in reading these verses that genealogy does not make anyone "specially elected of God." The "elect" are found only in Christ, and that is "by grace through faith" (Ephesians 2:8). Let's get back to the narrative in Genesis 17.

"And he that is eight days old shall be circumcised among you, every man child in your generations, he that is born in the house,

---

7. "Now to Abraham and his seed were the promises made. He saith not, And to *seeds*, as of many; but as of one, And to thy *Seed*, which is Christ." (Galatians 3:16, emphasis supplied).

or bought with money of any stranger, which is not of thy seed. He that is born in thy house, and he that is bought with thy money, must needs be circumcised" (Genesis 17:12, 13). The "eighth day" element of this commandment shows the wisdom of our Almighty Creator God. Science has proven that circumcision on the eighth day of life is the medically best time. At that point, the baby's body is producing clotting factors that prevent excessive bleeding, and discomfort to the infant is minimal.

The point God is making here concerning all who dwelt with Abraham, is that there is no distinction between "Jews" [8] and "Gentiles" who came into Abraham's camp either through purchase as slaves or born to servants already in Abraham's camp. Just as Paul would later write there is "neither Jew nor Gentile" for "all are one in Christ Jesus, and if ye be Christ's, then are ye Abraham's seed and heirs according to the promise" (Galatians 3:28, 29), God was here in Genesis 17 telling Abraham not to make a distinction between his own children and those that came to live with him. God views them all alike "in Christ."

Returning to the definition of circumcision, God went on, "My covenant shall be *in your flesh* for an everlasting covenant," to forever remind you that your "works of the flesh" will not accomplish anything except heaping up more unbelief concerning My power to do what I say I will do.

Focusing on our "good works" keeps us looking at ourselves and not looking at God who alone can save us from sin, give us the eternal treasure of Christ's righteousness, and finally restore our inheritance that was lost "in Adam" when he fell, i.e., the whole earth made new. Without recognizing this fact, and attempting to live a "righteous life" without faith, whether or not circumcised in the flesh, "that soul shall be cut off from his people; he hath broken My covenant" (Genesis 17:14). The everlasting covenant is based on God's grace and Jesus' faith, not "faith *plus* works" or "faith plus" our human efforts, or "faith plus" the sacraments of the church or prescribed acts of penance.

Unbelief is "breaking" the covenant of promise that God gave to all of humanity (Genesis 3:15). In that first statement of His promise,

---

8. Technically speaking, "Jews" didn't exist at this point in the Biblical narrative, and the term does not apply to Abraham. Isaac had not yet been born, and the name Jew was not used of this ethnic group until after their return from Babylonian captivity, when they were known as the people from Judah—"the Jews."

the declaration of God's everlasting covenant, God said that *He* would transform our heart of unbelief into a heart of appreciation and love for Him. *He* would change the enmity [hatred] toward God that Satan instilled in Adam and Eve's hearts, that has been passed down to us all through our fallen nature, into hatred for sin and Satan.

Unbelief is "breaking the covenant" because it prevents God from accomplishing what He wants to do in our lives. Unbelief in God's promise to place hatred for sin in our hearts is what will cause people to end up in the lake of fire and be eternally destroyed.

Unbelief is the "unforgivable sin" because God cannot get through the barrier erected by it. The barrier of unbelief is what prevents the Holy Spirit from doing His work in convicting us of sin, of bringing us into righteousness, so that we may stand uncondemned—naked and unashamed—before our holy God in the final judgment.[9]

---

9. "Because thou sayest, I am rich, and increased with goods, and have need of nothing; and knowest not that thou art wretched, and miserable, and poor, and blind, and naked: I counsel thee to buy of Me gold tried in the fire, that thou mayest be rich; and white raiment, that thou mayest be clothed, and that the shame of thy nakedness do not appear; and anoint thine eyes with eyesalve, that thou mayest see. As many as I love, I rebuke and chasten: be zealous therefore, and repent." (Revelation 3:17-19).

20

Abraham Laughed

Genesis 17:15-22

Yes, it is awesome indeed that we are all called "children of God," adopted from the foundation of the world by the mighty Monarch of the universe, Who knows us personally, knows every hair on our head (Matthew 10:30), and is acquainted with our every experience. For this reason, Jesus became one with the human race, so that He was qualified through His experience to become our great High Priest in the heavenly sanctuary.[1] Jesus Christ gave up all of His heavenly glory to be our Redeemer.[2] If we could get a grip on how much God loves us and how much was given to redeem us from sin, then we might better understand the Gospel's message of righteousness by faith.

God knews us intimately: "You have known my reproach, and my shame, and my dishonour: my adversaries are all before You." (Psalm 69:19). "You know my downsitting and my uprising, You understand my thoughts afar off." (Psalm 139:2).

---

1. "For verily He took not on Him the nature of angels; but He took on Him the seed of Abraham. Wherefore in all things it behoved Him to be made like unto His brethren, that He might be a merciful and faithful high priest in things pertaining to God, to make reconciliation for the sins of the people." (Hebrews 2:16, 17).

2. Christ Jesus, "Who, being in the form of God [having the same nature as God], thought it not robbery to be equal with God [because He is God]: but made Himself of no reputation, and took upon Him the form of a servant, and was made in the likeness ["sameness"] of men: and being found in fashion as a man, He humbled Himself, and became obedient unto death, even the death of the cross." (Philippians 2:5-8).

"According as He hath chosen us *in Him* before the foundation of the world, that we should be holy and without blame before Him in love: having predestinated us unto the adoption of children by Jesus Christ to Himself, according to the good pleasure of His will" (Ephesians 1:4, 5, emphasis supplied). "For ye have not received the spirit of bondage again to fear; but ye have received the Spirit of adoption, whereby we cry, Abba, Father. The Spirit itself beareth witness with our spirit, that we are the children of God: and if children, then heirs; heirs of God, and joint-heirs with Christ" (Romans 8:15-17).

WOW, did you catch that!! Joint heirs with Christ!! Absolutely mind-blowing to realize that, as insignificant as we are in the vast universe, mere specks in the gigantic ocean of trillions times trillions of stars and other fantastic celestial creations that populate God's measureless domain, we are the supreme interest of this Almighty God! And He was willing to lay everything on the proverbial "line" to win our allegiance back from Satan.

From this perspective, the question in the final judgment will be, "What did you do with the gift of My Son?"

The conversation in chapter 17:1-22 was between the LORD and Abraham, no one else. Not meaning to leave his wife out of the discussion (because the two were "one flesh" in marriage), God now addresses to Abraham, Sarah's need of faith. Just as He told Abraham that he would be "the father of many nations" and "kings shall come out of thee," (Genesis 17:5, 6), now God tells Abraham the same thing about Sarah. "And I will bless her, and give thee a son also of her: yea, I will bless her, and she shall be a mother of nations; kings of people shall be of her" (vs. 16).

And just as God changed Abram's name to signify the promise to him, He now changes Sarai's name for the same purpose. "And God said unto Abraham, As for Sarai thy wife, thou shalt not call her name Sarai, but Sarah shall her name be" (vs. 15). The meaning of Sarai is "she that strives, a contentious person," which she proved herself to be in our previous studies. Her new name means "princess," and foreshadows God's prophecy that "kings of people" will come from her.

But we still have the problem of advancing age and continual barrenness. And so, in considering these seemingly preposterous proposals that Sarah will the mother of many nations and a princess who gives rise to kings, "Abraham fell upon his face, and laughed, and said in his heart, Shall a child be born unto him that is an hundred years old? and shall Sarah, that is ninety years old, bear?" (Genesis 17:17). If it was impossible 25 or 50 years ago, how could it happen now? God still has to deal with an unbelief that looks only to man for the solution.

"And Abraham said unto God, O that Ishmael might live before thee!" Ishmael has reached the "age of accountability," being now in his fourteenth year. He has been raised as the heir, the only son of Abraham, the one whom all the camp looks to as the inheritor of all that their master owns. Everyone expects Ishmael to be the father of all of Abraham's descendants. How could it be otherwise?

But God insisted, "Sarah *thy wife* shall bear thee a son indeed; and thou shalt call his name Isaac: and I will establish My covenant with him for an everlasting covenant, and with his seed after him." God emphasized that Sarah was the "wife" through whom the promised son would be born, not a concubine. It was as though God were saying: Abraham, I keep telling you, over and over, what I am going to do for you! Why won't you believe Me? And this time, with the restatement of the promise of a son *through Sarah*, God gives the true heir his name: Isaac. The Hebrew root from which Isaac comes means "to laugh." Abraham laughed at God's promise, and the son Sarah will bear to him will forever remind him that he laughed at God.

God had no intention of casting off Ishmael. He was after all, a child of Abraham, and loved by God. So another promise is given. "And as for Ishmael, I have heard thee: Behold, I have blessed him, and will make him fruitful, and will multiply him exceedingly; twelve princes shall he beget [cf. Genesis 25:12-16], and I will make him a great nation" (Genesis 17:20; cf. 21:18). The tribes that came from Ishmael ended up being as numerous as a plague of locusts when they swarmed up out of the Arabian Peninsula under Islam's conquering zeal (see Revelation 9:1-3).

"But My covenant will I establish with Isaac." The covenant here is not referring to circumcision, but the everlasting covenant given from the foundation of the world (Genesis 3:15). The everlasting covenant concerns the Messiah who would come through Isaac's descendants, through the tribe of Judah. Christ descended from Judah, the fourth-born son of Jacob, because Reuben, Simeon and Levi disqualified themselves through inexcusable behavior. Jacob prophesied this as he lay dying. "The scepter shall not depart from Judah, nor a lawgiver from between his feet until Shiloh [the Messiah] come; and unto Him shall the gathering of the nations be" (Genesis 49:10). The everlasting covenant concerned the Messiah, not a political nation or territory in the Middle East.

"Which Sarah shall bear unto thee at this set time in the next year" (Genesis 17:21). Watch this. Now things have been pinned down to "within the next year." God has His plan marked and timed. By stating the time frame to Abraham, He is once again putting His integrity on the line. Can He accomplish this thing in a year, when nine months will be consumed in the pregnancy? This means only three months until the promised conception will take place.

There is a lot of work that needs to be done in three months to overcome Sarah's unbelief so that she will be receptive to God's promise. For the last 25 years things have crawled along, but now it's zip-zap and it's done? What miracle does God have up His divine sleeve that can transform Sarah's thinking?

This question propels us forward in the narrative in anticipation of seeing how God is going to solve the seemingly impossible: to get unbelieving Sarah to believe in Him.

"And He left off talking with him, and God went up from Abraham." I just find this sentence so very encouraging and personal. God was "talking" with Abraham as Friend to friend, in Abraham's very presence. After He finished, He "went up" and left Abraham, so God must have been personally present before Abraham when speaking to him. God is our personal Friend, and willing to communicate with us One to one, if we will learn to listen to Him.

21

Abraham Explains His Mistake

Genesis 17:23-27

Now we pick up again the theme from verses 10 to 14 concerning circumcision. The commandment was given, but not carried out at that point. The rite was initiated later in the day. First God had to finish His conversation with Abraham concerning the son before He let Abraham take care of the business regarding circumcision.

Circumcision was not unheard of to Abraham. The Egyptians had been performing it on adult males for about 300 years, as attested by a bas-relief depicting circumcision found in Pharaoh Ankhmahon's tomb from 2345 BC. Papyri illustrating the procedure in full color have also been found from that time. The Ethiopians, Syrians, and Phoenicians, all practiced circumcision before the time of Abraham.

So God took another known ritual, as He did with the Canaanite method of making a covenant in chapter 15, and He turned it on its ear, giving it an entirely new meaning. Deuteronomy only mentions circumcision as a "spiritual" rite of the faithful who had a heart-appreciation and love for God (Deuteronomy 10:16; 30:6). This is echoed in Jeremiah 4:4.[1] As the apostle Paul would later write to the Galatians, circumcision had to be of the heart, not the flesh; it was the sign of faith in the coming Messiah, or it had no meaning at all.

---

1. "Circumcise yourselves to the LORD, and take away the foreskins of your heart, ye men of Judah and inhabitants of Jerusalem." (Jeremiah 4:4).

After the LORD (Christ, the Word of God in His pre-incarnate form) had finished His conversation and disappeared back into the heavens, Abraham had to gather all the male members of the tribe, all the servants, herdsmen and shepherds, and then explain this thing about "cutting the flesh." It was going to very painful (no anesthesia back then), and it would take a week before they were healed (cf. Genesis 34:22-25).

Humbly, Abraham had to explain that this thing was his fault for doubting God's promise concerning the real son, the true heir who would be named "to laugh," that was yet to be born of his 90 year old wife, Sarah. Convincing the men of these incredible things was going to take some talking. After all, for 25 years Abraham had been telling them that God was going give Sarah and him a son, and nothing had happened yet. And now the old man was asking all the males in the camp to submit to a painful ritual simply because *he* did not believe the Word of God? That would seem a bit over the top, a bit too much for the men of the camp to have to endure because of Abraham's unbelief in God's promise.

Abraham also had to humbly admit that he had made a terrible mistake in taking Hagar as his concubine in an attempt to produce the heir through his own (well, okay, Sarah's) ingenuity and physical strength. And he had to explain the "faith thing" concerning the symbolism of this new ritual that would be carried on "perpetually" for no telling how long into future generations. After all, who knew when the Messiah would come to bring the rituals to an end? All Abraham could offer by way of explanation was that God told him that if you were part of the tribe, then circumcision would be performed, no matter how you came about entering the tribe.

The amazing thing is, all of Abraham's men and male children submitted to this rite, evidently without much questioning. Well, they might have had questions, but they didn't resist him. They had confidence in Abraham's leading, even when asked to do something as quirky as this idea. By faith in Abraham, and believing what he told them about the Creator God, they submitted. Does this indicate that the servants had more faith in God than Abraham himself had?

"And Abraham took Ishmael his son, and all that were born in his house, and all that were bought with his money, every male among the men of Abraham's house; and circumcised the flesh of their foreskin in the selfsame day, as God had said unto him." (Genesis 17:23). He began with Ishmael, his own son, and then proceeded through the assembled men and boys until he reached the last. Then after all that bloody work on others, he had to circumcise himself.

But during this speech explaining what he was going to do to them, Abraham also had to reveal that Ishmael was not the "promised son" and was not the heir. All the promises God gave concerning the future generations though which the Messiah would be born, did not figure Ishmael into the scheme. Now Ishmael who once believed that he *was* the heir, and all the circumstances surely supported this assumption, was left out in the cold. Dashed dreams of greatness and wealth would fester in Ishmael's heart, blossom four years later into scorn and mockery, and result in his expulsion from the clan.

"And Abraham was ninety years old and nine, when he was circumcised in the flesh of his foreskin. And Ishmael his son was thirteen years old, when he was circumcised in the flesh of his foreskin. In the selfsame day was Abraham circumcised, and Ishmael his son. And all the men of his house, born in the house, and bought with money of the stranger, were circumcised with him." (Genesis 17:24-27). Abraham exactly carried out the instructions given by God concerning the rite of circumcision.

And this must have left the wives a bit concerned regarding the mental status of their leader. He was an old man, and now he demanded that all the men and boys in the camp be cut like this? He must be getting crazy or demented in his old age to order the mutilation of all the males! It was left to each man to explain the meaning of the ritual to his wife. And Abraham had to explain it to Sarah and Hagar, too. Four hundred years later, Moses' wife would call him a "bloody husband" because he insisted on the circumcision of his son (Exodus 4:24-26). Even after four hundred years, the women seemed to have difficulty in understanding it.

And now the scene is set for the next incredible theophany.

22

Visitors at Mamre

Genesis 18:1-8

The first eight verses set the tone for the story that follows. Hospitality was very important in the Middle East. No stranger was allowed to pass by without taking them in for refreshments. In the arid regions where water was scarce, even your worst enemy could not be denied water, if he asked for it.

"And the LORD appeared unto him in the plains of Mamre: and he sat in the tent door in the heat of the day" (Genesis 18:1). Abraham is still encamped in Mamre, where he had been for some time. It is noon, and the day is hot. Abraham is sitting under the shade flap of his tent door. Perhaps there is just a ruffle of a breeze that shakes the leather of the tent over his head, making it snap and pop in protest. "And he lifted up his eyes and looked, and saw three men standing by him." (vs. 2). Squinting against the noon sunlight, he noticed three strangers standing near his tent. They materialized from nowhere, and Abraham had not heard them walking up on him. No crunching sandals shuffling in the sand had brought them to his attention before he noticed them standing there.

But when he saw them, he hurried from his tent door to where they stood, and bowed himself toward the ground, saying, "My Lord, if now I have found favour in thy sight, pass not away, I pray thee, from thy servant." Abraham presented himself to these strangers as a humble servant who bows before persons of honor. We are not told at this point whether or not Abraham immediately recognized that "my

Lord" was the LORD Himself, even though it is presented from the beginning to the reader that the Person who appeared before Abraham's tent was the LORD—Christ in a pre-incarnate manifestation.

Abraham continues, speaking rapidly, not giving any time for responses from these three men. "Let a little water, I pray you, be fetched, and wash your feet, and rest yourselves under the tree." One of the primary means of showing hospitality was washing of the feet. Wearing only sandals and shuffling through the hot sand meant that the feet suffered from the dry conditions and could become painful.

We find this also in the Gospels as a sign of humility and honor to the guest. Jesus criticized Simon the Pharisee for not performing the customary role when Jesus attended Simon's party that, supposedly, was meant to show honor to the One who had healed him from his leprosy.[1] Jesus also showed the importance of humility in foot washing when He washed the disciples' feet in the upper room the night He was arrested for treason.[2]

"Rest yourselves under the tree" because the tree was nearby Abraham's tent and offered shade for all. Abraham continues to rapidly state his offerings, "And I will fetch a morsel of bread." Just a "morsel of bread" because Abraham doesn't want to be seen as though he is making an arrogant statement of his wealth. It will only take a moment to "fetch" a small amount of bread, so don't think that you are putting me out by accepting it from me.

And, please "comfort ye your hearts; and after that ye shall pass on: for therefore are ye come to your servant." Please, make me happy by taking this morsel of food from me. Refresh yourselves by eating the bit bread and sitting under my tree. In the Hebrew there is a subtle play between the words bread and heart, both of which come from the same root word, *leb*. Abraham is telling his visitors "Eat my morsel of *bread* and make your *heart glad* because I am your servant, and you have come especially to visit me, and that has made me *glad*."

---

1. "And while He was at Bethany in the house of Simon the leper, as He was reclining at the table ... He said to him, "I entered into your house, you gave Me no water for My feet ... you gave Me no kiss ... My head with oil you did not anoint" (Mark 14:3; Luke 7:44-47).

2. "So He got up from supper, laid aside His robe, took a towel, and tied it around Himself. Next, He poured water into a basin and began to wash His disciples' feet and to dry them with the towel tied around Him. (John 13:4, 5, HCSB).

Though none of the three men have yet spoken, Abraham may have by this time, figured out who his visitor is. He has, after all, previously had several personal encounters with the LORD, the last just a short time before this day, when they spoke face to face during daylight hours. Christ didn't need to speak to be recognized; His countenance and attitude would have been enough to allow Abraham to know who He was as He sat under the tree.

The polite response from these strangers is, "So do, as thou hast said." And now Abraham, "hastened into the tent unto Sarah, and said, Make ready quickly three measures of fine meal, knead it, and make cakes upon the hearth." Abraham doesn't delegate this project to any of the servants, and certainly not to Hagar, but tells his wife to make these flatbreads from "fine meal"—finely ground grain so the breads would have a tender, open crumb with a crisp surface texture. These breads would be thin unleavened bread baked on a flat stone placed over a fire to create the hearth. The breads were made from finely ground whole meal flour, water and salt, similar to lavash. The recipe was the same as the one later used in the sanctuary services.

Then, Abraham "ran unto the herd, and fetched a calf tender and good, and gave it unto a young man; and he hastened to dress it." Abraham chose the "fatted calf" from the herd, the young animal always reserved for the most special meal. No matter how fast you are at butchering, it would take at least an hour to slaughter, gut, skin and quarter a small calf to ready it for the roasting spit. Abraham has to let "a young man" carry out this part of the meal preparation because it was much too hard for a woman to accomplish. He did not want to do it himself because he needed to get back to his guests; didn't want to neglect them for very long.

And when everything was ready, Abraham "took butter, and milk, and the calf which he had dressed, and set it before them; and he stood by them under the tree, and they did eat." Abraham continued in the role of humble servant, attending his guests himself, instead of letting the usual housemaids do it. "And they did eat" indicates that when angels take human form, they act like humans, even being able to consume food and drink. It is a pretty awesome thought that we don't know when we may have had heavenly angels among us and not recognized them, because they looked and acted like humans while carrying out the task God sent them to accomplish.

The preparation of this meal took several hours, during which time Abraham and his guests conversed about we are not told what. But wouldn't it have been interesting to have been a maid behind the tent wall listening in on this conversation between God and His humble, faithful servant Abraham? These three men took the time to be patient while waiting for their food. We can imagine that the conversation was easy between these three heavenly visitors and Abraham. He had no duplicity in his character, but was open and very friendly toward them. And, since they were of heavenly origin, they already knew Abraham well. Sitting there under the tree, camaraderie would have been natural as they returned the kindness and cordiality.

The afternoon was drawing on toward evening, and their task was yet before them on down the road at Sodom.

23

Sarah Laughed

Genesis 18:9-15

"And they said unto him, Where is Sarah thy wife? And he said, Behold, in the tent." One of these strangers now asked about Abraham's wife, and called her by name. How did they know her name? Well, Abraham's clan was well known in the area where he had been more or less settled for about 20 years. While women were not socially prominent at that time, Abraham had had some interesting events take place while living in Hebron, and these were part of Abraham's fabric as a character living there among the native peoples of the land.

One strange event in particular that would have been a topic of discussion among the people who occupied that area, was when the God of Abraham came flaming out of the sky like a meteor, and consumed the animals laid out to make the parity covenant. Who had ever heard of anything like that before? And the almost mythical rumor that Sarah was still supposed to have a child, even though she is now ninety years old, certainly would have provoked some discussion around the campfires in the evenings. Who or what was this God of Abraham's who insisted that He could cause an old barren woman to become pregnant? Not even Baal, the god of life and fertility, could do anything like that!

Even though Abraham had the prominent role in hosting these visitors, the three had not come for Abraham, but for Sarah. The LORD's visit this time, was for her. This is why He appeared at the tent where He knew she would be. He did not come in the night time when it would have been inappropriate for a woman to be interacting with a strange man, when a conversation between them would have been more difficult to carry out. The Word of God came in the "heat of the day" when Sarah would have been in the tent seeking relief from the baking hot sun.

As He sat outside the tent, the LORD was continually conscious of Sarah's presence within a few feet of where He was resting while eating His lunch. And He knew she was listening, too. So His next words are aimed directly at her heart. "And He said, I will certainly return unto thee according to the time of life; and, lo, Sarah thy wife shall have a son." This now makes eight times that Abraham had been told by God that He would give him *and Sarah* a son of their "own bodies"—both of them, not Abraham and a concubine, but both Abraham and Sarah.

Before this encounter with the LORD, Sarah had always gotten the promise secondhand, from Abraham. The promise had always been given to him, even though it included his wife. It is a distinction that opened the door for Sarah in the past to have doubt whether the promise really meant that she was included, or whether Abraham was the one, the only one, to whom the promise was given. Maybe the female side of it didn't really matter, and that thought brought Hagar into the picture with disastrous results.

Now this stranger is making a personal promise to Sarah. "I will" do this thing—"your wife Sarah will have a son." A declaration with no hint of indecision on the part of the One who made the statement. "I AM" said it, firmly and openly and with conviction. The I AM that spoke everything in the universe and this world into existence said, "*I will give* your wife, Sarah, a son." At Creation Christ, the Word of God, spoke, and *it was*. All things came into existence by His spoken Word. Now He is speaking again with just as much certainty that the event would come to pass. He would give the son to them. It would be a gift from Him. They had no power to generate it on their own. The time of natural fertility was long past, and the promise could only be fulfilled by the God of the universe, Who alone can give life.

"And Sarah heard it in the tent door, which was behind Him." Sarah was sitting just inside the tent, listening to the conversation taking place between the three strangers and her husband. She had prepared the breads from finely ground flour, and receded back into the privacy of her tent, out of sight, but not out of hearing.

Listening in on a conversation is one thing, and we often do it, but then suddenly we hear our name come into the conversation, and we are startled. Maybe what is about to be said is going to be bad. Maybe we need to turn off our ears so our feelings are not hurt by what we are going to hear next.

It is easy to imagine that Sarah was surprised when she heard these words directed right at her. Nothing in the conversation thus far was particularly about her or any thing that concerned her. It was general conversation, perhaps complimenting the delicious food, and maybe some discussion about politics concerning Sodom, which is where the men were headed when they left Abraham's camp in just a few more minutes.

And then Moses, our author, throws this in: "Now Abraham and Sarah were old and well stricken in age; and it ceased to be with Sarah after the manner of women." It doesn't seem like Moses needed to remind the reader of this long-standing problem that has been the focus of four of the last six chapters. But as a literary device it does set the scene for Sarah's comment.

And the restatement of the problem makes the reader anticipate some new thing, since the LORD had just stated He was going to do the impossible. "I will return unto you, Sarah, the power to conceive a son." Not just a child, but a *son*. God was also going to control the gender of this miracle child. A son was necessary for the development of a tribe of people though which the Messiah would be born, and God was going to give Sarah a son.

Now it's Sarah's turn to laugh. "Therefore Sarah laughed *within herself*, saying, After I am waxed old shall I have pleasure, my lord being old also?" She did not speak these words out loud. She just thought them "in her heart." God knows our every thought and the intents of our hearts. Nothing is hid from Him with Whom we have to do.[1]

The LORD doesn't speak directly to Sarah, but to her husband. "And the LORD [Jehovah Himself, who is Christ pre-incarnate, the Word of God who personally interacts with men] said unto Abraham,

---

[1]. "For the word of God is living, and active, and sharper than any two-edged sword, and piercing even to the division of soul and spirit, of both joints and marrow, and able to judge the thoughts and intentions of the heart. And there is no creature hidden from His sight; but all things are open and laid bare to the eyes of Him with whom we have to do." (Hebrews 4:12, 13, NASB).

Wherefore did Sarah laugh, saying, Shall I of a surety bear a child, when I am old?"

There was no open laughter, not even an audible chuckle from Sarah, so Abraham could not have heard what the LORD was referring to when He asked, "Why did your wife laugh?"

And then the punch line. "Is any thing too hard for the LORD?"

Abraham, I have been telling you for twenty-four years that I would give you a son, and you always refused to believe My word to you. And now Sarah is laughing at Me, too. If you both would only believe that I can do the impossible, then things would be different.

But I am telling you right now that "at the time appointed I will return unto thee, according to the time of life, and Sarah will have a son." At the exact time, this very time next year, one year from now, you are going to have a son born to your barren and old wife!

But there is one more trial that I will give to you both, and that will convince you of My power to do what I say.

Caught in the act of denial, Sarah speaks out loud to those on the other side of the tent curtain. "Sarah denied, saying, I laughed not; for she was afraid. And He said, Nay; but you did laugh." You can't fool Me, Sarah. I know all things. And I will have the last laugh, one year from now when Isaac, the child of laughter, is born from your dried up barren, useless old womb to which I will "return the time of life."

24

Sarah Denies Her Denial

Genesis 18:12-15

"Then Sarah denied, saying, I laughed not; for she was afraid. And He said, Nay; but thou didst laugh."

Why was Sarah afraid of what she heard the Man say? Was she afraid of the omniscience of this Person who was sitting outside the door of her tent, casually eating her bread, a perfect stranger who knew so much about her? If He knew the things about her that He spoke out loud to the group, what else did He know about her? Was it His intimate knowledge of her that made her afraid, or maybe even made her feel threatened? How could He know these things?

It would have been unnerving to overhear someone you never saw before, talking so personally about you. Was she afraid that what He said about her having a son might come true, and that's why she laughed in the first place?—a nervous, incredulous laugh of denial of the facts?

Or was she afraid because she was caught in her sin of unbelief?

Like you said in one of your earlier comments, Abraham was willing to admit his error and obey God, no matter what humiliation he had to suffer through. Sarah didn't seem willing to do that, at least not yet. However, she could never get away with denying her sin of unbelief because the evidence was right there before her eyes every day, playing outside her tent attended by his loving mother, talking with her compliant husband who yielded to his wife's sinful suggestion. It was hard for her to deny what she had done concerning Hagar.

But she did deny it.

Our high and mighty self-righteousness just won't let God be God, because we want to be God in place of Him. Like Satan who coveted God's heavenly throne,[1] we don't want God sitting on the throne of our hearts. We want to control every aspect of our lives without submission to God. Abraham and Sarah both wanted to ground their essential being and personal identity in themselves, and we all do the same thing.

But the Bible reveals to us that this was the root of the first sin—Eve placed her own opinion above the Word of God concerning the tree of knowledge, and it caused her to fall into the sin of unbelief. Eve distrusted the word of God concerning the tree of knowledge, and instead unquestioningly accepted the voice coming from the spirit-controlled serpent in the tree that contradicted God's command.

Self-centeredness must be eradicated from our thinking before God can dwell upon the throne of our heart where He should be.

Unbelief is both subtle and bold. It is subtle in that it sneaks up on us, gradually transforming our mind. Before we realize it we have wandered away from things we used to believe were true. Small compromises push us inexorably into the sin of unbelief. Like Eve standing beneath that forbidden tree. She once believed what Adam told her about that tree, but subtly (granted, it was under the influence the most "subtle" of creatures, Satan himself) she began to doubt what she once knew to be true. And then bold unbelief allowed her to rebel even in the face of what she knew to true, justifying her sinful action at the same time. We are no different when tempted to sin.

So here is Sarah sitting in the coolness of her tent, serenely denying that she's in denial of God's power to do what He says He will do. "*I did not laugh!*" But her lie made her afraid because the One outside her tent already knew all things about her. And when without any contention He replied, "Nay, but you did laugh," she was more afraid because of His gentle rebuke, against which she had no denial or defense.

---

1. "How art thou fallen from heaven, O Lucifer, son of the morning! how art thou cut down to the ground, which didst weaken the nations! For thou hast said in thine heart, I will ascend into heaven, I will exalt my throne above the stars of God: I will sit also upon the mount of the congregation, in the sides of the north: I will ascend above the heights of the clouds; I will be like the most High." (Isaiah 14:12-14).

"And the men rose up from thence, and looked toward Sodom," leaving Sarah to ponder all that had been said *about* her and *to* her by this Stranger from nowhere. But the Holy Spirit would now get to work on that crack in her prideful façade, bringing to her mind all the times she had openly fought against the Word of God, her resistance strengthening her unbelief. Repentance begins with a recognition of our unbelief and the sins that it caused.

Sarah also now had to deal with the more real idea of becoming a mother at ninety years of age. The unmistakable authority in the Man's voice, speaking as the omniscient and omnipotent God when He pronounced that she would bear a son in one year, was hard to get out of her head. There was no room for doubt, even though she still wanted to disbelieve the possibility of it all.

It is tough enough to have a child come into your life when you're young and more flexible in your ways, but at her age there would be a massive disruption to her every day activities in having to care for a baby. Leisure time would evaporate as a mist before the hot sun when she had to give her time and attention to a totally helpless infant, upon whom so much depended. If all those promises to Abraham about a "great nation" were indeed to come true, this child would need special care and guarding, even spoiling, to protect him from childhood dangers and the harsh realities of life.

Yes, Sarah had so many things to think about, so many things were about to change in her life. And she was left alone to deal with them because "Abraham went with the men to bring them on the way" as they journeyed toward Sodom. In the quiet of the fading day, she had no one to talk to except the LORD who had just left her tent door. But she could follow Him in heart-felt prayer, and He would answer her.

25

Abraham Teaches Us Intercession

Genesis 18:16-33

Having completed their mission at Abraham's camp, the three men now turn toward Sodom, which was about ten, or a little more, miles east of Abraham's home in Hebron. This is a fascinating section of Scripture. It shows us that the LORD does not destroy without a thorough investigation into the facts concerning sin. Yes, the LORD is omniscient, and knows all things. But judicial investigation always precedes judicial action from the divine tribunal. All the facts in the case are laid bare before divine judgment takes place.

"The eyes of the LORD are in every place, beholding the evil and the good." (Proverbs 15:3). "Great in counsel, and mighty in work: for thine eyes are open upon all the ways of the sons of men: to give every one according to his ways, and according to the fruit of his doings" (Jeremiah 32:19). "Neither is there any creature that is not manifest in his sight: but all things are naked and opened unto the eyes of him with whom we have to do." (Hebrews 4:13).

When Adam and Eve sinned, Christ came to them asking questions, not because He did not know what they did, but to open before the watching universe all the facts of the situation. He did the same thing when Cain killed Abel. The investigation is not because God does not know what is going on, but to reveal to His creatures how careful He is in making His judgments. Here with Sodom, we also learn that God will do all that He can to save people. He is not willing that any should perish, but that all should come to repentance (2 Peter 3:9).

"And the LORD said, Because the cry of [from] Sodom and Gomorrah is great, and because their sin is very grievous; I will go down now, and see whether they have done altogether according to the cry of it, which is come unto Me; and if not, I will know." (Genesis 18:20, 21). The word translated "cry" in this verse has the basic meaning of "to cry out for help in a time of distress." In other places in the Bible it is used of a cry from a disturbed heart that is seeking some kind of help. It is expressing a felt need and is most frequently directed toward God. The same word is found in Psalm 22:5, where David prophetically reveals to us the cry of the Saviour as He hung on His cross, stretched between heaven and hell, taking upon Himself the sin burden of the whole world.[1]

The LORD already knew about the atrocious sins of Sodom and Gomorrah, but now He is investigating the situation because a cry for help had come to Him from that city. Someone there was terribly distressed by what was taking place there, and God was ready to intercede. Someone's personal outrage against the great wickedness of those two cities had provoked an outcry because the person could stand the situation no longer, and wanted relief. It is not here revealed to us who this person was, but the LORD heard his plea for intervention and salvation from the slimepit of sin called Sodom.

"And the LORD said, Shall I hide from Abraham that thing which I do; seeing that Abraham shall surely become a great and mighty nation, and all the nations of the earth shall be blessed in him?" (Genesis 18:17). Again, the LORD points us to His promise that a miracle son was soon coming to Abraham, through whom a nation would spring. "All the nations of the earth shall be blessed" is the same promise given in Genesis 12:3, which is referred to in this question.

"For I know him, that he will command his children and his household after him, and they shall keep the way of the LORD, to do justice and judgment; that the LORD may bring upon Abraham that which He hath spoken of him." Yes, the LORD knew Abraham,

---

1. "Our fathers trusted in Thee: they trusted, and Thou didst deliver them. ... But I am a worm, and no man; a reproach of men, and despised of the people. All they that see Me laugh Me to scorn: they shoot out the lip, they shake the head, saying, He trusted on the LORD that He would deliver Him: let Him deliver Him, seeing He delighted in Him. ... Be not far from Me; for trouble is near; for there is none to help." (Psalm 22:4, 6-8, 11).

understood his heart and mind. He read his motives. He saw how Abraham trained the people of his clan, and how all of them willingly followed Abraham's leading in spiritual matters.

"And the men turned their faces from thence, and went toward Sodom: but Abraham stood yet before the LORD." God does not come into the presence of evil, for His is a consuming fire, and all would have been destroyed as soon as He showed up at Sodom's gate (Deuteronomy 9:3; Hebrews 12:29). God does not destroy people; He destroys sin. The day is fast approaching when He will destroy all sin. If we cling to sin, unwilling to believe the LORD's assessment of our sinful condition, then we are certainly going to be destroyed when we come into the presence of the Almighty God. "Behold, they shall be as stubble; the fire shall burn them; they shall not deliver themselves from the power of the flame." (Isaiah 47:14).

As an example of how faith in God's promises will prepare us, the three Hebrew young men that Nebuchadnezzar threw into the fiery furnace were perfectly safe as they walked in the presence of the LORD, without receiving even the smell of smoke upon themselves. They knew the promise from Isaiah: "When thou walkest through the fire, thou shalt not be burned; neither shall the flame kindle upon thee. For I am the LORD thy God, the Holy One of Israel, thy Saviour." (Isaiah 43:2, 3). Long before they faced that trial of their faith, they had totally surrendered their minds and bodies to the care of their LORD, and when threatened by Nebuchadnezzar, they had no fear of him or his furnace.

But we've wandered off on a different path. Let's return to our story of Abraham and the three men.

Instead of all three men going down the hill, the two angels by themselves went down to Sodom to see if any persons could be rescued from the conflagration that was about to pour from the sky. And as they went on their way, Abraham showed his character of mercy and justice, which was a reflection of the character of his God. He begins to bargain for the persons living in wicked Sodom and Gomorrah. "And Abraham drew near [to the LORD who still stood by him], and said, Wilt Thou also destroy the righteous with the wicked?"

Abraham knew judgment was fast approaching those evil people, but his heart went out to them. Maybe there were some few who weren't so bad?

And so Abraham stepped in front of the LORD, slowing his pace in an effort to stay the execution a little longer. Abraham was not far away from the LORD as they were walking, but now he comes even closer, getting personal, perhaps reaching out and touching the Man's arm to help express the emotions in his humble heart. "Oh, let the LORD not be angry because I speak so boldly to You; I am not being irreverent. I am but dust and ashes in Your holy presence."

This is a lesson for us in intercessory prayer. God cannot intervene where He is not wanted. Our free will prevents Him from interceding when we have chosen to reject Him; He will never violate our freedom of choice, even if that choice ultimately brings us to destruction in the lake of fire.

But the "effectual fervent prayer of a righteous man" [person] (James 5:16) who humbly approaches the throne of grace in behalf of another, can open the door for God to step into the situation and bring a remedy. God can enter into the situation, not because the sinner wanted Him to come help, but because someone else requested the help from God in their behalf.

To implore God in an intercessory prayer we must first realize our total inability to accomplish what needs to be done. The intercessory prayer must be presented before the throne of grace from a humbled and contrite heart. We cannot *command* the Creator to do anything. We are nothing and He is everything, a totally sovereign Being. We can only *seek* His power to intercede in behalf of another if we first recognize our utter powerlessness and lay the glory of man in the dust.

In the next nine verses, the dialogue concerns how many righteous persons could be found in those wicked cities in the Siddim Valley, persons who did not commit the sins for which Sodom and Gomorrah were notoriously known. In incremental steps, Abraham decreases his number, until he gets to ten persons. With each number that Abraham named, the LORD acceded to Abraham's request. He was not in any hurry to destroy even the wicked, and was more than willing to save those who believed in Him.

Abraham pressed on, "And he said, Oh let not the LORD be angry, and I will speak yet but this once: Peradventure ten shall be found there. And He said, I will not destroy it for ten's sake."

Abraham had no idea how many persons living in Sodom and Gomorrah were free from the sexual sins so prevalent there, but he did know that Lot and his family numbered about ten persons, counting his wife, sons, daughters and in-laws. And when he reached that minimal number, and the LORD agreed that He would spare the city if there were ten persons who were not guilty of Sodom's sin, Abraham was satisfied. His only hope was to believe that his nephew and his family were going to be safe from the destruction. He had done what he could to intercede for them at the throne of grace. There was no need for begging or argument. The case was forth and the LORD said He would save the cities, if there were ten righteous persons living there.

God is willing to forego judgment, as evidenced by His revocation of the condemnation of the city of Nineveh, after the repentance of the people in response to Jonah's preaching (Jonah 3:10). However, unlike Nineveh, not even the minimal number of ten righteous people could be found in Sodom, and the LORD already knew it. Abraham was not able to read the hearts of Lot's family, but God could. "And the LORD went His way, as soon as He had left communing with Abraham: and Abraham returned unto his place."

We can imagine the thoughts Abraham had as he slowly made his way back to his tent that evening. Destruction was on its way, but the LORD had promised that He would spare the city if ten persons could be found who did not participate in the sins of that wicked place. There was hope, but also dread in Abraham's heart because he was not sure of the spiritual condition of Lot's family. He had prayed and done all he could to intercede for them, now he must be content to leave the situation in God's merciful and just hands, and humbly accept whatever was the outcome.

26

The Man in the Gate

Genesis 19:1-3

Yes, there are unfallen worlds out there in God's vast universe. The Bible has declared that we are not alone. The Book of Job opens its narrative by saying that on a particular day there was a council meeting in heaven and all the representatives from the unfallen worlds attended the meeting. "There was a day when the sons of God came to present themselves before the LORD." (Job 2:1). Those beings were not angels, nor resurrected humans who were given their own planet to rule (as some believe), nor any other creature from this world of ours. Those representatives were the "Adams" from other worlds that refused to listen to Satan's lies. They did not fall when presented with Satan's misrepresentation of God's character of love.

Yes, they were called "sons of God" but that Hebrew word is never applied to angels. In the Bible it is used of humans in the usual sense of the word "son" as referring to the biological off-spring of a man and a woman. Jesus was "born of a woman" and therefore is called the "Son of man" as well as the Son of God. "But when the fulness of the time was come, God sent forth His Son, made of a woman, made under the law, to redeem them that were under the [curse of] law,[1] that we might receive the adoption of sons." (Galatians 4:4, 5). Adam

---

1. "Christ hath redeemed us from the curse of the law, being made a curse for us: for it is written, Cursed is every one that hangeth on a tree." (Galatians 3:13). The "curse of the law" is disobedience that brings eternal destruction to the unrepentant.

was created to be the representative of this world, and he is called the "son of God" in Luke 3:38 because he was the first created being on this planet.

When Satan caused Adam to fall, he stole the headship position from Adam and became "prince of this world" (John 12:31; 14:30; 16:11; Ephesians 2:2). As the "prince of this world," Satan went instead of Adam to represent our world at that council meeting. There Satan laid out his challenge against God before all of those representatives from unfallen worlds and the heavenly angels that he had previously attempted to deceive. Job, and God, were placed on trial by that challenge. The trial would answer two important questions: Was God a loving beneficent Being who cared for His creatures? And would Job rely completely upon God's Word, no matter what happened to him, no matter how much he suffered and lost, even to his death?

Both God and Job were on trial for their faith. God was confident that Job's faith in Him would bring him through whatever Satan choose to pour out on the man. This was not a matter of God's omniscience prevailing over Job's freewill, or that God already knew what choice Job would make during his trials, and therefore had nothing to lose by letting Satan test Job. In allowing the test of His faithful servant, God was putting His own character on the line for all watching universe to see the demonstration of how righteousness by faith works in those who are submissive to Him in all things. Job could have failed. For all those watching, the trial was not a foregone conclusion.

A Quarantined World

Carl Sagan has been trying to make contact with "aliens out there" for nearly 50 years through the radio telescope at Arecibo, Puerto Rico. Scientists have been beaming an encoded interstellar radio message since 1974, giving basic information about human beings. The hope is that some day, some being "out there" will decode the message and signal back to earth that they have received it. Then Sagan and his buddies will be able to proclaim that "we are not alone!"

But as we've just seen, we are not alone in God's universe, the Bible tells us that in so many ways. We have been the spectacle of the universe ever since Adam fell. All those unfallen worlds have been watching us for 6000 years, observing us to see how we are going to handle the gift of Christ, who gave up His precious life to save us from sin.

And since these unfallen beings are very aware of what sin has done to us, how virulent and inexcusable sin is, they will never answer Sagan's message. Our wicked world has been quarantined to prevent the spread of sin's virulent influence.

Angels Arrive at Sodom's Gate

"And there came two angels to Sodom at even." This is the same day that the two angels and the LORD lunched with Abraham. They left Abraham's tent in the late afternoon, and the fact that they arrived "at even" at Sodom's gate tells us that they did not *walk* that distance from Abraham's camp to Sodom. They traveled there through their angelic abilities to be where they were needed when they were needed. When the LORD finished His conversation with Abraham "He went His way" and disappeared from the sight of Abraham. Gone in a flash. But Abraham was not surprised by this, because he had been with his LORD in earlier conversations and knew that when He was finished conversing with him, He vanished.

When the angels arrived within view of the city of Sodom, they approached in the usual manner for human beings, walking along the road that led to the city gate. "And Lot sat in the gate of Sodom." When Lot first decided to move from Hebron to Sodom, he originally planned on just living in his tents in the *vicinity* of that wicked city. His original intention was that he merely wanted the greener pastures for his many flocks and herds. He beheld "all the plain of Jordan, that it was well watered everywhere" and that was what he needed.

However, over the twenty years that he had been gone from Abraham's camp, Lot changed his mind, and he actually moved into the city. When Lot left Abraham, he was not married. He now is married and this is the most likely reason for his moving into the city. Sodom was his wife's hometown, and no doubt was where she wanted to live among her kinfolk in a regular house, instead of a shepherd's smelly tent among his noisy flocks.

Curiously, we will find that from Eve onward the women in these Genesis narratives seem to have an inordinate ability to negatively influence their husbands …

"And Lot seeing [the angels who appeared as men] rose up to meet them." The import here is that Lot *hastened* to meet them as the angels approached near to the gate. His action implies more than mere friendliness toward them. There is behind the action a sense of urgency. Lot must greet these two men and quickly get them safely into his house before they are assaulted by the men of Sodom. Lot knows the kind of people he has been living among for the last twenty or more years.

You asked about the identity of the person who sent up to heaven his cry of despair because of the terrible sins going on in Sodom. We are not told specifically, but from the actions of Lot toward these two strangers, I think it is safe to say that Lot was the man.

"He bowed himself with his face toward the ground." Lot showed respect for these two strangers and in doing so, he provides us with information about his own character. Courtesy and humility were a part of Lot's nature, just as they were of his uncle Abraham. Lot had learned his manners well during the time he lived in Abraham's clan, and he did not forget them.

There was a valid reason behind Lot's sitting in the gate. The gate of ancient cities served several purposes. It was a marketplace where people coming and going would be most likely to stop and make purchases. In the evenings, it was a favorite place for lounging and gossiping about what was going on in the city and its surrounding area. And public business, such as transfer of property, was conducted there (see Ruth:4:1-4ff; Genesis 34:20, 24).

It was also the place of judgment (see Deuteronomy 21:18-20; 22:13-17ff.). The most prominent citizens of the city who had proven themselves to be unbiased and fair-minded were chosen to be judges over disputes among citizens living in that place. These selected persons sat at the gate where people could bring their disputes and arguments to have them settled.

Any of these three reasons could be why Lot was sitting there. That he was there indicates for us that he had been in Sodom long enough to have proven his character to Sodom's citizenry, and gained their respect. The people of Sodom thought Lot was a worthy man and had appointed him as a judge over them, a fact that was later used against him.[2] One strong historical point in support of his acceptance and appointment as judge is the fact that Abraham rescued Lot and the

---

2. " 'Get out of the way!' they said, adding, 'This one came here as a foreigner, but he's acting like a judge! Now we'll do more harm to you than to them.' They put pressure on Lot and came up to break down the door." (Genesis 19:9, HCSB).

residents of Sodom that Chedorlaomer had carted off. After that event, Lot would have promptly gained prominence in the town.

Lot's house must have been located near the gate because as he hastened to get these strangers off the street, he said, "Behold now, my lords, turn in, I pray you, into your servant's house, and tarry all night." "Turn in" indicating that the door to the house must have been very close by. Then follows the common courtesy of washing the travelers dirty feet. Lot did not seek to detain these two men, but was just offering the shelter and protection. They were free to "rise up early, and go on their ways" in the morning.

"And they said, Nay; but we will abide in the street all night." It was not an unusual thing for travelers to find shelter near a building or a shed, and simply lie down with their animals for the night. Inns for lodging were not common in small towns in that ancient time, and towns then were generally safe places. A stranger could come inside the gates, which were shut at night against robbers, other nefarious persons, and the danger of marauding wild animals, and find themselves safe to sleep on the street wrapped in their outer garments.

But there was an additional purpose behind the refusal. The angels had come to the city to test the spiritual conditions of it—to see if "the cry of the city was great" because "their sin is very grievous." How they were treated while lying innocently in the street would give a final convincing assessment concerning Sodom's great sin.

"And he pressed upon them greatly." Lot was afraid for their safety, and he strongly urged them, pressing them, giving them no way to graciously decline his offer. He probably did not reveal to them what their fate would have been had they chosen to stay on the street after dark. How do you tell perfect strangers that they would in all likelihood be gang raped if they did not accept his offer of hospitality? Of course, the angels already expected this to be the outcome. They knew Sodom's reputation and were not afraid to confront it. That's what they came for.

But "they turned in unto him, and entered into his house." Lot gave a sigh of relief, thinking he had rescued these two young men from a horrendously wicked night on the street. "And he made them a feast, and did bake unleavened bread, and they did eat." The meal is the same as the one they ate earlier in the day sitting outside Abraham's tent, just simple fare, quickly made.

But the night is drawing on and the Evil knows there's fresh flesh to be had. These two men were not seen only by Lot. Other men had been sitting or standing around the city gate when the angels appeared as travelers seeking refuge for the night, and it didn't take long for word of the arrival of two strangers to spread around town.

27

Another Kind of Intercessor

Genesis 19:4-11

Ensnared, yes, that's a perfect word to describe Lot's predicament. He was ensnared in Sodom's wicked world. But he did it to himself by choosing to move to Sodom's vicinity in the first place. He knew beforehand what Sodom was like. Their reputation was long-standing. And after God set him free through Abraham's rescue from Chedorlaomer's clutches, incredibly, Lot went back! That capture by an enemy army was Lot's signal to escape, but he didn't heed the message. He was more in tune with his materialism than the spiritual lessons God was trying to teach him.

Upon his return, Abraham's scorn of the king of Sodom should have sent a strong message to Lot. Uncle Abe rightly assessed the character of Sodom, and it was meant to educate his nephew concerning the peril of his continued residence among those people.

You asked, how did the people of Sodom get so bad? A reputation is built over time according to the activities that went on there. All five cities on the plain were known for their homosexual activities, but Sodom and Gomorrah were the most vile. Sexual sin always brings the downfall of an individual, and of a people group or nation.

When sin takes control of a population, the restraining power from holy angels and the work of the Holy Spirit in convicting people of their sin is rejected. "Even as they did not like to retain God in their knowledge, God gave them over to a reprobate mind to do those things which were not convenient [were morally wrong]" (Romans 1:28).

God "gives them up" to the evil desires of their hearts. When God's holy restraints are rejected, He removes them, and then Satan has full control. The whole world is careening right now down that path to destruction for just this same reason—we have rejected God's saving message, freely chosen the evil and are reveling in it.

The evening was drawing on; the meal Lot prepared was finished. It was nearing bedtime. I can imagine that Lot was nervous about his visitors, wondering if he was going to get them through the entire night without incident. And sure enough, "before they lay down, the men of the city, even the men of Sodom, compassed the house round, both old and young, all the people from every quarter." Not just a few, but "all the men" from every part of the city.

There in Sodom those sex-crazed maniacs "compassed the house round" yelling to Lot and beating on the door. Men of all ages and every part of the city came out for the fun, if not to personally participate, they at least would watch the goings-on. It probably had been a long time since strangers wandered into Sodom, and having the opportunity to rape someone new was more than these wicked men could resist.

"And they called unto Lot, and said unto him, Where are the men which came in to thee this night? bring them out unto us, that we may *know them*" (literally, "have sex with them"). The men of Sodom did not veil their intentions. They stated outright that they came to rape those two men that Lot had given refuge to. Fear gripped Lot's heart. He had taken in the men to protect them from exactly this ill-fortune. And now he was helpless to fight off the men outside his door, who far surpassed his ability to restrain them.

In what seems like an insane decision, "Lot went out at the door unto them, and shut the door after him" to try to keep them from barging into the house. What he thought he was going to do against the entire city's male population, he didn't know. Being the reasonable person he was naturally, Lot thought he'd be able to reason with the mob. After all, they respected him as their judge and arbiter when other matters needed a sane assessment.

But you can't reason with mob mentality that is bent on having its way. People in a mob lose control of their usual inhibitions. Their mentality becomes that of the group, controlled by peer pressure so that no one would have been willing to lose face by backing down. Influenced by the behaviors of the people they were with, there was little chance that any of the men would heed Lot's plea for a logical and reasonable assessment of the situation.

With his heart racing and fear in his voice Lot said, "I pray you, brethren, do not so wickedly." He pleaded with them as their friend and fellow citizen to pause and think about what they were contemplating and turn from it. When tempted we don't have to follow through and commit the sin. Through the power of our risen Saviour, we can say no and turn away from it.

He had no other argument. All Lot could do was hold out his hands pleadingly, trying to reach some vestige of morality in the debased minds of those men. "Think about what you're doing here! This is a wicked thing! These two men are innocent strangers to this area and don't know what they've walked into tonight. I beg of you, please, leave them alone."

And then Lot said one of the most mind-boggling things in the entire Bible. "Behold now, I have two daughters which have not known man; let me, I pray you, bring them out unto you, and do ye to them as is good in your eyes: only unto these men do nothing; for therefore came they under the shadow of my roof."

Wait a minute here. Lot was more interested in preserving etiquette concerning hospitality and protecting those strangers who came under his roof, than he was in maintaining his duty as a father to ensure the safety of his two young virgin daughters?

What is Lot thinking?! The men outside his door are morally deranged and would probably kill those two girls in their furious sexual assault. Even if Lot assumed that the girls would come to no harm (a very unlikely outcome, considering the fierceness of the men's attitude), Lot's willingness to throw out his daughters like shark bait was a grievous violation of his duty as a father.

It gives us insight into how far Lot had compromised his moral sensibilities when we read that he was willing to offer up his daughters to the lust of the Sodomites. He may have spoken rashly under the pressure he felt to defend his visitors, and he probably hoped that he would be turned down, knowing that the men outside his door preferred men over women. But to offer his own flesh and blood to that sex-hungry rabble seems unimaginable and unforgivable to us.

In the house behind his closed door were his wife, the mother of those two young girls, and the daughters who were so recklessly being offered to the mob. What were they thinking about how their husband and father was handling the situation at their front door? Surely they were all terribly frightened by the roaring men circling the house like a pack of vicious lions, beating on the doors, and wondering how long Lot could stave the impending disaster by his words.

Lot's offer was promptly rejected, and the men threatened, "Stand back!" We're not going to be turned away by you or anyone. We're here to have our fun. Let us at those two men! But Lot stood his ground, barring the doorway. Afraid?—yes, but nonetheless, determined.

"And they said again, This one fellow came in to sojourn, and he's trying to be a judge over us." This man is a foreigner! He's not one of us, and he has always stood aloof. Who does he think he is, with his high and mighty attitude, challenging the ways of the whole city?

For a time after Abraham's rescue from Chedorlaomer, the people of Sodom had respect for Lot, and tolerated his (to them) aberrant sexual ideals. Because he had been just and reasonable in all his ways, they had chosen him to be a judge of ordinary things. That is why he was sitting in the gate that afternoon. But he was still considered an outsider, even after 20 years' residence in that city. And when provoked as at this time, the natives of the city turned against the man whom they always considered was a stranger in their midst.

Yelling obscenities and shoving toward the door, the men of Sodom menaced Lot with stronger words. "Now will we deal worse with you than with them!" Not that they wanted to rape Lot, but they were furious enough to kill him with their bare hands because he was preventing what they wanted to do. "They pressed sore upon the man, even Lot, and came near to break the door." Evidently, they had been standing at a little distance from Lot and his door, but now they began to swarm toward him, coming "near to break down the door." Lot lost his moral ground and was about to be overrun by the vicious mob.

And now the angels spring into action, and "the men put forth their hand, and pulled Lot into the house to them, and shut to the door. And they smote the men that were at the door of the house with blindness, both small and great: so that they wearied themselves to find the door."

With these actions, the two "men" reveal themselves for what they are—powerful holy angels sent by God to rescue Lot and his family. Lot's eyes are now opened to that reality. They were there to deliver "just Lot, vexed with the filthy conversation of the wicked." Yes, it was Lot who had sent up that cry for deliverance, that brought down the LORD to investigate the situation. Lot had been "that righteous man dwelling among them, seeing and hearing" the continual sins against his LORD and it "vexed his righteous soul from day to day with their unlawful deeds." (2 Peter 2:7, 8).

But he was the only one, and Abraham's prayer for the salvation of that wicked city if there were "ten righteous persons" in it, proved to be an unanswerable prayer.

28

Night of the Dead

Genesis 19:11-16

I've been thinking about Lot all weekend. If he was the "only good man left" in Sodom, that speaks volumes about the horrendous spiritually degraded condition of that city. And it says a significant amount about Lot's own spiritual condition, too. In contrast with his uncle, Lot does not display any spiritual fortitude when faced with this crisis. When he stepped out that door to his house, he did not go forth with courage built on a foreknowledge of God's power to protect him and his household. He did not display any faith in God at all, and that's why he was so afraid of the men yelling and threatening to kill him and rape his visitors.

And yet, God already sent Lot and his family a rescue team! There was no reason for Lot to be fearful of anything. His cry of distress had been heard by the LORD of all creation and was answered, but Lot didn't have faith enough to realize it. God's deliverance was there in the house with him, but he was too spiritually benumbed to see it.

In contrast, when Abraham was faced with the challenge of rescuing Lot and all the persons from Sodom that Chedorlaomer had hauled away, he had no doubt that he and his little band of 318 men would be able to defeat the five armies that were with Chedorlaomer. When he argued in favor of saving the cities on the plain, he also had no doubt that the "Judge of all the earth would do right" by those people. If there were any righteous, they would be saved. And Abraham was willing to accept the judgment even if they were not saved, because he had faith in the mercy and justice of the Judge. No one that *could* be saved would be lost because God failed to search for them and save them. "For the eyes of the LORD run to and fro throughout the whole earth, to shew Himself strong in the behalf of them whose heart is perfect toward Him." (2 Chronicles 16:9).

God would have saved the entire town, if they had been willing to repent and turn away from their wicked lifestyle. Sodom was not destroyed because God was wrathful and unforgiving, but because they refused the LORD's mercy and clung to their sin. Lot's confrontation with the men at his door was their last call from God to repent.

I find it interesting that the angels did not destroy the wicked men at Lot's door when they pulled Lot back inside the house. All those people were about to die anyway, so why not right then? Instead, the angels "smote the men that were at the door of the house with blindness, both small and great: so that they wearied themselves to find the door." This blindness was not that they *could not* see—that their eyes didn't have the *ability* to see—but that they were mentally confused. Their eyes could see, but could not see objects correctly.

In the story of the prophet Elisha and the Syrian army, we find a similar thing taking place. When the army in an attempt to capture him came down off the hill to attack the city where Elisha was staying, he "prayed unto the LORD, and said Smite this people, I pray Thee, with blindness." And when they had come to where Elisha was, he told them, "this is not the way, neither is this the city, follow me, and I will bring you to the man you seek." But he led them to Samaria and the king of Israel. And they didn't "see" where they were going until they got there, and didn't know they were being led the man they sought to capture (2 Kings 6:8-20).

The blindness inflicted upon the men of Sodom allowed them to return to their homes, and clear the streets so Lot could run unmolested to the houses of the other members of his family—his sons and sons in law who had married Lot's other daughters.

"And the men said unto Lot, Have you here any besides you?" Evidently during the entire evening while the men were with Lot, eating their supper and talking, the women of the household never made any appearance in the room. Lot must have prepared the meal for his guests without calling out his wife or daughters to help.

But the angels know Lot has family somewhere and they want to rescue them also, so they tell Lot go get your "son in law, and thy sons, and thy daughters, and whatsoever you have in the city, bring them out of this place. For we will destroy this place, because the cry of them is waxed great before the face of the LORD; and the LORD has sent us to destroy it." (Genesis 19:12, 13).

Now Lot knows for sure who he has been entertaining all evening. These "men" have finally fully revealed themselves as angels sent directly from God with the commission to destroy the wicked cities on the plain. His prayer for deliverance is answered. He must accept that the destruction of the city is impending and prepare to leave that wicked place.

Hurriedly Lot ran out into the streets to warn his family. When he got their homes, he "spoke unto his sons in law, which married his daughters, and said, Up, get you out of this place; for the LORD will destroy this city. But he seemed as one that mocked unto his sons in law." They had deaf ears, turned off by the sins they lived among every day of their lives, never challenging the wrongness of them.

Sin was so commonplace and so openly committed that it was no longer seen as sin, and was not in the last offensive to these young men and women. It was life as usual in that city. Like the postmodern world of today, they felt that everyone had a right to do as they wished and no one should be judged or condemned. There was no objective moral standard because the Law of God had been cast aside.

Through Lot's efforts to collect up his family, going door to door in search of them, God was giving Sodom its final appeal to "come out" and be saved from the impending destruction. As Lot went out into the city, to the houses of his sons in law and sons and daughters that were not in his house with him, he was warning everyone, one last time. But they laughed at him as though he were a crazy man, talking about destruction. Who ever heard of such a thing?

This is why the angels did not kill those men at Lot's door, but instead blinded them. The door of mercy was still open and God gave one more chance for them to be saved. Lot was God's final emissary to that doomed city and the people refused the message.

With a heavy heart Lot returned to his home without anyone coming back with him. Only the two daughters living with him and his wife would make it out of Sodom alive. Weighted with the miserable thought that he had brought destruction upon his family by choosing to live among the wicked, he joined the angels in their haste from the city.

The people of Sodom were so morally degraded that they didn't have the ability to appreciate God's final mercy call. It is without doubt that Lot's heart was heavy when he came back home. No one would listen to him. He wasn't the first man to experience this feeling of rejection. Noah experienced the same thing just before the Flood came upon the world. Noah had preached the message of Christ and His righteousness as the only means of salvation for 120 years, and no one listened to him either.

One by one the righteous were laid in their graves before the Flood came, Methuselah being 969 years old when he died "in the year of the flood" as his name implies. Of all the billions living on the earth at that time, Noah was only able to convince his own three sons and their wives to believe in the coming destruction of the world by rain falling from the sky, a phenomenon the world had never seen.

Christ Himself preached mercy to Israel for three and a half years, but His message was rejected by those He came to save. As He hung on that cross, He felt that His mission had failed. "I am a worm, and no man; a reproach of men, and despised of the people. All they that see Me laugh Me to scorn: they shoot out the lip, they shake the head, saying, He trusted on the LORD that He would deliver Him: let Him deliver Him, seeing He delighted in Him." (Psalm 22:6-8).

And now in our own day, at the end of this world's history, people are so blinded, deafened, and distracted by the prince of this world[1] and all that he has to offer them, that they do not want to learn the final message of God's mercy that is to be proclaimed with a loud voice to all the world.[2] People don't have time or the inclination to listen to words of living truth that will save them from eternal destruction because they are too busy listening to their iPods and playing with

---

1. "Now is the judgment of this world: now shall the prince of this world be cast out. And I, if I be lifted up from the earth, will draw all men unto Me." (John 12:31, 32). "Wherein in time past ye walked according to the course of this world, according to the prince of the power of the air, the spirit that now works in the children of disobedience: among whom also we all had our conversation in times past in the lusts of our flesh, fulfilling the desires of the flesh and of the mind; and were by nature the children of wrath, even as others." (Ephesians 2:2, 3).

2. "And I saw another angel fly in the midst of heaven, having the everlasting gospel to preach unto them that dwell on the earth, and to every nation, and kindred, and tongue, and people, Saying with a loud voice, Fear God, and give glory to Him; for the hour of His judgment is come: and worship Him that made heaven, and earth, and the sea, and the fountains of waters." (Revelation 14:6, 7).

their iPhones and Xboxes, tuning in to Satan's message continually while tuning out the voice of the Holy Spirit that is calling them to repentance. Distracted by "the lust of the flesh, the lust of the eyes, and the pride of life," and intensely enjoying all the "pleasures of sin for a season," we are no different than the people living in those wicked cities on the plain.

But there will be one more attempt made by God just before Christ returns, when the fourth angel of Revelation 18:4 cries out "come out of her My people, and be ye not partakers of her sins, and that ye receive not of her plagues."

Parallel pleas from God from Genesis to Revelation—"come out and be not destroyed!" God has always worked to save sinners from destruction! Our God is an awesome God of love and mercy!

29

It's Just a Little Sin

Genesis 19:15-22

That long night of terror was coming to an end as the sun rose over the hills to the east of those doomed cities on the plain. "And when the morning arose, then the angels hastened Lot, saying, Arise, take thy wife, and thy two daughters, which are here; lest thou be consumed in the iniquity of the city." Only the two daughters that Lot threatened to throw out to the sex-crazed mob were in the house with him and his wife. From wherever they had been hiding, Lot now gathered them as he was ordered by the angels.

But for some reason Lot lingered. Unsure of what to do; where to go? Was he afraid to go out the door for fear of the people of Sodom who were then awakening and would see him escaping? Afraid that they would resume their assault in clambering to rape the two visitors? Was he wondering what he needed to take with them? What he would need in the place where the angels were taking them? He didn't know.

Whatever the reason, "while he lingered, the men laid hold upon his hand, and upon the hand of his wife, and upon the hand of his two daughters; the LORD being merciful unto him: and they brought him forth, and set him without the city."

Two mighty angels sent by the Sovereign of the universe, taking control of the desperate situation. One angel leading forth two people tightly held in his powerful grip, as a parent would lead his young children to safety. The hourglass of Sodom's destruction was running out of sand. Sin was to be dealt with thoroughly, without any remnant who could take their poison elsewhere.

"And it came to pass, when they had brought them forth abroad, that he [the angel] said, Escape for thy life; look not behind thee, neither stay thou in all the plain; escape to the mountain, lest thou be consumed." Our God is "a consuming fire" and sin and its results cannot exist in His presence. All that was associated with Sodom and Gomorrah in the valley surrounding the cities was about to experience the "presence of God" that they had rejected for so long.

When the angels had hurried Lot and his family along to a safe distance from ground zero, they let go of their charge's hands and were about to return to their appointment in the city when Lot again showed his weakness and lack of faith in God's protection. When told to run on ahead without the angels he became more frightened. Being left alone to manage getting his family to the mountains that were some distance to the east of the city, it seemed to overwhelm him. Perhaps he had never in his life ventured into those places and was unsure of the environment and benignity of its inhabitants. We read farther down in the narrative that, according to his daughters, Lot is old and possibly feeble, which would have added to his insecurity.

And so when told to run to the mountains in the distance he complained, "Oh, not so, my Lord: behold now, thy servant has found grace in thy sight, and thou has magnified thy mercy, which thou has shown unto me in saving my life!"

Lot made sure that the rescuers knew how much he appreciated their assistance in saving him, but he was greatly alarmed by being told to go on alone. Crippling fear made him incapable of action. "I cannot escape to the mountain, lest some evil take me, and I die."

He didn't know exactly what he was scared of, but he was sure it was going to kill him, as if the One who had intervened for his rescue would not have protected him also in the mountain's desolate places! Oh, how quickly Lot forgot the events of just a few hours before when he was saved from the roaring mob outside his door! It is by remembering all that God has done for us in the past that we learn to walk forward without fear, relying only on Him who watches over us with tender loving care.

In this narrative it seems that Lot is devoid of any faith in God. No matter how much God does to protect him, he seems blind to what is really taking place. Whatever he had been saved *from* was not as terrible as the unknown that loomed before him. Living among the evil in Sodom with only wickedness as his "model" in life, he had not learned how to walk by faith and not by sight (see 2 Corinthians 5:7).

One has to wonder at this blatant misunderstanding of God's protection. Why does Lot fear the mountains, but not the city of Zoar that was contaminated with the same sins as Sodom? He is fully aware of its wickedness, and knows that is why Sodom is going to be destroyed. Why does he assume that he can find safety in the iniquitous town of Zoar rather than in the place that God Himself has selected for his shelter from the fire bombing that was soon to pour down from heaven?

Relying on his own ideas, he was really choosing to stay close to the cities of hell rather than running for the heavenly abode. He was suspicious and fearful of the mountains that were free from sin while opting to remain in a city that was overflowing with crime and vice, just as Sodom was. He was still desiring a place that was an abomination to God rather than seeking the shelter of the mountains that were free from the contamination of Sodom's wickedness.

Lot appealed to the mercy of the angels once more by saying, "Behold now, this city is near to flee unto, and it is a little one: oh, let me escape thither, (is it not a little one?) and my soul shall live." Earnestly appealing to the angels for even more from them than he has already received, he begged to be allowed to run to the nearby city of Zoar. This "little city" was located very near to Sodom, closer than the mountains, which reveals that perhaps Lot is a trifle lazy in not wanting to expend the effort to run the greater distance to the hills. Zoar was the easy way out.

Lot pretended that the city was "little" and therefore not as sin-filled, not as bad as Sodom, in hopes that this would justify his request of a more easily obtained asylum. He begged only a tiny corner there among the wicked instead of being alone in the rugged mountains to the east, a desolate place that would not afford him any creature comforts at all. This is a remarkable display of moral dull-headedness and lazy selfishness on the part of Lot. It is the same obtuseness he demonstrated when Abraham brought him back from Chedorlaomer, when he chose to return to Sodom instead of returning to Hebron and Abraham's godly abode.

God never forces anyone to keep His gift of mercy and salvation. He does all He can to convince the sinner, but in the end will give him what he wants most. And so the angel relinquishes, and "he said to him, Alright I will grant you this also, that I will not demolish the town that you have spoken about. Now hurry up! Run there, for I cannot do anything until you get there. Therefore the name of the city was called Zoar" which means "little one."

Lot's request to go to this "little town" was to the angel as a statement in favor of its continued probation. And God gave the angel a nod of acceptance to Lot's plea, and so he replied, "I will not overthrow it because you have spoken in its favor." The angel would never have made a decision such as this on his own when God had commanded him to destroy all five of the cities on the plain, none excepted. It was God's mercy to Lot that saved Zoar that day.

The angel was sent to destroy Sodom, but also to preserve Lot and his family, so he cannot do the former until the later is accomplished. The angels delayed their appointed task until Lot managed to make his way to the nearby town. And that took all of the day. Genesis 19:23 tells us that "the sun had risen over the land when Lot came to Zoar." The phrase means that "the sun had gone forth *over* the land"—passed overhead—by the time that Lot got to Zoar. In other words, the sun had completed its path through the sky and was in the process of setting in the west by the time Lot reached Zoar.

Thus, Lot had from dawn, when the angels physically hauled him out of Sodom, to dusk to travel the distance from where the angels left them, until he got to Zoar. Even a tired old man could walk five miles in about 10 hours. The nearby eastern mountains must have been located closer than that, and would have afforded more protection from what was about to come raining down out of the sky, for God told the angels to send Lot into the mountains, but he refused to go.

In 1973 solid archeological evidence emerged that located the remains of two cities, probably Sodom and Gomorrah, buried under the southern end of the Dead Sea. The five cities Sodom, Gomorrah, Admah, Zeboim, and Bela (Zoar, cf. Genesis 14:2) were about five miles from each other, in a cluster in the Valley of Siddim.

The conflagration that was about to erupt there on the plain would consume everything within several surrounding miles. It was imperative that Lot and his family get as far away, as fast as they could.

The guiding and protecting angel would not have told Lot to head for the mountains if that distance was too far for them to obtain it in a reasonable amount of time. The mountains to the east were within easy distance of the plain, or God would not have chosen them for Lot's refuge. God never asks of us more than He also enables us to accomplish through faith in His power.

But since Lot didn't think he could make it that far, nor endure the hardship of life in that craggy terrain, he was allowed to enter Zoar. That God was willing to spare the "little" wicked city of Zoar because it became a sanctuary for the object of His love, is a significant revelation of God's character of mercy and grace toward all, even the worst of sinners.

30

Don't Look Back!

Genesis 19:23-26

It was beginning to grow dark when Lot and his family finally arrived at Zoar's town gate. Twenty-four hours have passed since he was calmly sitting in the gate of Sodom, and welcoming his two visitors to his home. What a wild twenty-four hours it had been!

God is infinitely patient and merciful toward sinners, but probation does not go on forever. The clock was on overtime for Sodom and Gomorrah because of Lot's insistence that he needed to get to Zoar, but as Lot passed through the gates of that "little city," and was safely away from the danger zone, the "LORD rained upon Sodom and upon Gomorrah brimstone and fire from the LORD out of heaven; and He overthrew those cities, and all the plain, and all the inhabitants of the cities, and that which grew upon the ground." The timing of the destruction of those cities depended upon Lot getting away from their neighborhoods. Once he was clear of peril, the conflagration began.

But Lot's wife took one more look at her home as she was about to pass into safety, and instantly "she became a pillar of salt" (Genesis 19:26). When God asks you to leave all and follow Him to safety, remember His imperative: "Remember Lot's wife!" Don't look back upon what you have left behind of your sinful existence. That longing back-glance at the sins you love could cause your eternal destruction.

No one really can explain what happened to those cities that were located at the southern tip of the Dead Sea. Archeological surveys have found what appears to be the remains of structures buried deep, but work in these places is hindered by the thick, sticky petroleum slime or "tar" that continually bubbles to the surface of the sea in that area. The Bible calls this gooey stuff brimstone, which is a sulphurous bituminous tarry substance (aka natural asphalt) that is flammable. At ordinary temperatures it forms sticky clumps, but when it catches fire, it thins and runs in streams giving off suffocating fumes.

The La Brea tar pits in Los Angeles are an example of this type of natural formation where the asphalt seeps from the underground to the surface and forms pools or lakes. Excavation of the La Brea pits have brought up large mammalian bones, the remains of animals that got trapped in the sticky slime. The pit was known by Native Americans for thousands of years, and they used its goo to seal canoes.

In Trinidad and Tobago there is a large lake of natural asphalt that contributes tens of thousands of tons of pitch per year for use around the world in road building. It has been estimated that this huge asphalt lake has reserves of about six million tons. As the asphalt is mined, it is steadily replenished from below ground.

One thought that can be taken from this fact is that not all "petroleum" is "fossil fuel." How can that be the case when animals (according to evolution's theory) are not currently being buried in the ground, decaying over "millions" of years to produce "fossil" oil and asphalt? Evidently, from the very fact that the asphalt lake in Trinidad and Tobago is continually replenishing itself, the petroleum must have some other natural mechanism by which it is created.

Asphalt volcanoes have been discovered under the Gulf of Mexico, and several quite large asphalt volcanoes are located off the coast of Santa Barbara, California. Smaller asphalt volcanoes are located at Carpinteria, California, and at one time they were used as an asphalt mine. Both Santa Barbara and Carpinteria are earthquake-prone, being just to the west of the San Andreas fault. Often associated with underwater asphalt volcanoes, are mineral structures known as salt domes.

Palestine is also on a major fault line that runs down the middle of the Dead Sea. This fault line divides the Arabian Plate from the African Plate. Earthquakes are not infrequent along this rift, and a most notable one occurred in AD 31, when Christ died on the cross outside Jerusalem. Josephus reported that more than 30,000 people died in that earthquake. In 1927 there was a major earthquake with its epicenter located at the northern end of the Dead Sea.

All this diversion into geology has a point.

Though the Bible does not supply us with specific information about how Sodom and Gomorrah were destroyed, there is enough geological information that can be gathered from similar natural events in other parts of the world to be able to make a fairly accurate assessment about what occurred that day. All the necessary elements were in place at Sodom and Gomorrah—a fault line with volcanic potential (like we find in Santa Barbara), and naturally occurring semi-liquid flammable bitumen (such as in the La Brea "tar" pits). All God had to do was remove His protection and the place exploded into a massive fireball.

As the explosions began, Lot and his daughters scurried inside the city before the gates were closed for the night, but Lot's wife, running at a distance behind them, halted and turned around to see what was taking place at her beloved city, "and she became a pillar of salt," like those salt domes that are found associated with asphalt volcanoes.

"Remember Lot's wife" is Christ's admonition to His people at the end of time. "Likewise also as it was in the days of Lot; they did eat, they drank, they bought, they sold, they planted, they builded; but the same day that Lot went out of Sodom it rained fire and brimstone from heaven, and destroyed them all. Even thus shall it be in the day when the Son of man is revealed." (Luke 17:32, 28-30).

When that day arrives, Jesus told us not to look back in longing desire for what is about to come to an end. Don't turn around wishing that you could hang on to your material, earthly things and still gain the eternal promises.

With the destruction of Sodom, thus is ended the third period of Lot's life. He is first introduced to us as Abraham's nephew, then we know him as member of Abraham's clan, after which he makes his decision to live in Sodom. Twenty years pass with him living in that wicked environment, during which he acquires a wife and children. But in one day comes annihilation of his chosen home, his wealth, his companions of the city, and his family, except two daughters, who, it would seem later, are as morally corrupted as the rest who perished in the conflagration.

But even though negatively effected by his surroundings, we still find evidence of goodness in Lot's character. In his story recorded in Genesis chapter 19 we have found a man who means well, even if he can't always carry out his good intentions. He was a hospitable person, kind, courteous, generous, all of which were exhibited toward his two strange visitors. He was also a man who possessed natural shame for the sins that were so blatantly committed all around him. He never seemed to become inured to the sin that was always in his face, but "cried out" to the God of heaven because his home was so corrupted.

We learn more about Lot's repugnance of the sin of Sodom from what he said to the men who were attempting to beat down his door to get at the strangers. In kindness toward them hoping to divert the danger, Lot called these men "brethren" and admonished them, "do not so wickedly!" His pleading was from a gentle heart that wanted his "brethren" to repent of their wickedness and go home without committing the sin they came to do.

Lot's loyalty was demonstrated when he ran out after his other daughters and their husbands, unmindful of the usual nighttime dangers of the city. His only thought was to bring his family members into the safety of his angelic protectors. His humbleness is evidenced when the angels were about to leave him, and Lot poured out his gratitude for all that they had done to save him.

Outward actions that were provoked though fear, belie Lot's true heart condition. When He judges, God looks at the inward part, not the outward actions. He knows what has happened in our lives to shape the decisions we make. "I am He which searcheth the reins and hearts" (Revelation 2:23). Christ knows our mind and inmost motives. And so, in the end, the apostle Peter could write an epitaph of Lot saying that God "delivered just Lot, [who was] vexed with the filthy conversation of the wicked: (for that righteous man dwelling among them, in seeing and hearing, vexed his righteous soul from day to day with their unlawful deeds); the Lord knows how to deliver the godly out of temptations, and to reserve the unjust unto the day of judgment to be punished." (2 Peter 2:7-9).

But the wide contrast with Abraham's character is always before our mind. The most lasting impressions from the Lot narrative are made by what we see of Lot's selfishness and worldliness that cause vacillation and cowardice in him when he is faced with the trauma of having to give up his home, family and friends. This paves the way for the sad closing scene of his life's record.

31

A Tragic Life

Genesis 19:27-38

Okay, let's summarize Lot's history before we look at the final chapter of his bittersweet life. He was the son of Haran, Abraham's brother, and therefore represents that branch of the family descended from Terah. His grandfather, Terah, was an idol worshiper, and this seems to be a weak point in Lot's character, too. Lot may not have had statues and other objects of pagan worship in his home, but he did idolize his material possessions and the ease of Sodom's city lifestyle.

When he was instructed to flee to the mountains and told not to look back, because of his weak faith he found that command an impossibility. Living a life of comfort in the city, he never learned to rely completely upon God's protection. If we have not learned this lesson before we need it, it may be too late when we find ourself in a strait place without basic resources for survival.

"And Abraham got up early in the morning to the place where he stood before the LORD." This place was the same ridge overlooking the Siddim Valley where Abraham had argued with the LORD in favor of saving the all people of Sodom and Gomorrah if ten "righteous persons" could be found living in those wicked cities.

Counting up what we know from the narrative, Abraham was bargaining on the assumption that Lot's family would be found worthy. There was Lot, his wife, two daughters in the house with him, at least two sons and a son in law (Genesis 19:12), and the wives of those young men, making a total of ten persons in Lot's family. The LORD answered Abraham's argument with the promise that if He *could* find ten righteous persons, He would not destroy the city (Genesis 18:32). Even though the outcome was already known to Him, the LORD was gracious toward His faithful servant's request.

"And he looked toward Sodom and Gomorrah, and toward all the land of the plain, and beheld, and, lo, the smoke of the country went up as the smoke of a furnace." The cities had been burning all night and were not yet anywhere near being fully consumed, the wickedness was so great. Smoke still boiled upward into the morning sunlight and was quite visible at the distance from which Abraham was observing the destruction of Lot's former home. He had no knowledge of whether or not Lot had been rescued before the conflagration began.

But Abraham had faith in God, and that was enough for him. His prayer for Lot's safety was answered. "And it came to pass, when God destroyed the cities of the plain, that God remembered Abraham, and sent Lot out of the midst of the overthrow, when He overthrew the cities in the which Lot dwelt." The apostle James wrote that "the effectual fervent prayer of a righteous man avails much" (James 5:16).

It doesn't take much imagination to believe that Abraham prayed all of the previous night for his family living in Sodom. And seeing the devastation below him, Abraham believed that God had kept His promise, and Lot was indeed safely out of that city. Abraham could return to his home in peace, resting in the faith of God's promise.

It didn't take Lot long to regret his decision to take refuge in Zoar instead of the mountains, as God had originally commanded him. Looking out of the city upon the still smoking ruins of Sodom and Gomorrah, he came to his senses realizing that he could have been destroyed with all the wicked in Sodom, if God had not sent those two angels to rescue him.

As the aftershocks continued to rock the plain, Lot became fearful of staying in a city that was just as wicked as the one he had been rescued from. Zoar, too, might soon receive the same judgment. Twice he had been miraculously delivered from death, and now it was past time to follow God in leaving behind the evil of those cities.

"And Lot went up out of Zoar, and dwelt in the mountain, and his two daughters with him; for he feared to dwell in Zoar: and he dwelt in a cave, he and his two daughters." Doubtless, when Lot left Sodom that fateful night, he had with him some form of money, as any person normally would have in a pouch tied to his waist sash. It was enough for him to purchase victuals to sustain him and his daughters while they lived in the cave they found in the mountain on the eastern rim of the valley.

Then one day, the oldest daughter cooked up a plot. "And the firstborn said unto the younger, Our father is old, and there is not a man in the earth to come in unto us after the manner of all the earth: come, let us make our father drink wine, and we will lie with him, that we may preserve seed of our father."

They were not thinking of a purely sexual and incestuous encounter with their old father, but were intent on preserving the family name. After what they had seen concerning the demolition of the only home they had never known, it was natural for them to believe that "there was not a man on the earth to come in unto us"—to marry them and give them children. They had survived an Armageddon-like event and it was easy for them to believe it had been nearly universal, except for nearby Zoar. Lot was the only surviving male of their family. Conserving something of the family heritage seemed now to take priority over social convention.

"And they made their father drink wine that night," the implication being that Lot would never have willingly consented to incest with his daughters, unless they had gotten him drunk. "And the firstborn went in, and lay with her father; and he perceived not when she lay down, nor when she arose." Lot was in such a drunken stupor that he had no knowledge of what he had done. But one has to wonder what he thought of his hangover the next morning!

"And it came to pass on the morrow, that the firstborn said unto the younger, Behold, I lay yesternight with my father: let us make him drink wine this night also; and go thou in, and lie with him, that we may preserve seed of our father."

Somehow, the sly daughters were able the following night to cajole and convince their poor father to again drink too much alcohol. Perhaps the old man was having serious depression or post-traumatic shock from all that he had been through. Everything he owned was lost. His sons and other daughters and his wife were all dead in their sins and lost eternally. How much was he to blame for it all, since he chose to live in that wicked environment, exposing his family continually to terrible sin and violence? It would not be unreasonable to assume that Lot was in such a deranged state of mind that his moral compass was failing him. In that mental condition, the application of alcohol quickly overwhelmed his normal moral standards.

"And they made their father drink wine that night also: and the younger arose, and lay with him; and he perceived not when she lay down, nor when she arose. Thus were both the daughters of Lot with child by their father."

And so, Lot comes to an opprobrious end. His history is not told beyond these verses in Genesis 19. He fades away into oblivion, only being mentioned four more times in the entire Bible: twice as the father of Moab and Ammon (descendants of whom demonstrated shameful hostility toward the children of Israel); once in the reference by Christ to the overthrow of Sodom; and then by the apostle Peter, who calls him a "righteous man" when all the evidence seems to tell us otherwise.

And here in the closing scenes of Lot's life we also have a literary tragicomedy. Contrary to their Aunt Sarah who strove for sixty years to get pregnant, and still had not produced the promised heir, these two young girls are successful on the first try.

But their two sons were not conceived through faith in God, but by the works and contrivance of human flesh. What they told their father about their pregnancies is not revealed to us. Lot called them "virgins" when offering them to the sex-crazed mob outside his door. Yet now they are both pregnant at the same time. Since they were living in a cave in the mountains, far away from other people, Lot must have been told, or deduced, that he was the father of these two boys. "And the firstborn [daughter] bare a son, and called his name Moab: the same is the father of the Moabites unto this day. And the younger, she also bare a son, and called his name Benammi: the same is the father of the children of Ammon unto this day."

Moab and Benammi went on to be two great nations who possessed the territory on the east side of the Dead Sea beyond the mountains in which they were conceived. When the children of Israel entered into Canaan, God commanded them, "Distress not the Moabites, neither contend with them in battle: for I will not give thee of their land for a possession; because I have given Ar unto the children of Lot for a possession."

God was merciful to Lot's descendants through the sons conceived in that incestuous relationship with his daughters. "And when thou comest nigh over against the children of Ammon, distress them not, nor meddle with them: for I will not give thee of the land of the children of Ammon any possession; because I have given it unto the children of Lot for a possession." (Deuteronomy 2:9, 19).

However they were not to forever remain under the blessings of the LORD. Their immoral beginning and improper spiritual training learned from their mothers, contributed to their degradation as a people, so that they soon accepted the gods of the Canaanites, fell into an abominable lifestyle, and eventually became the enemies of the children of Israel.

Nevertheless, from this disgraceful beginning, comes two great mothers of Israel. Ruth the Moabitess was an ancestor of King David through her marriage to Boaz (Ruth 4:21, 22), and the Ammonite woman called Naamah became the wife of Solomon and the mother of King Rehoboam of Judah (1 Kings 14:21).

So we find that out of these squalid events recorded in Genesis 19:30-38, there arose the seed of messianic redemption through the Moabitess Ruth (Matthew 1:5). No matter how bad things appear, no matter how hard Satan works to destroy God's plan of redemption, God is able to bring to completion His divine will for mankind.

32

Abraham Does It Again

Genesis 20:1-13

Very true!—I did just jump right over Lot's wife and her demise. Though the language seems literal, we should not assume that her body literally became salt instead of flesh. With the violent events taking place just behind her, the sulphurous vapors and fiery explosions pouring from the earthquake's fissures, and the turbulence of the salty sea rising in great waves releasing mist into the air, it is reasonable that she was first burned to a cinder and was then encrusted with the salty mist that rained down as "salt snow" quickly covering her so that she resembled a statue made of salt. Even today, objects in close vicinity to the Dead Sea are quickly encrusted with a salt rime.

There is an entry in Josephus's works where he said that the "statue" was still standing in his day, and that he had seen it. "But Lot's wife continually turning back to view the city as she went from it, and being too nicely inquisitive what would become of it, although God had forbidden her so to do, was changed into a pillar of salt; for I have seen it, and it remains at this day." (*The Antiquities of the Jews*, Book 1, chapter 11, section 4).

Scripture does not tell us whether or not Abraham ever had any more contact with Lot and his daughters, or ever knew anything about where they ended up. Perhaps, like so many other things at that time, news of Lot traveled to Abraham via the trading caravans that came into Hebron from the King's Highway east of the Dead Sea. The last we heard about Lot, those mountains are where he was living in a cave.

"And Abraham journeyed from thence toward the south country, and dwelled between Kadesh and Shur, and sojourned in Gerar." (Genesis 20:1)

For some unexplained reason, Abraham struck camp and went about 50 miles southwest from Hebron into the district inhabited by the Philistines. Gerar is just on the northern edge of the Wilderness of Shur, which is located in the northern end of the Sinai Peninsula. Kadesh was the place where the children of Israel met their challenge of faith coming out of Egypt. And they failed there, numerous times. Kadesh is full of history for the people of the Bible.

When Hagar fled from Sarah's wrath, she ended up at the spring of Beer-lahai-roi which is between Kadesh and Bered where the Angel of the LORD appeared to her (Genesis 14:7; Genesis 16:14). As the children of Israel were about to enter the land of Canaan, they opted to send in twelve spies to reconnoiter the land. The returning spies found the twelve tribes camped at Kadesh, and when they gave their evil report of the inability of the people to conquer the land—again, they exhibited no confidence in God's promise or power—it was at Kadesh that they were condemned to stay for 38 years, until all the unbelievers were dead.

It was at Kadesh that they rebelled against Moses concerning the lack of water. And Moses failed there, too, because instead of *speaking* to the Rock, out of anger and frustration with the people, he *struck* it, and not just once, but twice—a lapse of faith that caused him to lose entrance into the promised land (Numbers 20:8-12). And Miriam died at Kadesh. A lot of Bible history occurred in this one place.

And here at Kadesh, once again, Abraham shows his lack of faith in God's power and promise.

"And Abraham said of Sarah his wife, She is my sister: and Abimelech king of Gerar sent, and took Sarah." This is the exact same ploy Abraham played in Egypt with Pharaoh! What is he thinking? That lie didn't work 25 years before, why would he think it would work now? And he tells this lie without provocation from Abimelech. No threat has been received from the king of that place. Yet, Abraham seems to have thought he was threatened for some reason, and again he is willing to throw out his old wife as a sacrifice to protect himself. And this action was taken soon after he was visited by the LORD who told them that Sarah would bear his son in one year! What a short memory he had.

It is really curious that these pagan kings of Egypt and Philistia thought that it was their "divine right" as kings to steal another man's wife or, in this case, "sister." In reality, it was probably a power play. Taking a man's wife, or the principle female in a tribe, without a fight showed their political power over the man from whom the woman was taken. This is the meaning when Absalom raped David's concubines (2 Samuel 15:16; 16:22). Amazingly, at the age of ninety, Sarah must still have been a very attractive woman, or no man would have looked at her twice to even consider her a political "prize."

But God was not going to let anything happen at this late date in the heir game, and so "God came to Abimelech in a dream by night, and said to him, Behold, thou art but a dead man, for the woman which thou hast taken; for she is a man's wife." In this verse we learn that God will talk with pagans just as well as a "righteous man," if it serves His purpose. He later spoke to Nebuchadnezzar in a dream that became one of the foundational prophecies of the history of the world.

God told Abimelech plainly, without mincing words: You're a dead man, Abimelech because you have taken another man's wife. Serious language. No denying the fact, and no offer of escape. "But Abimelech had not come near her: and he said, Lord, wilt Thou slay also a righteous nation?"

Obviously, Abimelech had heard about Sodom and Gomorrah's destruction for their wickedness, and knew that that destruction was by divine judgment upon those wicked cities who rejected the appeals from the God of the universe to repent. It is true that there was no daily newspaper or Internet news outlet or CNN, but news did travel through other means, and it travelled quickly. Everyone everywhere knew about the destruction of the cities on the plain.

Somehow, Abimelech was able to recognize the voice of the LORD in that dream, and he made the same appeal that Abraham did for the salvation of those cities on the plain: "Will You destroy the righteous with the wicked?" O righteous God, will you destroy me, who am innocent of your charges against me?

Then Abimelech laid out his defense. "Said [Abraham] not unto me, She is my sister? and she, even she herself said, He is my brother: in the integrity of my heart and innocency of my hands have I done this." He didn't know that Abraham and Sarah were both lying to him about their true relationship. He was an "innocent man" in this situation by the moral standards of his culture, but not by God's moral standard. Polygamy and adultery have never been God's standard. Abimelech was being judged by the higher standard, not that of his own society's customs and ethics.

"God said to him in the dream, "Yes, I know that you did this with a clear conscience. I have also kept you from sinning against Me. Therefore I have not let you touch her" (Genesis 20:6, HCSB). God Himself had taken out of Abimelech's mind any desire to take this women into his bed. Sarah had been brought into his camp, but not into his house. "Now therefore restore the man his wife; for he is a prophet, and he shall pray for you, and you will live: and if you restore her not, know you that you shalt surely die, you, and all that are yours."

Abimelech's entire tribe would die for his sin, if he did not hastily send Sarah back to Abraham. "Therefore Abimelech rose early in the morning, and called all his servants, and told all these things in their ears: and the men were sore afraid." Of course the men of his tribe were afraid! That they should be condemned to die along with their king for *his* sin, seemed the height of injustice.

God was making the point that there is corporate responsibility for sin and a need for corporate repentance.[1] We live in a sinful world, and because our basic human nature "is enmity against God" (Romans 8:7), we accept various sins as normal for the society in which we live. Hazy, indistinct ideas about what constitutes sin produces only a hazy, indistinct response to it when we're confronted by it. This is a major reason why there is so much apostasy and backsliding in the church.

---

1. "Corporate" guilt and responsibility, in the theological sense of the term, is Biblical. First Corinthians 12:12-26 teaches us that the church is "one body"—one "corpus"—and that the many "members" of the body are all answerable to and responsible for each other. "When one member [of the body] suffers, all the members suffer with it; or if one member is honored, all members rejoice with it" (verse 26). When King David sinned in calling for a census to determine the size of his army, all of Israel suffered for his lack of faith in God. David had a choice to make when the prophet Gad came to him declaring the punishment: seven years of famine on the entire land, three months of running from his enemies, or a pestilence on the land. He chose the pestilence, "so the LORD sent the pestilence upon Israel from morning even to the time appointed: and there died of the people from Dan even to Beer-sheba seventy thousand men." (2 Samuel 24:15). At Pentecost, with Jews gathered from every nation, Peter was led of the Holy Spirit to preach a sermon on their corporate guilt and responsibility in crucifying the Son of God. He gave indisputable evidence of their guilt and sin and 3000 repented. (Acts 2:22-24).

Lot's children, raised in a completely immoral society, succumbed to sin's seduction and could not discern the danger when their father warned them to flee in the night to avoid destruction. They had been so influenced by the society in which they lived, through mind working upon mind during their daily associations, that the "natural" enmity they had for God was stimulated into action. We may shake our heads in disbelief over their wrong decision, but we are of the same mind. We await only convenient circumstances to demonstrate our willingness to also commit the same sin that we frown on in others.

Through our neglect to call sin by its right name, we are constantly compromising our moral convictions, convincing ourselves little by little that "sin must not be so bad" since the whole of our society is committing it without apparent condemnation. By our silence and lack of moral outrage when confronted by evil, we are in essence condoning those sins committed by society. We become complicit through our silent acceptance of the evil.

Corporate responsibility and corporate guilt require corporate repentance for sins we would have committed had we been given the opportunity. We all have the same sinful heart of rebellion against God, and we are unaware of the depth of sin to which we would sink if given the chance. The counsel given by the Faithful and True Witness, who "knows our works" of evil is "be zealous therefore, and repent" (Revelation 3:19).

"Then Abimelech called Abraham, and said unto him, What have you done to us? and what have I offended you, that you have brought on me and on my kingdom a great sin? You have done deeds unto me that ought not to be done!"

Abimelech is justifiably angry over what had taken place, and what could Abraham say in his defense? Nothing. He knowingly tricked the king because of his self-centeredness and fear for his own safety, and most importantly, because of his lack of faith in God's power and promise. "And Abimelech said unto Abraham, What did you see, that you have done this thing?" What kind of threat was I to you when you moved into my territory? Did I or my people do or say anything to make you feel unsafe, causing you to lie to me like this?

"And Abraham said, Because I thought, Surely the fear of God is not in this place; and they will slay me for my wife's sake." As the narrative played itself out, it is obvious that Abraham's assumption was inaccurate. Abimelech did have some "fear of God" because he responded to God's voice when He spoke to him in his dream.

Abraham would not give up on his self-justification for his lying. "And yet indeed she is my sister; she is the daughter of my father, but not the daughter of my mother; and she became my wife." Yes, it is true that Sarah was his half-sister, but that does not minimize the greater fact that she is his wife, and very soon would conceive the promised son who would be heir to the blessings of God!

Abraham continues with his demonstration of false reasoning. He now states that this lie was a pact made between him and Sarah decades ago. It was their "habit" or custom to make the claim that they were brother and sister rather than husband and wife. "And it came to pass, when God caused me to wander from my father's house, that I said unto her, This is thy kindness which thou shalt shew unto me; at every place whither we shall come, say of me, he is my brother."

There is no consideration in Abraham's proposition for what this lie would bring upon Sarah who was laid wide open to the very real possibility of being taken from her husband and used as a concubine in another man's household.

It is the same song that he chirped for the pharaoh of Egypt. The same misinterpretation of the situation that he used to justify his lie. Nearly twenty-five years have passed and not one iota is diminished in Abraham's willingness to fall back on the same lie. You just have to shake your head in disbelief of Abraham's thick-headedness. How much does God have to do to prove to Abraham what must take place in his heart for him and his lawful wife to bring the promised heir into reality?

Just a couple months before this affair with Abimelech, the LORD had appeared at Abraham's tent door telling him, again, that Sarah would be the mother of his son before a year had expired. But here goes Abraham once more handing his wife off to another man, thus potentially threatening the reality of God's promise.

Like all of us, Abraham's enmity toward God that is the root of all unbelief, runs deep causing him to commit the same sin, over and over. His eyes where not yet fully focused on his LORD, but remained turned toward himself.

33

Sarah's Final Exam

Genesis 20:14-18

Well, we don't have any information about why Abraham moved from Hebron to Gerar, but being a shepherd with lots and lots of animals to keep fed, it probably was due to the need of fresh pasturage or water. At that time the Philistines didn't appear to be very hostile toward others living in Canaan. The Philistines were originally a sea-going people who traded with other peoples along the Mediterranean coasts. So the king here was not necessarily an enemy of Abraham.

But Abraham did move into his territory, and taking or giving a woman from the tribe was a traditional method of ensuring peace between two tribes or nations. Solomon's many wives were of this political order, his first wife being an Egyptian (1 Kings 3:1), but this was also the beginning of Solomon's downfall. His many foreign wives influenced his spiritual thinking turning him away from the one true God. None of Solomon's sons figure into the genealogy of Christ. Jesus was descended through David's third son by Bathsheba, who was named Nathan (2 Samuel 5:14; cf. Luke 3:31).

Marrying off daughters for political alliance was common even up to the 1800s when Queen Victoria married her five daughters to the various heads of state in Europe and Russia. It has been said that World War I was just a big family feud. There was so much German blood in the British royal house that after that war, the family changed their name to Windsor to appease the anti-German sentiments of England. But all of this is way off task, so we swerve back to Genesis chapter 20.

"And Abimelech took sheep, and oxen, and menservants, and women servants, and gave them unto Abraham, and restored him Sarah his wife." Just as pharaoh had done when God warned him about Abraham's married status, Abimelech now rewards Abraham with the same kinds of things—servants and livestock—making him richer than when he went down to Gerar.

This sort of makes it look like "you sin and you get great wealth," kind of a "prosperity" false gospel. In reality, it is more an action done by a pagan to appease what he understands as being the angry God of Abraham. Abraham's God threatened to kill him, so he better hand off lots of wealth to that God's earthly representative to make sure that the God of Abraham does not carry out His threat.

"And Abimelech said, Behold, my land is before thee: dwell where it pleaseth thee." Thus Abraham was able to dwell there in the vicinity of Abimelech without any fear of attack from the king or his shepherds and servants, who all now greatly feared him. Abraham had originally thought that the fear of God was not in that place (vs. 11). However, with Abimelech's generosity toward him, Abraham is assured that indeed, the "fear" of God *was* in that place. It is was not the "fear" of faith—awesome respect and honor due to God—but the very real apprehension of angering a most powerful God who promised to kill them all for their violation of the sanctity of His servant's wife.

"And unto Sarah [Abimelech] said, Behold, I have given thy *brother* a thousand pieces of silver: behold, he is to thee a covering of the eyes, unto all that are with thee, and with all other: thus she was reproved." We can almost hear Abimelech's sarcasm (though respectful) as he speaks directly to Sarah when he sent her away. "I gave your *brother* a thousand pieces of silver for you." The value here does not concern Sarah's worth, which would bring in a sense of harlotry on her part, but the value of all the livestock and servants. We can compare these verses with Exodus 21:32 to learn the value of animals and slaves, and thereby get an estimation of how many servants and animals were given to Abraham. A slave was reckoned to be worth 30 shekels.

Then he pointed to Abraham as Sarah's "covering." Both Abraham and Sarah had failed to put forth the "covering" of the marriage contract between them which, in the first place, led to the misunderstanding on Abimelech's part. And when neither Abraham nor Sarah complained about the abduction, Abimelech had no reason to believe he was doing anything more than making a peace pact between the tribes. So Abimelech's comment is a reproof of Sarah's lying to him by *omission* about her already being married. If she had declared up front that she was married to Abraham, Abimelech would have "covered his eyes" and never considered her as a woman to be brought as a concubine into his own household. In other words, if she had *acted* as a married woman, no one would have glanced her way twice.

The last two verses contain a great deal that must be placed back into the previous part of the narrative. Verse 18 must be read back to verse 6 for context. There was something that God did to all the people of Abimelech's tribe that prevented them from being able to conceive. "I withheld thee from sinning."

We do not know how long Abraham was encamped in that region, nor how long Sarah was in Abimelech's household before God spoke to him in that dream. But it was long enough that it became well known that no woman had been able to conceive, "for the LORD had fast closed up all the wombs of the house of Abimelech, because of Sarah Abraham's wife." Months must have passed for this inability to conceive to be noticed—but not too many months, because the clock is ticking toward the fulfillment of the LORD's promise that Sarah would have a son within the year.

As God plagued pharaoh's house because of Sarah, now He plagues Abimelech's house with barrenness—the curse that Sarah has borne all of her life was now the curse placed upon Abimelech's entire tribe. The barrenness continued long enough that it got the attention of the men and women in Abimelech's clan, long enough that they knew something had gone awry, and they were all effected by it. And the assumption was that it was due to that stranger in their midst and his weird God. In verse 7, God told Abimelech he must restore Abraham's wife and then His prophet would pray for him and he would be restored. A double play on the same word Hebrew word for "restore."

"So Abraham prayed unto God: and God healed Abimelech, and his wife, and his maidservants; and they bare children." This constituted the final lesson for Sarah's unbelief in God's power to give her a child. If God was strong enough to *close up* the wombs of that entire tribe, and then *open* them at His will, then He must also be strong enough to open her own dried up womb so that she could conceive the promised heir. This was what God had been working for all along, that Sarah would see and believe in His power to do as He promised. He alone could "open" her old dried up barren womb, restore to her the "time of life," and she would conceive the promised son.

And so, "the LORD visited Sarah as He had said, and the LORD did unto Sarah as He had spoken." (Genesis 21:1). Through the events that took place while they were in Gerar, Sarah was finally cleansed from all doubt, and God restored unto her "according to the time of life" as He had promised three months before (18:10, 14). Sarah birthed Isaac one year after the LORD made His promise to her; nine months after the incident with Abimelech.

After twenty-five years of struggling, it ended up being so simple! All Abraham and Sarah had to do was *believe* God's Word, the same Word that spoke every thing in the universe into existence from absolutely nothing. If He could create worlds and everything in them, then why would He not be able to fix a barren womb, and from it bring forth a son? The creative Word is powerful to accomplish just what He says He will, when we get ourselves out of His way.

When the LORD visited Abraham on His way to Sodom, He said, "Is anything too hard for the LORD?" No, nothing is too hard for Him. What *prevents* Him performing great things in each of our lives is the barrier *we erect* through our unbelief in His power to do just as He says He will in saving us from sin. The barrier of unbelief is impregnable to the power of the Holy Spirit,[1] because if we *will not believe*, then there is nothing the Holy Spirit can do. We drive Him away from our heart and mind and He is unable to bring us conviction and repentance, and through that, to transform our lives into a reflection of the character of our Saviour. By our unbelief, we make the active choice to throw away salvation so freely given to us.

---

1. "For it is impossible for those who were once enlightened, and have tasted of the heavenly gift, and were made partakers of the Holy Ghost, ... If they shall fall away, to renew them again unto repentance; seeing they crucify to themselves the Son of God afresh, and put Him to an open shame." (Hebrews 6:4, 6). "For if we sin wilfully after that we have received the knowledge of the truth, there remaineth no more sacrifice for sins, but a certain fearful looking for of judgment and fiery indignation, which shall devour the adversaries. He that despised Moses' law died without mercy under two or three witnesses: of how much sorer punishment, suppose ye, shall he be thought worthy, who hath trodden under foot the Son of God, and hath counted the blood of the covenant, wherewith he was sanctified, an unholy thing, and hath done despite unto the Spirit of grace?" (Hebrews 10:26-29).

34

What Is Faith?

What is faith? That's a good question. Many people are confused by this seemingly simple term. If you ask a half dozen people, you will get at least a half dozen different answers, maybe more. The current mantra seems to be "only believe and all things are possible"—but faith is not some magic formula. Faith is believing the Word only to do what that Word says He will do, yes, but it is more than that. Faith and "believing" must be grounded in a solid, Biblical concept of who it is we're "believing" in.

God is not some genie in a bottle who is simply waiting for us to make a wish so He demonstrate for us His power in granting that wish. God is the sovereign LORD and Master of the universe. He is not subject to anyone or anything. We are puny creatures and have no power to *command* God to *do* anything. "Faith" is not "power" or "authority" that allows us to *command* God to perform what we want Him to do for us just because we raise our hands in the air and mutter a few words. That is a very pagan concept of who God is.

In creation, the Word spoke and it was immediately accomplished, no time-lapse between His speaking and the appearing of what He spoke. At some point in the far, far distant past, there were no worlds, or stars, or suns, or creatures of any kind, but when He spoke there immediately appeared in the universe all of these things. When He spoke concerning this world, animals, fishes, plants of unnumbered variety appeared in their respective realms, fully formed and fully mature.

The same power that created everything can transform us when He speaks to our hearts that are fully surrendered to His love. Then all things are possible in our lives, too. This is why my favorite parts of the New Testament are the Gospels of Mark and John. They both are filled with Jesus saying, "just believe Me" and people were healed of their illness, crippled legs could walk, blind eyes could see, and some were even raised from the dead by the Word when He spoke. Those people who were healed *knew* that the Man standing before them *was* the Son of the Living God, that He is God Himself and that He alone has the power to perform what He says. The word of God is powerful and quick, but *our* word is *less than nothing* to accomplish anything.

If we think that "healing" from sin's problems in our lives takes a long time, then we really are acting like evolutionists—believing that change comes about only through long periods of time over which we continue to sin and repent and sin and repent until we get tired of the process and either give up on "religion" all together as a hopeless fake, or we finally *give up on ourselves* as the means of accomplishing that change in our lives. If we do the latter, *then* Christ can step in and do the work He has been wanting to do all along, just as with Abraham and Sarah. They had to get their unbelief out of God's way. Unbelief was creating a barrier for the work of God in their lives.

How the Living Word "Works" in Those Who Believe

Jairus's friends told him, "Thy daughter is dead: why troublest thou the Master any further? As soon as Jesus heard the word that was spoken, He saith unto the ruler of the synagogue, Be not afraid, only believe." And his daughter lived again, despite the scoffing of the man's friends and neighbors (Mark 5:35, 36).

To the woman who had a serious bleeding problem for twelve years, "He said unto her, Daughter, thy faith hath made thee whole; go in peace, and be whole of thy plague." And she went way immediately completely healed from her disease, not just the bleeding stanched, but her lost vitality was renewed (Mark 5:34).

To the father whose son was tormented by demons, "Jesus said unto him, If you can believe, all things are possible to him that believes." And the son was immediately set free from the devil that controlled him (Mark 9:23).

These examples of Christ's healing did not require long periods of time to effect the cure. The cure was immediate as soon the Word spoke to the needy person.

"When Jesus saw him lie, and knew that he had been now a long time in that case, He saith unto him, Wilt thou be made whole? The impotent man answered him, Sir, I have no man, when the water is troubled, to put me into the pool: but while I am coming, another steps down before me." This man had for many years been relying on the supposed "magic" that was thought to be in the spring of water when it bubbled up out of the ground. He had seen many other people climb down into the pool of water and apparently come up "healed."

But he was paralyzed in the legs and had "no man" to help him crawl into the water. This man's "faith" was focused on the wrong thing, whether in the water or in some person to help him get into the water. And now this stranger is standing before him asking him if he wants to be healed? Of course he wanted to be healed, but he didn't know how to accomplish it in his own power.

"Jesus said unto him, Rise, take up your bed, and walk. And immediately the man was made whole, and took up his bed, and walked: and on the same day was the Sabbath" (John 5:6-9). The man at the Pool of Bethesda went immediately from hopeless years of "faith" in the bubbling spring's water, to complete faith and confidence in Jesus' word spoken to him—rise up and walk! And he did; without questioning, contradicting or complaining, he rose up and walked.

In none of these stories or any of the others in the Gospels, does it take years—or even days or minutes—for the person to be healed from whatever is ailing them. Only the one blind man was sent away to *do* something else before he could see fully. In John 9:7, the blind man is sent to the Pool of Siloam to wash away the "mud" plaster that Jesus had put on the man's eyes. But this was done as a demonstration to all the neighbors and people who had known this man all of his life, so that they would also come to believe in the power of Jesus to heal us.

Like the old hymn says, "faith is the victory!"

The promise of God in sending Jesus is not about preventing colds or curing cancer, or putting money in our bank account. Material wealth or health is not the purpose of God's everlasting covenant. The everlasting covenant promise that was spoken by Christ to fallen Adam and Eve concerned overcoming their enmity toward their Creator so that He could *cure them of their disease of sin*. Sin brings death (James 1:15; cf. 1 Corinthians 15:56), and the only cure for death (the second death, which is eternal), is our own dying to self *now* "in Christ."

Romans 6:6, 7 tells us that the death of our "old man" of sin is what brings us freedom from that eternal death. The "old man" must be "crucified with Christ" (Galatians 2:20), and then we are resurrected "in newness of life" (Romans 6:4). When we learn to die to self, then we are a "new creature"—"therefore if any man be in Christ, he is a new creature: old things are passed away; behold, all things are become new." (2 Corinthians 5:17).

This is the whole point of the Gospel's message, that we become "new creatures" through Christ's power over sin and death (Revelation 1:18). But this is not magic or superstition or fantasy. Despite what agnostics and atheists say, there is nothing more *reasonable* than to believe in the power of God. It is the most profound truth, the depths of which, we will be studying throughout all eternity.

When we really learn to accept this truth, what logically follows is a *willing consecration* of the whole heart, and a *dedicated service* to God who gave His Son to redeem us from sin. When we understand that it is God who *moved* our heart in the first place, *drew* our mind to Him, and *stimulated* our intellectual powers to see the death of Christ on the cross in this light, then the *faith of Christ* (also His gift to us, Romans 12:3) begins to work in the transformation of our characters. *Then* we begin to live by the *faith of Jesus* through which we are justified freely (Galatians 2:16, 20; Romans 3:24).

God never promised us that life would be free of pain or suffering. In fact, what He promised Adam after the Fall was that life would involve endless toil and struggle. The apostle Paul gave us a list of the things he suffered throughout his ministry. In "stripes above measure," beaten with rods, stoned, shipwrecked, perils everywhere he went by land or sea. He was weary constantly, cold, hungry, thirsty, in pain from an unknown affliction that God would not remove even though Paul prayed for relief from it three times (see 2 Corinthians 11:23-27; 12:7, 8). And in the end, the Romans chopped off Paul's head (Emperor Nero ordered the deed to be done). What an ignominious death for the one who, in the Bible, wrote more about faith than anyone else! And yet, Paul suffered more than most of us ever have. The Gospel is *not* about healing disease or giving us our every demand.

Jesus Himself was not free of suffering while He walked this earth. He is called the "Man of sorrows" Who is "acquainted with our griefs" (Isaiah 53:3). He suffered for our sake that He might be a merciful high priest to all who come to Him for relief from the *pain of sin* (Hebrews 2:17, 18; 4:15, 16). Jesus' faith was sorely tried in the Garden of Gethsemane, and especially on the cross when, because of His suffering under the weight of the world's burden of sin, He could not see His Father's face. This caused Him to cry out to His Father, "My God, why have You forsaken Me?" (Matthew 27:46).

"Wherefore seeing we also are compassed about with so great a cloud of witnesses, let us lay aside every weight, and the sin which doth so easily beset us, and let us run with patience the race that is set before us, looking unto Jesus the Author and Finisher of our faith; who for the joy that was set before Him endured the cross, despising the shame, and is set down at the right hand of the throne of God. For consider Him that endured such contradiction of sinners against Himself, lest ye be wearied and faint in your minds. Ye have not yet resisted unto blood, *striving against sin*." (Hebrews 12:1-4). Not "striving" against some disease or poverty or some emotional problem. We are to "strive against sin" by rejecting the "lusts of the flesh, the lusts of the eyes, and the pride of life" (1 John 2:16).

What then was the purpose of all those people who were relieved from their bodily afflictions through the word of Jesus? Why were they healed by their faith, but we don't seem to be when we pray for healing?

Jesus healed and relieved suffering because by doing so He was proving His claim to be God. Everywhere He went, He left behind Him a village of people who knew that they had been in the very presence of God Himself. This is why the leaders of the Jewish people were so incensed. Jesus was proving His claim to be God and they could not deny it because the evidence was everywhere. Only God could do the things that Jesus was doing. God was daily walking among them, but they refused to believe in Him, no matter what He did. Miracles do not convince anyone.

Today, the religious world has many charlatans who claim to be able to heal the lame or blind, or cure cancer or some such disease. The term "faith cure" is commonly applied to the work of these frauds, about which there is, in strict truth, neither faith nor cure. The only "faith" that is present in such cases is a blind confidence in the powers of the "healer," and the only "cure" that follows is a product of the imagination, or the work of the unseen spiritual agencies of evil who caused the "disease" in the first place. Satan will do anything to divert people's minds into the path of spiritism where he can better control them through his deceptions, while promoting the deception as being the "product" of their faith in God. We are a very gullible people.

So, I guess the lesson for us about what faith is, is this: God desires to shape our character through the things He allows to happen to us, whether accidents or disease or loss of wealth or death of loved ones. Faith sees through and reaches through all these trials and tragedies, trivial or major. Through all that comes upon us to afflict us and make us miserable, we are to steadfastly look to Jesus and know that nothing in this earth can truly hurt us. "What shall separate us from the love of Christ? Shall tribulation, distress, or persecution, or famine, or nakedness, or peril, or sword? ... No! In all these things we are more than conquerors through Him who loves us" (Romans 8:35, 36 ff.).

35

Abraham's "Two Sons"

Genesis 21:1, 2

Twenty-five years were covered between chapter 12 and chapter 21. When Abraham and Sarah finally realized that the power of God will accomplish what He says He will do, and surrendered to Him their minds and bodies, they then were empowered to overcame all their self motivated schemes that generated the unbelief that had produced Ishmael. After the fiasco with Abimelech, they were enabled to stand upon faith alone, and Isaac the true child of the promise was born. "And the LORD visited Sarah as He had said, and the LORD did unto Sarah as He had spoken. For Sarah conceived, and bare Abraham a son in his old age, at the set time of which God had spoken to him."

"At the time God had spoken to him" refers us back to Genesis 18:14 when the LORD, sitting there around the campfire after their meal, rebuked Sarah for laughing and said, "*Is anything too hard for the LORD?*" Nothing is too hard for God, except our stubborn unbelief. He cannot work in us to accomplish what He wants to do, until we believe fully in His power to change our lives. He always works *for* us in protecting us and providing for our needs, but He cannot do the work He wants to do *in us* until we get rid of all vestiges of unbelief.

And this phrase "at the time God had spoken to him" verifies for us that the Man visiting Abraham that day three months before was truly Christ pre-incarnate, the second Person of the Godhead, the Word of God who openly communicated with Abraham, face to face. He was *not* a created angel, but is truly the divine Son of God.

Abraham's "old age" was now 100 and Sarah was 90 when the child of promise was born to them—*husband and wife*. Husband and wife represents the *new covenant* that is founded in complete faith in God's promise, while man and concubine was man's striving to perform the work of God in their own power, and that illustrates the "old covenant."[1] And it utterly failed for Abraham and Sarah. The old covenant will always fail because it is based on the theory of assumed merit inherent in human effort to accomplish the "work" that God wants us to do—assuming *we can do it* if we just try a little harder or pray a little more earnestly.

Biblical Illustration of the Two Covenants

"For it is written, that Abraham had two sons [Ishmael and Isaac[2]], the one by a bondmaid, the other by a freewoman. But he who was of the bondwoman was born after the flesh [Sarah's scheme in Genesis 16:1-4]; but he of the freewoman was by promise [Genesis 18:10; 21:1, 2]. Which things are an allegory [an illustration]: *for these are the two covenants*; the one from the mount Sinai, which genders to bondage, which is Agar [Hagar]. For this Agar is [figuratively] mount Sinai in Arabia [where the children of Israel placed themselves under the old

---

1. Considerable confusion exists concerning what constitutes the "old" and "new" covenants. Many people use the term "old covenant" to apply to the events that occurred at Sinai with the children of Israel, including the sacrificial system as part of that "old covenant" agreement between God and Israel. From this idea the claim is made that the Ten Commandments are part of that "old covenant" and that they were "nailed to the cross" when Jesus died, and are no longer "binding" on those who "believe" in Jesus. This view makes the "old covenant" a "dispensation" that applies only to the "Jewish" nation prior to the cross. Everything after the cross is considered to be the "new covenant era." However, there is no Biblical support for this position. The "old covenant" idea began at the gate of Eden with Cain thinking his fruit/vegetable offering that was the work of his own hands in growing the produce, was sufficient for a sin offering (Genesis 4:3, 5).

Dispensationalism was a system developed by John Nelson Darby, who strongly influenced the Plymouth Brethren of the 1830s in Ireland and England. Darby's view was promoted in America by James Inglis beginning in the mid-1800s. C. I. Scofield developed it into footnotes for a Bible he printed in 1909.

2. Abraham had six more sons born to him by his second wife, Keturah. These sons were the fathers of the Arab tribes living in the south and east of Canaan and Arabia (Genesis 25:1-6). Through the offspring of Keturah Abraham became "the father of many nations" (Genesis 17:4, 5; Romans 4:17, 18). Keturah must have been taken from the women living among Abraham's large clan. He would not have married a woman from among the native tribes of the pagan Canaanites.

covenant promise, "all the LORD has said, *we will do!*" and assumed full responsibility to accomplish God's promise by themselves; see Exodus 19:8; 24:3, 7], and answers [corresponds] to Jerusalem which now is [the "earthly" city], and is in bondage with her children [all who persist in unbelief or have confidence in their "works" for salvation]. But Jerusalem which is above [the "new" heavenly city, see Revelation 21:1, 2] is free [from sin and the "works" of the old covenant], which is the mother of us all." (Galatians 4:22-26, emphasis and explanations supplied).

In these verses Paul makes a clear statement about what the two covenants are. Using Hagar and Sarah as his illustrations, he tells us that the child produced through Hagar was a product of man's own thinking and self-centered motivation, and that kind of thinking has always produced people who live under the old covenant. It cannot be otherwise.

Then Paul points us to Sinai as a further illustration of the old covenant. What happened at Sinai that created an old covenant?

After God (Christ, the Word of God) spoke from the mountaintop telling the children of Israel that if they would *remember* ("obey" = Hebrew *shemea* = "listen to" or "heed" what previously had been stated) and *cherish* ("keep" = Hebrew *shamar* = "cherish" [3]) the covenant He *had already given* to Adam, Noah, and Abraham ("remember" must point back to something already established),[4] then the same gift of faith given to Abraham, for faith is a gift from God, (Romans 12:3),

---

3. When Adam was created, God commanded him to "cherish" the Garden of Eden. "And the LORD God took the man, and put him into the garden of Eden to dress it and to *keep* [*shamar*] it." (Genesis 2:15, emphasis supplied). The Hebrew word *shamar* means to guard, watch, protect, cherish.

4. "And Moses went up unto God, and the LORD called unto him out of the mountain, saying, Thus shalt thou say to the house of Jacob, and tell the children of Israel; ye have seen what I did unto the Egyptians, and how I bare you on eagles' wings, and brought you unto Myself. Now therefore, if ye will obey My voice indeed, and keep My covenant, then ye shall be a peculiar treasure unto me above all people: for all the earth is mine: and ye shall be unto me a kingdom of priests, and an holy nation. These are the words which thou shalt speak unto the children of Israel. And Moses came and called for the elders of the people, and laid before their faces all these words which the LORD commanded him. And all the people answered together, and said, All that the LORD hath spoken *we will do*. And Moses returned the words of the people unto the LORD." (Exodus 19:3-8, emphasis supplied).

would work in their lives, just as it did in Abraham and Sarah's lives (and in Abel, Enoch, and Noah before them).[5]

When the people who were gathered at the foot of Mount Sinai heard these words, they were terrified by the thundering voice, and the fire, smoke and lightning on the mountaintop. They were frightened because they had learned nothing through their experiences during the plagues poured out on the Egyptians. Faith was not part of their thinking.

Under pharaoh's dictatorship, they had had to satisfy him through their own efforts, and now here's this new Master telling them to "obey." Harkening back to their days in Egypt, they assumed that this new Master must be satisfied through the same method that brought peace with pharaoh—their own hard work. Therefore, they rashly made a promise to obey when they had not an ounce of power to fulfill that promise. They had not even heard the "conditions" of the "covenant," and yet they hastily promised to obey in their own power. (Exodus 19:8; 24:3, 7).[6]

In all that God did to preserve the children of Israel through the terrible plagues poured out on Egypt, and did to keep them safe during their passage through the Red Sea—*walking on dry land* between two walls of water being held back by the Word of God!! (Exodus 14:16). And did for them in raining food from heaven, and giving them water from a *solid rock* (Exodus 16:12-15;17:5-7). Through all those many amazing miracles, they had not seen the loving God that was taking them *out of slavery* to be His special people, to be a witness for His power to save them from sin. Their slave mentality blinded them to the truth of who God is.

Therefore, when they made that promise to obey through *their own power* ("*we will do it!*"), the promise consisted merely of a promise of

---

5. "By faith Abel offered unto God a more excellent sacrifice than Cain … by faith, Enoch was translated … by faith Noah prepared an ark to the saving of his house." (Hebrews 11:4, 5, 7).

6. "And Moses came and told the people all the words of the LORD, and all the judgments: and all the people answered with one voice, and said, All the words which the LORD hath said *will we do*. … And he took the book of the covenant, and read in the audience of the people: and they said, All that the LORD hath said *will we do*, and be obedient." (Exodus 24:3, 7, emphasis supplied). Their promise of "perpetual obedience" lasted forty days, and then they forced Aaron to build them a golden calf to worship.

the people to keep the law that they actually had *not yet heard spoken!* And that promise had, therefore, no power to make them free. No, instead, their promise "gendered to bondage" (Galatians 4:24, 25) since their making it was simply the making of a promise to make themselves righteous *by their own works*. However, man in himself is "without strength" (Romans 5:6) and can do nothing to effect salvation through "good works" (Titus 3:5).[7]

Since the covenant made *by the people* was not disavowed by God, but stood as they stated it, many people therefore conclude that God *gave* the children of Israel that binding suzerain contract there are Sinai. But did God Himself really lead them into bondage? Would He do such a thing? Not by any means. Since He did not induce them to make that covenant at Sinai, God cannot be accused of being the originator of that old covenant. It originated in the people's stony hearts and with the assumption that their own efforts would be sufficient to accomplish God's purposes.

Right here it needs to be stated that the Ten Commandments were not and never have been part of the "old covenant." When I was a teenager attending church with my father, the preacher's constant claim was that the Ten Commandments were part and parcel with the "old covenant," that the old covenant law was "nailed to the cross" and was no longer binding upon anyone. My unsophisticated and uneducated teenaged mind wondered if this meant that it was okay to kill or steal or lie or commit adultery.

When that preacher absconded with $20,000 from the church bank account and ran off to Texas in the Mercedes Benz that the church bought for him, I concluded that such must the result of the law of God being nailed to the cross. That preacher considered himself free to do what he wanted, and no one sought to prosecute him. I quit going to church shortly thereafter. Why bother myself with "religion" if the result of it amounted to the same kind of life I could live without going to church and making a hollow claim that I was a Christian?

---

[7]. "For when we were yet without strength, in due time Christ died for the ungodly." (Romans 5:6). "But after that the kindness and love of God our Saviour toward man appeared, not by works of righteousness which we have done, but according to his mercy he saved us, by the washing of regeneration, and renewing of the Holy Ghost; which he shed on us abundantly through Jesus Christ our Saviour; that being justified by his grace, we should be made heirs according to the hope of eternal life." (Titus 3:4-7).

The truth is that the everlasting covenant made with Adam, Noah, and Abraham meant that they were Commandment-keepers by faith in God's power to keep them from sinning. This we know to be the truth concerning Abraham from reading Genesis 26:5.[8] God's Ten Commandments are the foundation of His royal throne in heaven; they are His character put into ten sentences. When we believe His word to us, then those ten sentences become ten promises. When He said, "You will not" He was telling us that if we love Him above all things, then we *will not* have any other gods before Him, we will not worship idols, we will not lie or steal or kill or covet, and we will "keep" or *cherish* His holy seventh-day Sabbath as the sign of the covenant between us and God.[9]

According to the apostle Paul, whoever looks to the present Jerusalem situated on the hill in Palestine for blessings or any fulfillment of God's promise, is looking to the old covenant from Mount Sinai that was predicated on man's promises to obey, and therefore that person remains in bondage to sin, and legalism as an attempt to "obey" the word of God. But whoever worships with his face toward the New Jerusalem which is in heaven and who expects blessings from God alone, is looking to the new covenant wrought in Christ alone. He is looking to the heavenly Mount Zion, to freedom, for "Jerusalem which is above is free."

From this learn that the promise made to Abraham four hundred and thirty years *before* Sinai, was sufficient for all purposes. It needed no modification. That original covenant was confirmed (or ratified) in Christ through His life and death on the cross and, therefore, is a "covenant from above," as Paul wrote in Galatians 4:26. In John 8:23, Jesus stated that He was not "earthy" or earth-focused/self-centered in His spiritual thinking, as were the Jews and Gentiles, and all pagan

---

8. "Because that Abraham obeyed My voice, and kept My charge, My commandments, My statutes, and My laws. (Genesis 26:5). Abraham knew the Ten Commandments because they have always existed. They did not come into being at Sinai, and they do not "belong" exclusively to the Jewish people. The Ten Commandments are the eternal revelation of God's own character of love. "And he that keeps His commandments dwells in Him, and He in him. And hereby we know that He abides in us, by the Spirit which He has given us." (1 John 3:24).

9. "And keep My Sabbaths holy that they may be a sign between Me and you, that you may know that I am the LORD your God." (Ezekiel 20:20, ESV).

peoples, but that He was *from above*. He was "not of this world," but kept Himself focused on the things above, the eternal things.[10]

Jesus ever kept His eyes focused on His heavenly Father and followed His will explicitly. "Then answered Jesus and said unto them, Verily, verily, I say unto you, the Son can do nothing of Himself, but what He seeth the Father do: for what things soever He doeth, these also doeth the Son likewise. (John 5:19).

"Believest thou not that I am in the Father, and the Father in Me? the words that I speak unto you I speak not of Myself: but the Father that dwelleth in Me, He doeth the works. (John 14:10).

"I can of Mine own self do nothing: as I hear, I judge: and My judgment is just; because I seek not Mine own will, but the will of the Father which hath sent Me." (John 5:30).

The life of Jesus exemplified the meaning of the "new covenant" through His obedience wrought out by faith in the power of His Father to keep Him from sinning.[11] We will to do the same when we finally learn what "faith" really means.

We are all unrighteous, and all of our "works" are in the eyes of God the same as "filthy rags." "But we are all as an unclean thing, and all our righteousnesses are as filthy rags; and we all do fade as a leaf; and our iniquities, like the wind, have taken us away. (Isaiah 64:5).[12]

The old covenant can only produce more unrighteousness in those who attempt to keep the law of God in their own power, and all such attempts are repulsive to God because they are a rejection Him as a loving Person who has already given us the gift of salvation.

---

10. "And [Jesus] said unto them, Ye are from beneath; I am from above: ye are of this world; I am not of this world. I said therefore unto you, that ye shall die in your sins: for if ye believe not that I am He, ye shall die in your sins." (John 8:23, 24).

11. "Though He were the Son, yet learned He obedience by the things which He suffered; and being made perfect, He became the author of eternal salvation unto all them that obey Him." (Hebrews 5:8, 9).

12. The Hebrew word here translated "filthy" literally means "menstruation rags." Isaiah's use of this word conveys just how repulsive our sin is to God. Menstruating women were cast out of the camp and were to be avoided to prevent contamination. "When a woman has a discharge, and it consists of blood from her body, she will be unclean because of her menstruation for seven days. Everyone who touches her will be unclean until evening. Anything she lies on during her menstruation will become unclean, and anything she sits on will become unclean. Everyone who touches her bed is to wash his clothes and bathe with water, and he will remain unclean until evening." (Leviticus 15:19-21, HCSB). The bloody discharge was a symbol of sin's contamination.

Any attempt to substitute man's feeble "strength" for the power that created the universe and all that is in it, is in reality attempting to put that man (or woman or child) above the Sovereign LORD of all.

The law of Love, which is embodied in the Ten Commandments, is presented to us through the life and death of Jesus Christ. The love of God for lost humanity is so great that He was willing to lay down His own life that we might live. "For when we were yet without strength, in due time Christ died for the ungodly. ... For if, when we were enemies [of God], we were reconciled to God by the death of His Son, much more, being reconciled, we shall be saved by His life." (Romans 5:6, 10).

Christ "being in the form of God, thought it not robbery to be equal with God: but made Himself of no reputation, and took upon Him the form of a servant, and was made in the likeness of men: and being found in fashion as a man, He humbled Himself, and became obedient unto death, even the death of the cross." (Philippians 2:6-8). "Even the death of the cross" means that Jesus willingly took upon His sinless nature that sinful human nature that is condemned by God and consigned to eternal destruction. In *that* human nature, Jesus "condemned sin in the flesh" (Romans 8:3) and put that condemned "flesh" to death on the cross of Calvary, effecting salvation for all who will believe in His power to save them from sin.

In His life on earth Christ exemplified for us how to be a Commandment-keeper by faith. "I can of Mine own self do nothing: as I hear, I judge: and My judgment is just; because I seek not Mine own will, but the will of the Father which hath sent Me." (John 5:30). "Then said Jesus unto them, When ye have lifted up the Son of man, then shall ye know that I am He, and that I do nothing of Myself but as My Father hath taught Me, I speak these things." (John 8:28). Jesus' life was one of total commitment to the will of His Father. We can live the same life of obedience through surrender to His power.

The law of love promises Christ's own righteousness as a free gift of God effected in our life through the free gift of His faith (Romans 12:3), which "works in us to will and to do of His good pleasure" (Philippians 2:13). The love and power of God manifested in the life of fallen humanity is the summation of what the "new" covenant is all about.

36

More on Faith

Been thinkin' some more about faith and what it is and is not. In the process of composing a further answer to your questions about faith, I had to take it all the way back to heaven before the fall of Lucifer. In heaven, all the angels knew who God was. They had "angelic" Christ, who was then known as "Michael" the "archangel" (the chief or "captain" of the angels, who was their leader [1]) to show them who God was by demonstrating His character to them. The angels all knew God's character as loving, kind, and patient because Christ is the Word who reveals God's character to all creatures everywhere in the universe. So we could say that the angelic hosts and all the creatures who populate the unfallen worlds, "believed" in the benevolent nature of God. They had the evidence before them all the time.

When Lucifer decided that he wanted to be god sitting on the throne of heaven, he knew that he would need to supplant the Monarch of the universe to gain that coveted seat (Isaiah 14:13, 14; Ezekiel 28:16:14-18). Lucifer began the trouble by spreading lies

---

1. Three verses are sufficient to prove that "Michael" is the name Christ was known by before He became incarnate in human flesh. Jesus Himself said that He would raise up from the grave all who believed in Him (John 6:40). First Thessalonians 4:16 tells us that "the LORD Himself shall descend with a shout, with the voice of the archangel" and the righteous dead shall come forth from their graves. Jude 9 says that Michael is that "archangel" who raised Moses from his grave. In Daniel 12:1, Michael is identified as the "Prince" that stands for the children of God on the day when "everyone that is found written in the book of life" are delivered from this wicked world.

about God's character. When the angels heard these lies, they began to doubt whether what they already knew about God was really true. Maybe He *wasn't* as loving as they had always assumed.

Maybe Lucifer was right in saying that God had a dark side that most of them had never seen. After all, Lucifer was the highest, most beautiful created being, and held a position that placed him next to the throne of God (Ezekiel 28:13, 14). His proximity to the throne might make him privy to information that was not made obvious to all the rest of the army of heavenly angelic beings. Lucifer promoted the idea that the only reason no one had seen God's dark side, was because everyone had been blindly obeying God's arbitrary rules without thinking for themselves. It was easy to begin to doubt God's word if looked at from this viewpoint. Well, Lucifer might have said to his fellow angels, he for one was tired of being treated arbitrarily. He was going to do his *own* thinking, and make his own rules to live by.

His insidious accusations against God's character of love caused all the angels to wonder about the situation, and eventually, one third followed Lucifer into full-blown rebellion against God, causing "war in heaven" that got them cast out, down to this world.[2] Lucifer turned his love for God and his fellow angels into love for self, trusting only his own mind. Once self became the object upon which he relied, then everything else became suspect as unreliable and untrustworthy. The result was unbelief in the Word of God.

And through these twisted notions, unbelief was born in the universe. The same twisted insinuations also worked to cause Eve to doubt the Word concerning the tree of knowledge of good and evil, and that doubt brought sin and death into this world.

Unbelief breeds hatred (enmity).[3] Questioning and doubt soon created the idea in Lucifer's mind that the now un-credible Being

---

2. "And there was war in heaven: Michael and his angels fought against the dragon; and the dragon fought and his angels, and prevailed not; neither was their place found any more in heaven. And the great dragon was cast out, that old serpent, called the Devil, and Satan, which deceiveth the whole world: he was cast out into the earth, and his angels were cast out with him." (Revelation 12:7-9).

3. Enmity means intense hostility and comes from the same Latin root word that we get the word enemy. Enmity means the state of being an enemy. It is stronger than antagonism or animosity, both of which imply competitive feeling but do not go all the way to enemy status. As a result of the Fall, the human mind is "friends" with sin and Satan, and an enemy of God and righteousness. "Because the carnal mind *is enmity* against God for it is not subject to God, neither indeed can be." (Romans 8:7).

(at least in Lucifer's mind) who called Himself God could never be trusted, no matter what He said or did. Unbelief is a very stubborn condition because it accepts nothing that is presented contrary to its preconceived opinion on a subject.

In Eden, Adam and Eve both knew their Maker personally, just like the angels all knew Him in heaven. Adam and Eve talked with their Creator face to face every afternoon when He visited them in the Garden.[4] But one day, that snaky liar now called Satan, tricked Eve with his insinuations (just like he did with the angels in heaven), and consequently through Eve's influence, Adam also fell into unbelief. They both accepted Satan's lies that birthed unbelief in their hearts and minds about the character of God. That fateful afternoon unbelief and its ensuant enmity for God entered into this world.

And ever since, the Godhead has been working to turn around that terrible situation, and to turn man's hatred into love for their Creator and Redeemer.

What all this tells us is that once upon a time, God was known without any veil of unbelief obscuring His character. After the entrance of sin, first in heaven and then here in our world, that seed of doubt birthed unbelief and its cohort enmity, and they have infected the human race ever since. And so, we "naturally" don't think we can truly trust God to be who He says He is, nor can we trust Him to do to what He says He will.

How often have we experienced doubt caused by unanswered prayers? How many times in our lives have we asked and not received?— usually because we "ask amiss" to "consume the blessing upon our own lusts" (James 4:3). How many times, when we find ourselves in terrible straits and there was no one to get us out except ourselves, have we managed to "survive" by using our own will-power and native skills? And, very often those things we did through our own power and ingenuity did "save" us from our troubles, reinforcing to us that we *can* take care of ourselves without any "help" from God.

Thus, in our subconscious, and through self reliance, we drift gradually farther away from God, until we reach the point in our

---

4. "For by Him [Christ] were all things created, that are in heaven, and that are in earth, visible and invisible, whether they be thrones, or dominions, or principalities, or powers: all things were created by Him, and for Him: and He is before all things, and by Him all things consist." (Colossians 1:16, 17).

thinking where we assume we don't need Him at all—"Yes, sir, I can do it!"—and God is left out all together. If we manage to hold onto a vestige of what we think is "faith," we may perhaps come to accept the old adage, "God helps those who help themselves," and thereby justify our own "ability" to remedy our problems, including our sin problem. We "can do it" if we just try a little harder.

But this idea is rooted in old covenant thinking—we do our part in "working out our salvation" and then God will take care of all those "pesky things" that we never manage to fully conquer. But this is *not* the "overcoming" that Jesus is talking about in Revelation 3:21—"to him that overcometh will I grant to sit with Me on My throne, even as I also overcame, and am set down with My Father in His throne." [5]

However, one day perhaps we "wake up" in our drifting spiritual condition and decide that life is not what it should be. Perhaps we think, maybe church isn't such a bad idea after all. Maybe we have some friends who attend a church, and they tell us of the lively music, good fellowship, and how happy and up-lifted they are when they leave the service. So we start going to church with them. Maybe week by week we do come away really feeling invigorated by the praise music and shouting and singing and "glorifying God." We may not hear much preached from the Bible, but we accept that "good feeling" as being His will revealed to us, and we call that feeling "faith."

But as we continue to attend, we find that a mental assent to some facts about God and the Bible cannot erase that niggling doubt about whether He really loves us. When push comes to shove in our daily lives, we still fall back on ourselves and our ability to get ourself through troubles. Yes, we might pray about the situation and we certainly will ask our church friends to pray for us, too, thinking maybe they have a better "connection" to the throne of grace than we do.

But one day we find ourselves in some really deep trouble that has no earthly answer. All of our wonderful "experience" in church notwithstanding, we suddenly realize that we have no personal

---

5. It was Lucifer's desire to sit upon God's throne, to assume the power and position of God, and for this reason he challenged God's authority to be God. "For thou hast said in thine heart, I will ascend into heaven, I will exalt my throne above the stars of God: I will sit also upon the mount of the congregation in the sides of the north: I will ascend above the heights of the clouds; I will be like the most High" (Isaiah 14:13, 14). Lucifer's desire will never be realized for him. Instead that privilege of sitting on Christ's throne will be given to those who live by Jesus' faith and overcome all sin, just as He overcame sin.

resources through which we can solve the problem we're facing at that moment. And that causes us to pray harder, to beg God, and we cry our hearts out … and nothing happens to change the situation.

This is where I was when my father was dying of cancer. I begged God not to take my father from me; I needed him too much. He was my anchor in life and without him I didn't know what in the world I would do. I turned my face to the wall and cried myself to sleep. Two days later my father died. My strong crying and seeking God for help went unheeded. Where was God when I needed Him to fix my problem? Sure, I had been out of church a long time, but didn't God love me anyway? Isn't that what all those "feel good" sermons had been telling me—that I could claim to love God and do as I pleased, and He would still be there for me in a time of need? All I had to do was "ask" and pray a little harder!

And that unanswered prayer set me adrift into paganism. At least I thought it was unanswered, but God always hears us and He does answer us, just not always the way we want Him to answer. There are so many things that my father's death put into motion, that ended up really bringing me to Christ, that it would take another book to tell of them all! Mary Magdalene and I will have a lot in common when we both are able to sit down in heaven and discuss the transforming power of Jesus' love for us.

As a teenager I had learned in church that God could heal. I was told that Jesus had raised people from the dead. When I prayed that night, I really believed He could do it. So why didn't He save my father, who was really too young to be dying. I needed my father so much, why wouldn't He preserve him for me?

When He didn't, then God seemed to me to be a very distant God who did not care about someone as insignificant as I was. Or more probably, what the Bible said about Him was not a reality. Those miracles were no miracles at all, but just a bunch of pleasant stories to entertain kids. Why should I have any faith at all in the Being people called God?

From that point for the next ten years, I learned to take care of myself, wandering in a state of unbelief, getting farther and farther away from God. But all through that time, God never left me. I was running away from Him, but He never left me to myself. I didn't realize it at the time, but after I returned to Christianity (I don't say "faith" because that came later), I remembered all the times when things "happened" to help me, like the man I told you about who met me on the road one Christmas day and fixed my truck. At the times when those things "happened" (and there were more than a few such interventions), I assumed I had very good luck. Now I know that "luck" had nothing whatsoever to do with it. In my years of unbelief and rebellion, I was actually failing to recognize the evidence of God's love for me that was clearly before my eyes all the time in those "miracle" interventions that three times literally saved my wretched life.

Shortly after I married a Christian man, we met a retired preacher who had been a missionary in Africa for two decades, and was an evangelist in this country for many years. Alex taught me the real meaning of the Bible. Through his patient instruction he opened my eyes to the truth of God's character of love, and how that divine, self-sacrificial love reached down to the depths of human wickedness to bring me up into the sunshine of Christ and His righteousness.

Alex also introduced me to two men who were prolific writers and preachers of the Gospel in the late 1800s. It was from those two men and Alex, and a couple other gentlemen we subsequently became friends with, that we began to understand what faith really is. It is not a work. It is especially not "trust" like a person might have in their insurance company or fire department, or their best friend to come to their rescue when needed.

Faith, true faith, is a gift from God. It is the full measure of *the faith of Jesus Christ*[6] that He perfected while living in this wicked world and coming face to face with Satan's temptations every day of His earthly life.[7] This *tested and proven faith* is the only faith that will save us from sin and "present us faultless before the throne of God" (Jude 24).

One of those two men that we came to appreciate was named Alonso T. Jones. He was a profound Bible student and historian who presented the precious truth about the righteousness of Christ that

---

6. "Knowing that a man is not justified by the works of the law, but by the faith *of Jesus Christ*, even we have believed in Jesus Christ, that we might be justified by the faith *of Christ*, and not by the works of the law: for by the works of the law shall no flesh be justified." (Galatians 2:16, emphasis supplied). "According as God hath dealt to every man *the measure of faith*." (Romans 12:3).

7. "Though He were a Son, yet learned He obedience by the things which He suffered; and being made perfect, He became the author of eternal salvation unto all them that obey Him." (Hebrews 5:8, 9).

I had never heard before. It was a clear presentation of the Bible's teaching on justification, faith, and salvation from sin.

Along with his many written works, Jones also became editor of several international magazines, and a staunch defender of our First Amendment rights. He even went before a Senate subcommittee in 1888 to testify against the passage of a bill that would have undermined our Constitutional right to religious freedom.

In 1907 he penned what I think is the best definition of what faith is and how it works in our lives. Here it is for your consideration:—

> Righteousness, whether to men, to angels, to bright seraphim, or to exalted cherubim, comes not by obedience of their own. It comes only from the grace of God through the *faith of Jesus Christ*; never their own righteousness which is of the law, but always only "that which is through the faith of Christ, the righteousness which is of God by faith."
>
> And in this word "faith" I mean not a mere theoretical notion, but "faith" in its only true meaning of the *will submitted* to Him, the *heart yielded* to Him, and the *affections fixed* upon Him. This only is faith; and this itself by the grace and gift of God. And this faith, of the will submitted to God *through Christ*, of the heart yielded to God *in Christ*, and the affections fixed upon God *by Christ*—this is the faith of angels as truly as of men. And by this faith and in this faith of the Lord Jesus, all the glad array of holy angels, bright seraphim, and beatified cherubim, as well as men, empty themselves of all thought of *self*, of all thought of any righteousness of self or of law, and receive the righteousness of God, which is *by the faith of Jesus Christ*, through His boundless grace.

True faith is rooted in a personal knowledge of God, like the unfallen angels have and Adam and Eve had before they fell unto unbelief. It is rooted in an intimacy with the Man who made the everlasting covenant promise that He would save *from* their sin all who believe in Him. Jesus Christ gave His life to prove He meant what He said, and He will perform what He promised.

When we truly believe that He did all that for me, even *for little ol' me*, who am nothing at all but a fly speck in His universe, then we can begin to know how faith "works by love" (Galatians 5:6). This was the experience of Mary Magdalene after she was condemned by the self-righteous Pharisees who threw her at Jesus' feet. When Jesus looked on her lying there in the dust and said, "Neither do I condemn you, go and sin no more" (John 8:11), Mary was released from her self-hatred and her enmity for God who had seemed to abandoned her to a life of continual sin. After this gift of forgiveness she gave everything to Jesus, surrendered to Him completely. Her love for Jesus caused her to perform the most extravagant and extraordinary act of worship recorded in the whole Bible (see John 12:1-8; Luke 7:36-50).[8]

Faith, therefore, is a *heart appreciation* of the cost of our salvation from sin. It is a motivation change in our heart from a self-centered-

---

8. "Then Jesus six days before the Passover came to Bethany, where Lazarus was which had been dead, whom He raised from the dead. There they made Him a supper; and Martha served: but Lazarus was one of them that sat at the table with Him. Then took Mary a pound of ointment of spikenard, very costly, and anointed the feet of Jesus, and wiped His feet with her hair: and the house was filled with the odour of the ointment. Then saith one of His disciples, Judas Iscariot, Simon's son, which should betray Him, Why was not this ointment sold for three hundred pence, and given to the poor? This he said, not that he cared for the poor; but because he was a thief, and had the bag, and bare what was put therein. Then said Jesus, Let her alone: against the day of My burying hath she kept this. For the poor always ye have with you; but Me ye have not always." (John 12:1-8).

"And one of the Pharisees desired Him that He would eat with him. And He went into the Pharisee's house, and sat down to meat. And, behold, a woman in the city, which was a sinner, when she knew that Jesus sat at meat in the Pharisee's house, brought an alabaster box of ointment, And stood at His feet behind Him weeping, and began to wash His feet with tears, and did wipe them with the hairs of her head, and kissed His feet, and anointed them with the ointment.

"Now when the Pharisee which had bidden Him saw it, he spake within himself, saying, 'This man, if He were a prophet, would have known who and what manner of woman this is that toucheth Him: for she is a sinner.' And Jesus answering said unto him, 'Simon, I have somewhat to say unto thee.' And he saith, 'Master, say on.'

"There was a certain Creditor which had two debtors: the one owed five hundred pence, and the other fifty. And when they had nothing to pay, He frankly forgave them both. Tell Me therefore, which of them will love Him most?"

"Simon answered and said, 'I suppose that he, to whom he forgave most.'

"And He said unto him, Thou hast rightly judged. And He turned to the woman, and said unto Simon, Seest thou this woman? I entered into thine house, thou gavest Me no water for My feet: but she hath washed My feet with tears, and wiped them with the hairs of her head. Thou gavest Me no kiss: but this woman since the time I came in hath not ceased to kiss My feet. My head with oil thou didst not anoint: but this woman hath anointed My feet with ointment. Wherefore I say unto thee, Her sins, which are many, are forgiven; for she loved much: but to whom little is forgiven, the same loveth little.

"And He said unto her, Thy sins are forgiven. And they that sat at meat with Him began to say within themselves, Who is this that forgiveth sins also? And He said to the woman, Thy faith hath saved thee; go in peace." (Luke 7:36-50).

what's-in-it-for-me attitude, and from self exaltation and self-love, to a total commitment to God. "The love of Christ motivates us" and we come to love Him more than life itself, just as He loved us and gave His life for us. It is a willing assent of our understanding of God's words to us found in the Bible that will bind our hearts to Him in willing consecration and service to God—the *will submitted*, the *heart yielded*, and the *affections fixed* upon Him—to the point that we are willing to declare like Job, though He slay me, yet will I love Him!

37

Still More on Faith

Perhaps my verbose discussion in the last letter confused you, but the two covenants are not difficult to understand. So, let me try again, and hopefully I will be less confusing this time.

The "new" (aka "everlasting") covenant is God's promise to save us from sin and restore us in the "image of God" in which we were created. The "old covenant" is our promise to attempt to accomplish the promise of God through our own efforts, or through our efforts combined with God's "help." But the old adage of "God helps those who help themselves" is not the Gospel! That idea assumes that "faith" (or "trust") is a work, something we "do," and added to God's help, it saves us. The old covenant idea is in essence a co-equal equation, with us doing "our part" and God doing His. This is a fallacy from beginning to end.

The new/everlasting covenant is salvation through Christ alone. The old covenant is any attempt at salvation through "*faith*" plus our added efforts (faith + works = salvation). I say "attempt" at salvation because the second idea will never gain salvation for anyone, no matter how hard one "worked" at attaining it. And I put faith in italics because if we're striving to work out our salvation without relying completely on Christ's power, then it is not true faith that we are exercising. We are exercising self-confidence, which is confidence in the flesh, which is why Abraham and Hagar failed. Confidence in our own abilities to "appease an angry god" through our "good works," or through "human" sacrifice ("I gave up so much!"), is the basis of all pagan religions. Paganism believes (even today) that it is through human work/effort/sacrifice that we attempt to appease the angry god that condemns us. But the pagan god is never satisfied and we must continually bring more human effort hoping to win that god's favor.

The new/everlasting covenant teaches us the truth about the LORD whose love is active, not passive. Christ is called the Good Shepherd for a significant reason. He left heaven and came looking for His lost sheep rather than the lost sheep being left to hunt for its Shepherd. When Jesus told that parable in Luke 15, He said, though a Man have a hundred sheep, if one went astray, He would go after that one lost lamb, searching until He found it. And when He found it, He laid it upon His shoulders to carry it back to the fold where He would restore it in its rightful place in His flock. The parable is about our fallen world. We're the only "sheep" in God's universe that has gone astray. And the Shepherd came here for just that one purpose, to find us and bring us home, restoring us to His fold.

This is the story of Genesis 3:9: "And the LORD God called unto Adam, and said unto him, Where are you?" The LORD knew perfectly well where Adam and Eve were hiding, but He asked the question because it was necessary for Adam to learn two things: (1) he was not condemned by God (there was not even a hint of anger in the LORD's voice when He called for them), and (2) the Good Shepherd came looking for His lost lambs. Adam didn't have to run around the Garden looking for salvation from the sin he committed. Freedom from his sin was not hiding under a rock somewhere, and neither was it found in his fig leaf garment that he made for himself. Salvation came looking for him, and that very afternoon when Adam and Eve fell, the Gospel's everlasting covenant went into effect when Christ promised them that He would put enmity between them and Satan (Genesis 3:15). Fear, shame, and distrust of God would be replaced by a heart appreciation of the love God for the lost.

Romans 5 confirms this when the apostle Paul penned, "But God commended His love toward us, in that, while we were yet sinners [without being repentant or seeking salvation], Christ died for us." (Romans 5:8). Christ is the "Lamb slain from the foundation of the world" (Revelation 13:8; 1 Peter 1:18-21; Hebrews 4:3). And referring back to the Fall of Adam and the everlasting covenant promise given there in the Garden (Genesis 3:15), the apostle Paul goes on to say, "For if, when we were enemies [of God through disobedience, and having the mind of Satan working in us, which is enmity toward God, cf. Romans 8:7], we were reconciled to God by the death of His Son, much more, being reconciled, we shall be saved by His life." (Romans 5:10; cf. 2 Corinthians 5:19).[1]

Salvation does not depend on our struggling to find and then hold on to God's hand, but on our believing that He is holding on to ours (Isaiah 41:13; 42:6).[2] Isaiah 42:1-7 is a prophecy of the coming Messiah, but as the Father "held" Jesus' hand to strengthen Him during His ministry on earth, He will also hold our hand as He leads us along the path to righteousness as He restores our character into the image of His own righteousness (Psalm 23:3).

The good news of the everlasting covenant is that the Gospel is a practical message of salvation through faith alone—the gift of the *full measure of Jesus' faith* to each of us (Romans 12:3). And the gift of Jesus' faith is the faith which works in us recreating us as Commandment-keepers. It is not faith *and* works, but the faith *which* works *by love* (Galatians 5:6)—that heart appreciation for the cost of our salvation from sin provides our motivation. The Greek word for "works" here means "energize." We are "energized" by our new-found love for God and it motivates us to follow Him wherever He calls us.

Reading on down a few more verses we find Paul's practical application of the Gospel's power. "This I say then, Walk in the Spirit, and you *will not* fulfill the lusts of the flesh. For the flesh lusts ["wars"] against the Spirit, and the Spirit against the flesh; and these are contrary to one another, so that *you cannot do* the things that you would." (Galatians 5:16, 17, emphasis supplied).

---

1. "For the love of Christ constrains us; because we thus judge, that if One died for all, then were all dead: And that He died for all, that they which live should not henceforth live unto themselves, but unto Him which died for them, and rose again. ... To wit, that God was in Christ, reconciling the world unto Himself, not imputing their trespasses unto them; and has committed unto us the word of reconciliation." (2 Corinthians 5:14, 15, 19).

2. "For I the LORD thy God will hold thy right hand, saying unto thee, Fear not; I will help thee." (Isaiah 41:13). "I the LORD have called thee in righteousness, and will hold thine hand, and will keep thee." (Isaiah 42:6).

Now, right here many people stumble by thinking that the "things that you would" are good things, and they think that these verses are saying that since we are at war with the Holy Spirit, then we cannot do the good things "that we would," but instead continue to do the *bad* things that we don't want to do. That is taking the defeatist's attitude and denying the power of the Spirit! If that theory is true, then it ultimately means that Satan is stronger than God, and no one can ever be free from sin or Satan's power.

If the Holy Spirit is *not capable* of bringing us into obedience to all the Commandments of God, then He indeed must be considered as being less powerful than Satan who is the one who causes us to sin. Despite Satan's own claims, he is NOT more powerful that the Almighty LORD who created all heaven and earth! Satan is only "more powerful" in our lives because we *let* him be more powerful, instead of letting the Holy Spirit lead us. Through our own choices we can let God or we can let Satan direct our daily lives.

The apostle John wrote, "Greater is He that is in you [Christ in you], than he that is in the world [Satan]. And Paul wrote, "where sin abounds, grace does much more abound" (Romans 5:20). "If Christ be in you, the body is dead because of sin; but the Spirit is life because of righteousness." (Romans 8:10). Paul declared that he was "dead," spiritually crucified with Christ, but he added "nevertheless I live; yet not I but Christ lives in me: and the life which I now live in the flesh, I live by the faith of the Son of God, who loved me, and gave Himself for me." (Galatians 2:20).

It is Jesus' strongest desire that we let Him dwell in our hearts and minds, and thus He will be able to restore the image of God in us, as it was at Creation. This truth was the focus of His last lesson to the disciples, and of His last prayer before He was crucified. "Yet a little while, and the world will see Me no more; but you see Me: because I live, you shall live also. At that day you shall know that I am in My Father, and you are in Me, and I am in you" (John 14:19, 20).

"If a man love Me, he will keep [cherish] My words: and My Father will love him, and We will come unto him, and make Our abode with him" (John 14:23).

To His Father, Jesus prayed, "I in them, and Thou in Me, that they may be made perfect in One; and that the world may know that Thou hast sent Me, and hast loved them, as Thou hast loved Me. And I have declared unto them Thy name, and will declare it: that the love wherewith Thou hast loved Me may be in them, and I in them" (John 17:23, 26).

So, the good news of the everlasting covenant found in Galatians 5:16, 17 is that the Holy Spirit *is* more powerful than Satan and sin, and He works *in* us as we "walk in the Spirit." With Him fighting our battles against Satan, we cannot lose! When we fully accept the marvelous truth of the everlasting covenant's promise to save us *from our sins* (Matthew 1:21)—which is the whole reason why Jesus came to this world in the first place—and we surrender our hearts and minds to the control of Christ and the Holy Spirit, and *let* His "mind" direct our thoughts and actions (Philippians 2:5), then we will be walking by *the faith of Jesus*, and He never lost a battle against Satan!

And that's how the new covenant "works," while the old covenant of man's way of striving for salvation through his own efforts can never work to produce the necessary righteousness that will fit us for heaven. The real gospel message transcends theological hair-splitting, and brings powerful good news to the sinner.

38

Justification By Faith

Genesis 21:1-8

The reason it is so vitally important to get the two covenants figured out is because the everlasting covenant is all about justification within the Gospel's framework. As a newspaper man, you know about justification because you had to justify the typeset in the columns. Full justification means that the text in the column is evenly lined up on both right and left sides, perfectly aligned within the parameters of its column or page, with no ragged edges.

That's one type of justification. Then there is justification used as a legal term meaning to make right something that was wrong; putting right, making a crooked thing straight, vindicating the right (the truth). And most importantly, legal justification is an acquittal of charges against an individual who had been accused.

This last definition of justification fits the legal aspect of the Gospel's message and the everlasting covenant promise to save us from our sin. Christ *legally justified* all the human race from the foundation of the world through His promise stated in Genesis 3:15. It was this promise that extended Adam and Eve's probation. They did not die when they ate the forbidden fruit because Christ, as the Lamb of God, took their sin upon Himself, and by that, He justified them before the broken Law of God. Through the promise of the everlasting covenant, Christ placed His own blood over their transgression, thereby assuming their eternal punishment. This covenant promise of Christ shedding His own blood for the human race was ratified on the Cross four thousand years later. If Adam and Eve had died that day, there would have been no resurrection for them; they would have been eternally lost because of their sin. And neither would there be a human race filling all the earth today.

The sacrifice of Christ, promised in Eden, and given once on Calvary's cross, freely gave legal justification to the entire human race. What Adam did in bringing sin and death upon the human race, was undone by Christ (the "last" Adam) from the foundation of the world. The apostle Paul stated this clearly when he wrote his letter to the Romans, particularly in Romans 3:24, 25, and chapter 5. Chapter 5 is Paul's most legally-framed statement of the Gospel found in any of his writings, and is therefore, the most legally-framed discussion of justification in the entire Bible. Paul hammers away at the truth that Christ undid all that Adam did when he sinned in Eden. In his legal beagle mind set, the erstwhile Pharisee summa cum laude comes at the problem and solution from every angle, making sure that the reader cannot misunderstand his point: Christ *legally justified all mankind*; the entire human race was freed from condemnation,[1] and Adam did not die the day he rebelled, but went on to produce the human race that is fallen in sin.[2]

I particularly like the way the *New English Bible* translates Romans 5:18—"It follows, then, that as the issue of one misdeed was condemnation for all men, so the issue of one just act is *acquittal and life for all men*" (emphasis supplied). "Acquittal" is a legal term meaning that the person accused of a crime (sin against God) has been declared "not guilty" and is released from all penalty.

---

1. "So then, as through one trespass there is condemnation for everyone, so also through one righteous act there is life-giving justification for everyone. For just as through one man's disobedience the many were made sinners, so also through the one Man's obedience the many will be made righteous. The law came along to multiply the trespass. But where sin multiplied, grace multiplied even more so that, just as sin reigned in death, so also grace will reign through righteousness, resulting in eternal life through Jesus Christ our Lord." (Romans 5:18-21).

2. The human race is fallen but not *guilty* of Adam's transgression. We do not "inherit" Adam's guilt nor condemnation for Adam's sin. That is the Augustinian false idea of "original sin," for which, infant baptism is thought to be the remedy. Christ's justification from the "foundation of the world" (Revelation 13:8; 1 Peter 1:18-20; Hebrews 4:1-3), eliminated the curse that transgression brought. As soon as Adam sinned, Christ became his Saviour, and Adam did not die that fateful afternoon in Eden. Through the everlasting covenant promise (Genesis 3:15) we are born "legally justified" and without guilt and condemnation until we willfully commit sin.

Paul's argument in Romans chapter 5 is that Adam's one sin brought condemnation upon the entire human race because he is the father of the entire human race. When he sinned, all the generations yet unborn fell right along with him. After his sin, all Adam had to give to his children was fallen flesh and a mind full of enmity against God. But the "one just act" of Christ's death on the cross (promised in Genesis 3:15) cancelled Adam's guilt and condemnation, and the human race, though born with fallen sinful flesh, stands "acquitted" before the throne of God in Christ Jesus.[3]

Christ remedied the problem by taking upon His sinless nature, our fallen nature, and in that nature that we all have, Jesus, through faith in His Father's power over sin, worked out a perfect life.[4] Then He took that perfect life to the cross and died corporately *as* the human race He came to save, thus paying the penalty for the entire human race (2 Corinthians 5:14, 15).[5] Whoever is eternally lost will have thrown that gift of justification way—spurned it as a worthless thing, and thrown it away. Those who will live eternally have recognized the immense value of the gift of Jesus' precious life surrendered for our sins. And that recognition will transform their thinking, and subsequently bring them into alignment with God's eternal law of love.

Justification by faith is the other side of the justification "coin." It is the repentant sinner's believing and appreciating what Christ

---

3. Christ is the sacrifice for sin that God gave from the foundation of the world. The promise was made in the Garden of Eden and ratified 4000 years later on Calvary's cross. The fact that there were 4000 years from the promise to the act does not in any way negate or diminish the power that was in that promise of God when spoken to Adam the day he sinned. The entire human race was placed on probation "in Adam" and it remains for us to decide what we want to do with that gift: keep it or throw it away.

4. "Who in the days of His flesh, when He had offered up prayers and supplications with strong crying and tears unto Him that was able to save Him from death, and was heard in that He feared; though He were a Son, yet learned He obedience by the things which He suffered; and being made perfect, He became the author of eternal salvation unto all them that obey Him." (Hebrews 5:7-9). "Looking unto Jesus the Author and Finisher of our faith; who for the joy that was set before Him endured the cross, despising the shame, and is set down at the right hand of the throne of God." (Hebrews 12:2).

5. "For the love of Christ constraineth us; because we thus judge, that *if One died for all, then were all dead*: and that He died for all, that they which live should not henceforth live unto themselves, but unto Him which died for them, and rose again. …To wit, that God was in Christ, reconciling the world unto Himself, not imputing their trespasses unto them; and hath committed unto us the word of reconciliation." (2 Corinthians 5:14, 15, 19, emphasis supplied; "all" means "all," not "some.").

has already accomplished for them through the everlasting covenant promise and its fulfillment in the life and death of Christ. Thus it involves a *change of heart and mind* in the one who learns to appreciate it. When we surrender to God's love poured out in the life and death of Christ, then we are agreeing with God that we are abject sinners in need of His remedy—Christ's atoning blood.*

We need a divinely implemented heart and mind transplant performed by the Great Physician. If we *let* Him then He will give us His mind and His heart of love. Paul caught this wonderful idea when he penned, "Let this mind be in you which was also in Christ Jesus" (Philippians 2:5). The admonition is to "let" it happen; stop blocking the Surgeon's knife! *Let* Him transform you!

Justification by faith is a heart-reconciliation with God and His righteousness. And as Galatians 5:16, 17 says, when we "walk in the Spirit" we will fulfill all the Commandments of God, and "love, joy, peace, longsuffering, gentleness, goodness, faith, meekness, and temperance" will be the living testimony of the transformation of our characters. The *faith of Jesus* will make the believer a "doer of the law."

On the other side of the theological aisle, I now present some questions that illustrate how some people think about God's justification:—

Was justification only a legal *pronouncement* that God made, millions of light years away from us, "up there" somewhere in the starry reaches of His universe? And being so far removed from us, was it ever meant to actually touch our hearts and lives?

Or is legal justification just an *adjustment* in the record on God's heavenly supercomputer that erased our sin when we confess, but does not have any subjective component that effects our life day to day?

Or is justification what happens when *we make the decision* to "accept Jesus"? Does that "acceptance" start the heavenly machinery rolling so that eventually we obtain justification out the other end of

---

* I am not teaching the "moral influence" theory of the atonement! The moral influence theory claims that sin is not the problem and that Christ did not die the equivalent of the second death to pay the penalty for sin. This twisted view of the atonement claims that without Christ's sacrificial death, mankind was forgiven; sin is forgiven and there is no need for punishment. Further, this theory maintains that "sin" is just an estrangement from God, a "broken relationship" that can be remedied when humans look upon Christ's broken and bleeding body hanging on the cross. Viewing the suffering there, the human heart is pricked and the broken relationship is healed.

the chute, like spitting a candy bar out of the machine when we put the right coins in and push the button?

Or maybe, is it when we finally repent and then our name is entered in God's heavenly computer, that our eternal social security benefits get credited to our account for time and eternity?

None of these theological theories can afford us any *security* or assurance of salvation because they depend on us doing something first. And therefore, they all lead us to believe that salvation is partly God's "provision" that we must grasp "through faith," and that "grasping" part is our "work" in securing the provision to our benefit.

However, if any of these propositions are true, then it would follow that it is our *decision* which initiated this process of "legal acquittal" from our sin. And that opens wide the door for our pride to step up to the front of the stage and take a bow. An element of pride can enter here because we feel that *we initiated* the process which made our salvation effective. Therefore, when we get to heaven we can boast that we are there because we made the "decision for Christ," and our good choice earned us the right to be there.

All of that is rooted deeply in the old covenant idea of "we can do it." And this is the last bastion of legalism that seems so difficult for conscientious Christians to recognize. Self dies hard, kicking and screaming for recognition right up to the very end (see poem page 233).

In contrast, the Bible teaches that the "saints" are saved because of the Godhead's decision to save them from the foundation of the world. "God so loved the world [all the human race] that He gave His Son" (John 3:16) to take the sin of the world upon Himself (John 1:29).[6] When we finally get this figured out and we simply chose to *stop resisting* His work in us, then He will transform our characters into His likeness—just as simply as He opened Sarah's barren womb when she finally got things figured out after the fiasco with Abimelech.

The Biblical truth of what it means to be "under grace" is this: We are under a new *motivation* initiated by a deep heart-appreciation of Christ's love for us, as He demonstrated it by coming to this dark world to save us from sin, thus fulfilling the everlasting/new covenant stated in Genesis 3:15. Jesus, taking fallen human flesh upon His

---

6. "The next day John seeth Jesus coming unto him, and saith, Behold the Lamb of God, which taketh away the sin of the world." (John 1:29).

own sinless nature, facing Satan's every challenge with a "thus saith the LORD," overcoming and "condemning sin in the flesh,"[7] was the fulfillment of His promise to Adam, "I will crush Satan's head."

An appreciation of this truth will so motivate us that we will not stop to count the cost of giving up anything and everything for Him. Nor will we ask questions about how much or how little He expects of us, or what's the least we can "do" in order to get our "heavenly reward." No such thoughts will be in our mind as we "follow the Lamb whithersoever He goeth" (Revelation 14:4).

Our childish questions whether this or that is a "sin that will keep me out of heaven" shrivel up into the pettiness that they are. When we rightly understand the height and depth of the gift of the Son of God to us, we will forget about striving for reward, and will abandon our old covenant attempts to save ourselves. We will no longer be asking how many "stars will be in my crown," because all we want to do when we get to heaven is "cast our crowns" at the feet of the One who gave so much to and for us (Revelation 4:10).[8] Our only concern will be to help crown Him "King of kings and LORD of lords" (Revelation 19:16).

But, we've strayed again; let's get back to our Genesis study where we find the application of these vital truths concerning the everlasting covenant and faith "which works by love."

"And the LORD visited Sarah as He had said, and the LORD did unto Sarah as He had spoken. For Sarah conceived, and bare Abraham a son in his old age, at the set time of which God had spoken to him. And Abraham called the name of his son that was born unto him, whom Sarah bare to him, Isaac." This naming was in accordance with the instructions they received from the LORD when He visited Abraham to confirm His promise to give him a son by Sarah (Genesis 17:19, 21). "And Abraham circumcised his son Isaac being eight days old, as God had commanded him" in Genesis 17:12.

---

7. "For what the law could not do, in that it was weak through the flesh, God sending His own Son in the likeness of sinful flesh, and for sin, condemned sin in the flesh." (Romans 8:3).

8. "The four and twenty elders fall down before Him that sat on the throne, and worship Him that liveth for ever and ever, and cast their crowns before the throne, saying, Thou art worthy, O LORD, to receive glory and honour and power: for Thou hast created all things, and for Thy pleasure they are and were created." (Revelation 4:10, 11).

"And Abraham was an hundred years old, when his son Isaac was born unto him" and Sarah was ninety. And this fact caused Sarah to say, "God hath made me to laugh, so that all that hear will laugh with me," not just from the absurdity of the whole thing, but from joy that the desire of her heart had finally been fulfilled. She had suffered all of her life as a barren woman. In that culture, being unable to produce a male child as an heir was justification for the man's divorce from the barren woman. (Curious that it was always the woman's fault!)

The prophet Samuel's father had taken a second wife because Hannah could not produce a child, and she suffered terribly from the inability and shame of it. David's first wife, Michal (daughter of King Saul), was also unable to give him a child, but she scorned her husband because of it, blaming him for the problem.

And everyone knows the predicament of the English crown when Henry VIII couldn't produce a male heir and the Catholic Church refused him a divorce from Catherine of Aragon. Who, by the way, was the daughter of Isabella and Ferdinand who were responsible for establishing the Spanish Inquisition in 1478, to enforce religious uniformity in Spain, and were the ones who sent Columbus to the New World to claim the lands for the Catholic Church. Henry VIII's obsession to gain a son brought on the English Reformation!

"And Sarah said, Who would have said unto Abraham, that Sarah should have given children suck? for I have born him a son in his old age" of one hundred years. Abraham was the last of the patriarchs to produce children in an advanced age. Before the Flood, most everyone was about 100 years old when they had their *first* son, and went on to have "sons and daughters" in large numbers after that. But Isaac was "only" 40 or so when Rebekah finally got pregnant (she was also called barren, Genesis 25:21).

"And the child grew, and was weaned: and Abraham made a great feast the same day that Isaac was weaned." A child was weaned at the age of three, quite a bit longer than most women nurse their children these days, if they do it at all. And because weaning was a rite of passage, the feast was given to bring everyone in to celebrate the first "coming out" of the son. In this feast, Isaac was presented as the heir apparent to Abraham's massive estate.

More importantly, Isaac established the beginning of the fulfillment of the promise of the coming Messiah, who would "save

His people from their sin" (Matthew 1:21), and "bless all the families of the earth" (Genesis 12:3) through His life and death as the only remedy for sin. Isaac's birth was the fulfillment of God's everlasting covenant promise to Abraham, that through him and his *ultimate* [9] descendant, Jesus Christ, God would "bless the world" through the work of the Saviour. The birth of Isaac proved that God could do what He says He will when man finally takes Him fully at His word, and gets out of God's way. God was vindicated in the birth of this son, just as He will be ultimately vindicated through the life work of His "only begotten Son" as He transforms a group of people of whom He will declare: "Here are they that keep the Commandments of God, and the faith of Jesus!" (Revelation 14:12).

---

9. Ultimate is a precise word that conveys the truth of finality and completion of a series of events that have lead to this end. Nothing extends beyond the "ultimate" point. It is the terminal end, the utmost, the final. Christ's life and death fulfilled all the promises of God to humanity that He would give the Saviour to redeem mankind. In Christ all things are complete.

Self Dies Hard

The last inward enemy of the believer
to be destroyed is self.
It dies hard;
it will make any concession, if only allowed to live.
Self will permit the believer to do anything,
bear any crosses,
afflict soul or body to any degree—anything,
if only it can live.
It will allow victory over pride, poverty, and passion,
if only it is not destroyed.
It will permit any number of rivals,
so long as it has first place.
It will consent to live in a hovel, in a garret,
in the slums, in far-away heathendom—if
only it can be spared.
It will endure any garb, any fare, any menial service
rather than die.
Dying to self is a poetic expression—it
sounds romantic, chivalrous, supernatural, saintlike.
It is beautiful to read about, easy to talk about,
entertaining to theorize about.
Yet it is hard to do.
But it must be done.
There is no abiding peace,
spiritual power,
or prosperity without it.
We must die to good deeds and to bad deeds,
to successes and to failures, to superiority
and to inferiority,
to exaltation and to humiliation—to
every manifestation of self, and to self itself.
The Saviour said, "I, if I be lifted up from the earth,
will draw all men unto Me."
Self lifted up repels. Self crucified with Christ draws;
for only then is Christ lifted up in the yielded life.
Happy those who can say with Paul,
"I am crucified with Christ ...
the life which I now live
I live by the faith of the Son of God."

— Selected

39

Ishmael's Banishment

Genesis 21:6-21

And the child grew, and was weaned: and Abraham made a great feast the same day that Isaac was weaned. And Sarah saw the son of Hagar the Egyptian, which she had born unto Abraham, mocking." "Hagar the Egyptian" is thrown in just to make sure that the reader is fully aware that we're talking about the same mother and her snobby son who is now "mocking" Isaac, the three year old son that has replaced him as heir of Abraham's vast estate. His sneering arrogant attitude is not much different from his mother's toward her mistress when she realized that she was pregnant with Abraham's son.

There's an interesting play on words here. The Hebrew word that is translated as "mock" is the same word translated as "laugh" in Genesis 17:17; 18:12, 13; 21:6, and is Isaac's name. In the first instance, Abraham found it amusing that God still maintained that Abraham and Sarah would have a child. In the second, Sarah is laughing at the ridiculousness of her becoming pregnant at ninety years of age. In the third reference, Sarah is laughing for joy that she *did* become pregnant and successfully birthed the promised heir (no complications from childbirth and no birth defects caused by her advanced age—pretty amazing evidence of God's protection!). And Isaac's name would be a forever reminder of her laughing at God's promise to give her a son.

However, here in Genesis 21:9 where Ishmael is laughing, it is not for joy or incredulity, but for true derision of the little boy who was being celebrated at that feast.

Let's put some more perspective on this incident. Ishmael was thirteen when he was circumcised (Genesis 17:23, 25). Shortly after that the LORD personally appeared to Abraham and Sarah, and promised that Isaac would be born one year later. The feast for Isaac's weaning took place when he was three, which makes Ishmael 17 years old at that time. In this scene we have a young man of seventeen laughing at a baby of three. Envy is no doubt at the root of his feelings toward this toddler. Ishmael was definitely aware of the profound change in his own circumstances as Abraham's firstborn son.

What does this tell us of Ishmael's spiritual and emotional development? What does it tell us about how Ishmael was raised by his mother and his mother's attitude toward Sarah and her son?

Probably, due to the animosity that existed between the two women, Hagar and Ishmael were not regular visitors at Sarah and Abraham's tent. For this reason, perhaps Sarah had not before noticed the cruel streak in Ishmael's nature. But now she sees it. "Wherefore she said unto Abraham, Cast out this bondwoman and her son: for the son of this bondwoman shall not be heir with my son, even with Isaac." This is not just petty jealousy on the part of Sarah. She detected the very real enmity that was being demonstrated by Ishmael toward her little son, and it was portentous. Sarah recognized this mocking attitude as persecution.

And it wasn't just that Sarah was wanting to protect the *material* estate for her own son, but more importantly that she wanted Abraham to cast out the Egyptian slave woman and her son so that they would not benefit from the covenant blessings. The Hebrew word used here for "heir" has a direct connection to the inheritance of the covenant blessings. Sarah didn't have the global mind set of God concerning the everlasting covenant that is to be *a blessing to the whole world* (Genesis 12:3; 18:18; 22:18; 26:4; 28:17; Acts 3:25; Romans 4:11).[1] She wanted to exclude the Egyptian and her son as unworthy of *any* blessing.

---

[1] "Ye are the children of the prophets, and of the covenant which God made with our fathers, saying unto Abraham, And in thy seed shall all the kindreds of the earth be blessed. Unto you first God, having raised up His Son Jesus, sent Him to bless you, in turning away every one of you from his iniquities. (Acts 3:25, 26). "Then Paul and Barnabas waxed bold, and said, It was necessary that the word of God should first have been spoken to you [the Jews]: but seeing ye put it from you, and judge yourselves unworthy of everlasting life, lo, we turn to the Gentiles. For so hath the Lord commanded us, saying, I have set thee to be a light of the Gentiles, that thou shouldest be *for salvation unto the ends of the earth*." (Acts 13:46, 47, emphasis supplied).

"And the thing was very grievous in Abraham's sight because of his son." Abraham loved Ishmael as much as he loved Isaac. He didn't want to send him away. He had listened to his wife when she counseled him about her barrenness and it's earthy solution by using Hagar, and now he is not wanting to listen to her concerning sending his son away to who knows what kind of life alone in the desert. We can easily imagine that Abraham went into passive mode concerning this request. Perhaps if he just waited, when the feast was over, Ishmael would settle down and everything would fix itself. Sarah would forget this rash and harsh demand, and life would return to normal.

Not so. This time Sarah was speaking in concert with God's mind. "And God said unto Abraham, Let it not be grievous in thy sight because of the lad, and because of thy bondwoman; in all that Sarah hath said unto thee, hearken unto her voice; for in Isaac shall thy seed be called." How God communicated this to His friend, we are not told. God Himself does not appear in the scene as in previous communications with Abraham, but Abraham came to accept that what Sarah said was God's will. Maybe after he thought about it he realized the impossibility of raising both sons in his household. Conflict would be constant between the boys and their mothers, and an unhealthy home environment would result. Abraham would be caught in the middle every time.

Then God repeated His promise concerning Ishmael. "And also of the son of the bondwoman will I make a nation, because he is thy seed [son]." Ishmael *was* Abraham's son, and God was not going to cast him away like trash. He was going to bless and provide for him. The same promise God told Abraham when he begged the LORD to allow Ishmael to be his heir, is being reinforced here. "As for Ishmael, I have heard thee. Behold, I have blessed him and will make him fruitful, and will multiply him exceedingly; twelve princes shall he begat, and I will make him a great nation" (Genesis 17:20). Eventually, Jacob, Abraham's heir through Isaac, produced twelve tribes. God promised Abraham that Ishmael would also have twelve tribes descended from him. God blessed the one son equally as well as the other.

And so, with this blessing promised upon his son Ishmael, Abraham was comforted. And he "rose up early in the morning, and took bread, and a bottle of water, and gave it unto Hagar, putting it on her shoulder, and the child, and sent her away: and she departed, and wandered in the wilderness of Beersheba." Both Hagar and "the child" were given bread and water. Interesting that even though he is seventeen, Ishmael is referred to here as a "child." He had been acting childish at the feast and now he is sent away as a misbehaving child would be sent to his room to think about what he had done.

Abraham rose early in the morning to carry out this banishment. Leaving about sunrise would give Hagar and the lad time to get some distance from Abraham's camp before the noon sun began to beat mercilessly down on their heads. There is no intimation that Abraham provided fatherly instruction to the mother and her child about where they should go, where to seek shelter in their journey, or a final refuge. He left the results of their wandering to the LORD who had promised to provide for them.

"And the water was spent in the bottle, and she cast the child under one of the shrubs. And she went, and sat her down over against him a good way off, as it were a bowshot: for she said, Let me not see the death of the child. And she sat over against him, and lift up her voice, and wept."

Weary and faithless, that is what Hagar was when she got to this place in the wilderness at the extreme southern region of Canaan. Friendless and not knowing where else to go, she headed back toward her Egyptian homeland. Where else could she go with any hope of finding family and security?

Where they stopped to rest was on the western edge of the great Arabian wilderness that borders the coastal area that leads down to Egypt. She was certain that she had been banished from her home to die in the desert, rejected and unloved by anyone. All her years of service in Sarah's tent brought her no security. Now she sits down, and without water she expects to die.

Most of her life since she had been given nearly thirty years before as a handmaid to Sarah in Egypt, had been spent in the pleasant encampment of her mistress. She had never known privation, even if there had been times of distress after she became Abraham's concubine. Now, she could not bear to see her beloved son die of dehydration, so she placed him under a bush to shade him while she went a little way off and sat down with her back to him. Not having any experience in these things, in her mind death would come quickly. They just needed to sit and patiently wait for it.

Beersheba is a place that appears elsewhere in the Scriptures. The name has two parts. "Beer" means well of water, and "sheba" is the number seven, so the name means seven wells. The reality of the situation is that God brought the travelers to seven wells of water before they ran out of what Abraham had sent them way with in their water skins. But they didn't know His merciful heart as Abraham did, and so they were discouraged.

"And God heard the voice of the lad; and the Angel of God called to Hagar out of heaven, and said unto her, What aileth thee, Hagar?" What are you bellyaching about? Did I not take care of you when you, on your own, ran away into the desert to escape Sarah's wrath before Ishmael was born? Did I not protect you then, both from the elements and from Sarah's wrath? What I have done in the past, I am capable of doing now and in the future. I am the same yesterday, today and forever, so, "fear not; for God hath heard the voice of the lad where he is."

Evidently the young man was weeping and praying to the LORD that his father worshiped. During his seventeen years living in Abraham's camp he had learned something of who God was and how powerful He was, even if his Egyptian mother had not.

To Hagar God continued His conversation, "Arise, lift up the lad, and hold him in thine hand; for I will make him a great nation." The promise is repeated to Hagar that God would bless and multiply the descendants of her son. She had nothing at all to fear. God made the promise to Abraham, and He would not renege on that promise. Ishmael would grow up to be a great man with twelve sons.

"And God opened her eyes, and she saw a well of water; and she went, and filled the bottle with water, and gave the lad drink." Again we see the pitiful helplessness of this seventeen year old "child" who could not even fill up his own water bottle. He had been so pampered and petted all of his life, that his mother was to him as a slave, constantly waiting on him hand and foot as though he was royalty. No wonder Ishmael was envious of the newcomer who would usurp his position as the heir of the estate! He had been raised as the "king's" son, and now he was cast out like the trash.

But Hagar's lack of faith and her certainty that they were soon to die, blinded her from seeing what was right before them—seven springs of water gushing abundantly in that desert place. Her inexperience hid from her the truth that in the desert, if there was vegetation, there had to be water near by. Her focus was on their privations and not on the LORD's blessings. Self-centeredness blinded her to God's blessings. All she had to do was "open her eyes" and look around her. There it was, all the water they could ever need. God already had provided for them, guiding them to that place of vegetation and abundant water, even though in their lack of faith they did not recognize that it was His hand leading them there.

"And God was with the lad; and he grew, and dwelt in the wilderness, and became an archer. And he dwelt in the wilderness of Paran: and his mother took him a wife out of the land of Egypt." How they managed to exist there in the wilderness we are not told, but there must have been some means whereby they could make a living. Ishmael's abilities as an archer would have provided food from the wild antelopes that lived in the region around them. Date palms surrounding the spring gave them nourishing fruit. The wells provided plenty of water. There were no doubt other nomads living in the area who came to the wells to water their flocks. From them they could purchase or trade for grains like barley and wheat to make their bread, and obtain other things they needed to establish their home there.

To seal her reconnection with her homeland, Hagar found an Egyptian girl to marry Ishmael. All of his descendants would be at least three-quarter Egyptian. She didn't have to return to Egypt to obtain this wife, because with the springs nearby where they were staying, plenty of caravans would stop at the oasis to water their animals. People would come to them and she could communicate her desire for a wife for her son.

And so began the fulfillment of God's word concerning Ishmael: "and he will be a wild man; his hand will be against every man, and every man's hand will be against him; and he shall dwell in the presence of his brethren." "He dwelt in the wilderness of Paran," never traveling very far from where they landed when expelled from Abraham's camp.

40

The Well of the Oath

Genesis 21:22-34

As we begin the last section of this part of the narrative, there are some interesting things we should be careful to note. Seven appears four times in these verses: once as the number itself describing the gift of the lambs, twice hidden in the words "to swear," and in the name Beersheba (seven wells). Both Abraham and Abimelech's names are used seven times. Beersheba is doubtless the same area of the Negev that Hagar and Ishmael found themselves exiled to, which means that they did not move very far away from Abraham and his clan.

From the narrative itself, we have no idea the reason why Abimelech came to have this conference with Abraham. Perhaps because Hagar and Ishmael settled there, Abimelech felt that Abraham was establishing an "outpost" of sorts and extending his territorial claims further into Abimelech's lands. He must have felt threatened for some reason for him to come with the chief captain of his army, desiring to make a long-lasting peace treaty that would extend at least through Abimelech's grandson's lifetime.

"And it came to pass at that time, that Abimelech and Phichol the chief captain of his host spake unto Abraham, saying, God is with thee in all that thou doest: Now therefore swear unto me here by God that thou wilt not deal falsely with me, nor with my son, nor with my son's son: but according to the kindness that I have done unto thee, thou shalt do unto me, and to the land wherein thou hast sojourned."

Abraham's tribe had been living near Abimelech for some few years now. The story of Abraham's expulsion of his concubine, making the exclusive heir the second born son—who was born of a ninety year old barren woman that he himself had previously taken as a concubine—was the talk of the region. And the opening of the wombs of Abimelech's women was a tale that was repeated around the campfires when the gods of the area were discussed. Abraham's God was superior to all their gods, and they feared Him through their pagan superstitiousness. To make a treaty with Abraham was to make peace with his most powerful God.

There was no reason for Abraham not to be willing to agree to Abimelech's request, and so he said, "I will swear." His laconic reply with no elaboration, indicates that there was something more important on Abraham's mind, and that soon came to the forefront of the conference.

"Abraham reproved Abimelech because of a well of water, which Abimelech's servants had violently taken away." Water wells were always a source of dispute in that arid land. Throughout the Genesis narrative wells and arguments over water rights appear frequently. In this case, the well had been dug by Abraham's own men, and belonged exclusively to him and his tribe.

Abimelech replied, "I don't know who did this thing. You didn't report anything to me, so I hadn't heard about it until today." (Genesis 21:26, HCSB). He was innocent of any charge of conspiracy to defraud Abraham. He had come in peace, and now was told that there had been a dispute between Abraham's men and his own shepherds. Why didn't Abraham tell him? Probably because he didn't want conflict. Abraham always shied away from conflict.

We witness this characteristic in Abraham in his dealing with Lot over grazing lands, with Sarah telling him to take Hagar as his concubine, and again with Sarah concerning the expulsion of Hagar and Ishmael into the wilderness. The only time Abraham stepped out to fight was when Chedorlaomer captured Lot and his family. Abraham was a peace-loving man, a man after God's own heart, and never sought a quarrel with anyone.

"And Abraham took sheep and oxen, and gave them unto Abimelech." If these were a reciprocate gift to Abimelech's when he sent Abraham and Sarah away (Genesis 20:14), it is significant that there were no servants or slaves included in the gift. Abraham was not one to participate in human trafficking. The people living in his clan knew they were safe from being sold away from their home.

"And both of them made a covenant." This covenant was of the parity type; a covenant between persons of equal stature. It is the same type of covenant in which God demonstrated His everlasting promise in Genesis 15:17, 18. Remember, in that study we learned that God the Father and God the Son passed between those animals and burned them to ashes. Abraham sat on the sidelines as a witness.

Here in this instance of the parity covenant ritual, Abimelech was king in his realm, and Abraham was viewed as the nomadic king of his own wandering village made up of hundreds of herdsmen and shepherds, and their large families. When he returned from fighting Chedorlaomer, Abraham had been recognized as king by both the king of Sodom and by Melchizedek, king of Salem.

The animals used in this Canaanite covenant ritual were killed and then slit down the length of their bodies, dividing the carcass into halves, which were then laid out on the ground a little distance from each other. The ritual required both swearing parties to walk between the animal halves together, at the same time, each saying, "Let what happened to these animals happen to me, if I do not uphold my part of the agreement made between us this day." In effect, it meant putting their own lives on the line if either one should violate the terms of the peace treaty.[1]

Even though Abimelech came to Abraham desiring the treaty, it was Abraham who provided the sacrificial animals. Doing so showed both his willingness to have peace between them, and his superiority over the pagan king. The greater always gives blessings to the lesser.

When they had completed the ritual, "Abraham set seven ewe lambs of the flock by themselves. And Abimelech said unto Abraham, What mean these seven ewe lambs which thou hast set by themselves? And he said, For these seven ewe lambs shalt thou take of my hand, that they may be a witness unto me, that I have digged this well." These lambs

---

[1]. "Covenants in which the two parties step between cloven animal parts are attested in various places in ancient Near East as well as in Greece. The idea is that if either party violates the covenant, his fate will be like that of the cloven animal. The Hebrew idiom karat berit, literally, 'to cut a covenant', may derive from this legal ritual." Robert Alter, *Genesis: A Translation and Commentary* (New York: W.W. Norton, 1996), page 65.

were not part of the covenant but a witness that Abraham's men had dug the well. By accepting them, Abimelech officially acknowledged Abraham's true ownership of the well.

Abraham did not purchase the well from Abimelech, but through the gift of the seven lambs was proving his ownership. Wells were of great importance to a pastoral chief with many hundreds of flocks of sheep and goats, and cattle. In that part of the world, rain ceased from March to November, which meant that the water-bearing wadis in the land went dry. Without wells at strategic places, they could not successfully manage their herds during that season.

Digging a well took much time and effort and therefore was a prized possession. Sinking a new one also meant that the person responsible for the work was claiming ownership of the surrounding unoccupied fields, where he would pasture his flocks in close proximity to the water. If the one who dug the well should move away and the well fall into disrepair, then anyone who restored it acquired the right to use it and claim it as his own.

"Wherefore [Abraham] called that place Beersheba; because there they sware both of them. Thus they made a covenant at Beersheba: then Abimelech rose up, and Phichol the chief captain of his host, and they returned into the land of the Philistines." Satisfied with their agreement and the resolution of the dispute over the well, Abimelech returned to the coast, where the Philistines had their towns.

This well dug by Abraham's men is not the same place as the seven natural springs that God led Hagar and Ishmael to in the southern end of the Negev. Abraham's name of the place has to do with the seven lambs and the covenant promise.

This place called Beersheba is about twelve hours' journey south of Hebron on the road between Egypt and the Dead Sea. Archeological inspection of the place has determined that there are still stones in this area that are believed to be relics of an ancient town that was built up around two deep wells. The largest of these wells has an internal diameter at the mouth of more than twelve feet across, or a circumference of nearly forty feet. Imagine the effort and time it took to dig such a well. No wonder a well was a prized possession! The area is today called *Bir es Seba*, the "well of the oath."

"And Abraham planted a grove in Beersheba, and called there on the name of the LORD, the everlasting God." The word "grove" is used to describe a tamarisk tree. This long-lived species of tree has a wide spreading growth pattern, which provides abundant shade to all that gathers beneath it. It survives in that arid region by sending down deep roots into the subterranean water source and thereby flourishes in places unsuited to any ordinary vegetation.

Planting the long-lived tree that would send its roots deep into the barren ground and bring up life-giving water, can be symbolic of the "everlasting God" that Abraham worshiped at that place. The title "everlasting God" only appears three times in the entire Bible, here, and in Isaiah 40:28 and Romans 16:26. Isaiah's use of the title is appropriate for Abraham's situation also, as he recognized the true Source of his strength and safety. "Hast thou not known? hast thou not heard, that the everlasting God, the LORD, the Creator of the ends of the earth, fainteth not, neither is weary? there is no searching of His understanding. He giveth power to the faint; and to them that have no might He increaseth strength." (Isaiah 40:28, 29).

"And Abraham sojourned in the Philistines' land many days." Later, the Philistines would become unassailable enemies of the children of Israel, and never defeated by them, but now there is perfect harmony and peace between them and Abraham's clan. Abimelech learned the power of Abraham's God, and he respected it.

41

"Take Your Only Son"

Genesis 22:1, 2

It came to pass after these things, that God tried Abraham, and said to him, Abraham! and he said, Here am I. And He said, Take now thy son, thine only son Isaac, whom thou lovest, and get thee into the land of Moriah, and there offer him up for a burnt-offering on one of the mountains which I will tell thee of."

WHOA!! God worked for twenty-five years getting Abraham and Sarah to develop the faith necessary for them to begat a child from a dead womb, and now that same God is telling Abraham to take that promised child to a distant land, and there kill that son and burn him up on an altar. What a totally mind-blowing thing to say!

No other narrative in Genesis is so terrible to read, so profoundly powerful and mysterious as this one. Abraham has been through so much since entering the land of Canaan that it hardly seems possible that at his advanced age he should have to endure an additional trial, especially one of this magnitude.

To begin our journey in understanding the trial of Abraham, we need to notice something significant. Looking back to the many times that God spoke to Abraham, we find that when He first spoke to him in Genesis 12:1, God gave a simple imperative command: "Go forth," and Abraham did as he was told. In chapter 15 God came to Abraham in a vision, and also began with an imperative: "Fear not!" When the LORD appeared to him to restate the covenant promise in chapter 17, He began by identifying Himself as *El Shaddai*—the "Almighty God."

(17:1), the One with all power in heaven and earth. After identifying Himself, the LORD then, again, gave an imperative command: "Walk before Me and be perfect."

Never did God begin His address to Abraham by first calling his name; never before was Abraham spoken to in this most personal manner. Here, and only here, in Genesis 22:1 does God call to Abraham by his name.

And the name God uses is not Abram, but Abraham—the "Father of a Multitude." To produce that "multitude" God gave Abraham and Sarah the promised son, Isaac. In the previous chapter, God assured Abraham that he must banish Ishmael from his clan, because "in Isaac shall thy seed ["offspring"] be called." The everlasting covenant of the promised Messiah hinged on the promised son through whom the Rightful Son would be manifested in the world in human flesh (Genesis 49:10; Jeremiah 23:5, 6; Hebrews 2:14-16)

This is the theme that the apostle Paul picked up when he wrote in Romans and Galatians that it was through Isaac that the ultimate Seed would come. "Know ye therefore that they which are of faith, the same are the children of Abraham. And the Scripture, foreseeing that God would justify the heathen through faith, preached before the gospel unto Abraham, saying, In thee shall all nations be blessed. So then they which be of faith are blessed with faithful Abraham. ... Now to Abraham and his Seed were the promises made. He saith not, And to seeds, as of many; but as of one, And to thy Seed, which is Christ." (Galatians 3:7, 8, 9, 16).

"Not as though the word of God hath taken none effect. For they are not all Israel, which are of Israel: neither, because they are the seed of Abraham [literal genetic descendants], are they all children: but, In Isaac shall thy seed be called. That is, They which are the children of the flesh [literal genetic descendants], these are not the children of God: but the children of the promise are counted for the seed." (Romans 9:6-8).

In these verses Paul is using Isaac as a symbol of all faithful people throughout time. They are those who believe in the promise of God. No claim concerning a special election of God, or of righteousness and salvation, can be made on the basis of carnal descent through the literal nation descended from Isaac. The only way a person is saved is through the everlasting covenant promise of God through Christ.

Those who believe in Jesus are "the children of the promise" who are "counted as the seed" of Abraham.

The true "seed" of Abraham are not those who are genetically descended from Isaac, but those who by faith follow Christ are His children, and "heirs according to the promise." True children of the promise are heirs of everlasting life and of the new earth in which we will dwell for all eternity.

In the rite of circumcision Abraham learned the lesson that "the flesh profits nothing." (John 6:63). All schemes of the "flesh" through which we might think we can be saved are nothing, and less than nothing. Only in the promised Son of Righteousness can true righteousness be found. Only He, the Great Physician, has the necessary cure for our sin problem (see Malachi 4:2).

And now, all of a sudden, totally "out of the blue" as it were, God tells Abraham to take that long-awaited heir through whom so much would be realized, and offer him as a whole burnt offering. Nothing of that precious son was to remain but ashes when the all-consuming fire had extinguished itself.

Would you not be confused by this? Would you not question your sanity? Perhaps your imagination is running amok, Abraham; maybe the heat is warping your mind. Maybe you really didn't hear anything from God at all. Maybe it wasn't really God speaking to you, but some devil in your head. How can you tell?

No, none of these thoughts went through Abraham's head. We know this because he immediately answered God by saying, "Here I am!" Look, here I am, just as You named me—the "Father of Multitudes." I know Your voice, I have heard it many times over the years. And now I am inclining toward You, listening for Your voice, and wholly ready to follow Your word, no matter what You ask me to do. I have learned to be totally surrendered to You.

After Abraham, the Father of the Faithful, responded with an open heart to his LORD's call, then God said, "Take that beloved son of yours, and go to a mountain I will show you which is in the land of Moriah. And there, I want you to kill that son and burn him up on an altar of stones."

Here we need a little help from the Hebrew language because a substantial point is lost in translation into English. In the original Hebrew there is a tiny two letter word—*na*—that we miss in the

English. Added to the imperative "take" is this tiny but powerful word *na*, which means "*please*." God is not *commanding* Abraham to kill his son, but He is saying, "*please* take your son and do this thing." The *please* softens the imperative, giving Abraham the free choice to do as requested, or refuse to do it. Should he refuse, he would not incur any guilt for "disobedience."

The test is now seen as a loving response—a faith response—to God's request that Abraham could agree to do, or he could say no. It tells us just how large Abraham's faith had grown, and just how sure God was that Abraham truly did love Him.

42

Bitter Deed

Genesis 22:2-5

He said, Take now thy son, thine only son Isaac, whom thou lovest, and get thee into the land of Moriah; and offer him there for a burnt offering upon one of the mountains which I will tell thee of."

Moriah was north of where Abraham had been for some years living "in the land of the Philistines," in the far southern region of Canaan (Genesis 21:34). Moriah can reasonably be described as about a three-day trek from Beersheba where Abraham was encamped and where he disputed with Abimelech over the wells (Genesis 21:32, 33).

Some modern Biblical scholars of the higher critical persuasion [1] doubt that we can accurately locate this mountain, but the writer of 2 Chronicles 3:1 informs us that that mountain was the same place where Solomon built the temple.[2] Chronicles also links this mountain to another significant event at the end of David's reign.

---

1. Higher criticism views the Bible as a text created and written by humans during a later time period than Biblical historians had previously stated. The claim is that the writings served various human motives. The position assumes that men can decide whether a piece of Scripture was written by Moses, or was redacted (edited) at a much later date, the "redactors" adding material that seemed pertinent to that later time. Higher criticism does not view the Bible as the inerrant word of God, written "by holy men of God [who] spake as they were moved by the Holy Ghost"; it denies the word of God that says, "for the prophecy came not in old time by the *will* of man." (2 Peter 1:20, 21).

2. "Then Solomon began to build the house of the LORD at Jerusalem in mount Moriah." (2 Chronicles 3:1).

David committed a grievous sin in numbering the people so he could ascertain how many were available to form an army. It was a sin because David thought he needed to rely on the power of the size of his army, instead of relying on the power of God to win the battle. After that sin, God sent a plague upon the nation, but David realized his sin, pleaded with the LORD for mercy, and his prayer was heard (2 Samuel chapter 24). As a result of his prayer, the prophet Gad appeared to him telling him to "go up, and erect an altar to the LORD upon the [threshing] floor of Aravnah the Jebusite." David was to build the altar and offer burnt-offerings upon it and the plague would then be averted from Israel.

The Jebusites had occupied that mountain at least 400 years before David arrived there, and their name for the fortified city built on the southeastern ridge of that mountain was Jerus. After it was captured, the citadel became known as "the City of David" and "Zion" (1 Chronicles 11:15, cf. 2 Samuel 5:7).

Today Mount Moriah is occupied by the Dome of the Rock, an impressive Muslim structure erected in AD 691 over the ancient site of Herod's Temple that was destroyed in AD 70 by the Roman army under Titus. A large outcropping of rock inside the Muslim temple is still revered as the traditional site of the original altar upon which Isaac was to be sacrificed.

This site was chosen for the Muslim mosque because supposedly, Muhammad traveled from Mecca to Jerusalem in a single night on a strange winged creature called Bura. It is further claimed that from the same rock outcropping in Jerusalem where the Temple was built by Solomon, Muhammad ascended alive into heaven, and received there from God Himself, the command that all faithful Muslims should pray toward Mecca five times a day.

The name Moriah is associated with a Hebrew verb meaning "to see" or "to provide," which connects it theologically to the phrase that is repeated throughout Genesis 22:1-19. From the time of this narrative of Abraham and Isaac until the time of the sacrifice of Christ on the Roman cross, the site was the focal place where God "saw" and "provided" for His people, until the Ultimate Sacrifice of His Son was made on that same mountain in AD 31.

Despite what higher critics of the Bible present in their arguments, through evidence from Scripture and history we are assured that this

Mount Moriah is indeed that same place where God sent Abraham to sacrifice Isaac.

"And offer him there for a burnt offering upon the mountain." Human sacrifice was common among the Canaanites living in the land at the time of Abraham, and continued through the time leading up to the Babylonian captivity of the children of Israel. Molech, also known as "Milcom" among the Ammonites, was the national god of the people living in Canaan. Though they were polytheists, Molech was the main god and they worshiped it by putting their infant sons and daughters alive into the fire that burned in the metal idol. The innocent victim was literally roasted alive. Four hundred and seventy years later just as the Israelites were entering Canaan, Moses wrote in Leviticus and Deuteronomy strict prohibitions against falling into the abominable worship of the Canaanite god Molech (see Leviticus 18:21; 20:2-5; Deuteronomy 12:31; 18:10-13).[3]

But this is the very place and the method that the God of heaven chose to test Abraham's faith. Abraham was well aware of the forms and rituals of the pagans that lived around him. No doubt he abhorred the sacrificing of infant children to this abominable god, but after hearing God's plea to sacrifice his own son, he "rose early in the morning, saddled his donkey, and took two of his young men with him, and his son Isaac. And he cut the wood for the burnt offering and arose and went to the place of which God had told him."

Abraham went ready to make the sacrifice, preparing all the necessary items before he left. He did not go anticipating that there would be dry firewood on that forested mountain, but carried with him dry materials so he would not have to waste time hunting for what was needed. He would go where he was directed, and would swiftly carry out what he was asked to do there. Then just as quickly, Abraham planned to return home. Speed of action hopefully would reduce the bitterness of the deed.

---

3. "And thou shalt not let any of thy seed pass through the fire to Molech, neither shalt thou profane the name of thy God: I am the LORD. (Leviticus 18:21). "And I will set My face against that man, and will cut him off from among his people; because he hath given of his seed unto Molech, to defile My sanctuary, and to profane My holy name." (Leviticus 20:3). "Thou shalt not do so unto the LORD thy God: for every abomination to the LORD, which He hateth, have they done unto their gods; for even their sons and their daughters they have burnt in the fire to their gods." (Deuteronomy 12:31).

43

No Laughing Matter

Genesis 22:4-6

God tested Abraham and said to him, 'Abraham!' And he said, 'Here I am.' He said, 'Take your son, your only son Isaac, whom you love, and go to the land of Moriah, and offer him there as a burnt offering on one of the mountains of which I shall tell you.' So Abraham rose early in the morning, saddled his donkey, and took two of his young men with him, and his son Isaac. And he cut the wood for the burnt offering and arose and went to the place of which God had told him." (Genesis 22:1-3). Evidently, this "land of Moriah" was known to Abraham. He didn't need to ask anyone where it was or ask directions on how to get there. He just packed up and headed north.

We are not told if Abraham said anything to Sarah about where he and Isaac were going, but we can be certain that he did not tell her what he was going to do when he got there.

If Sarah had been informed, a howl would have gone up such as never was heard in that land before or since, and Moses certainly would have recorded her reaction. "Take *my* son, the son that we waited for and struggled to conceive during all those long years?! You're insane Abraham! You will not take *my* son and kill him, not for anything will you do this! You are thinking like the pagans we have been living among for way too long!"

And God's request "take *your* son" might have elicited a query from Abraham: "*which* son, I have two?" But God would have answered, "your *only* son." But Abraham could have further responded, "but I have *two* 'only sons,' each the 'only son' of his mother. Which do You mean?" God again refining the specification, "the one that you *love*." Good hearted Abraham, "but I love them both, even if you told me to cast out the one!" Then God got pointed, "I mean for you to *take Isaac*, the son of the promise, the *only son that I promised you*."

Despite the name of the young man, this is now no laughing matter. Abraham must make a serious decision here: Submit passively to this request from God, or turn his back against his best Friend. It does not appear from the narrative that Abraham hesitated once he was settled in his mind about what God was asking him to do.

It would not have been usual for a man of Abraham's wealthy status to take with him two servant men to handle the donkey, and the tent setup when they camped for the night, and to do the cooking. And so, while he chopped the firewood his servants saddled a donkey to carry the needed supplies, and putting his first foot forward on this agonizing journey, they left Sarah and the rest of the tribe behind as they headed north to the slaughtering place.

The next three days were full of mental torture and perhaps even physical distress for Abraham as he walked along with his beloved son at his side. Each slap of his sandals in the sand sounded a death knell for Isaac, and each step added to the weight that Abraham was carrying in his heart.

Many things would have been running through his mind. Foremost would have been, What would he tell Sarah and the rest of the tribe when we returned home without Isaac? How could he explain that the God who promised them a son, had now asked for the life of that son to be sacrificed to Him? What was he going to tell Isaac, and how would *he* react? He was old enough to physically resist his old father's crazy actions, what then? And finally the horrible thought: How was he going to find the courage to raise that knife and bring it down to slit his precious son's throat to let his blood flow upon the ground?

But the biggest question mark was, How was God going to fulfill His promise that through *this* son, all the world would be blessed, if the son was burned up on the altar? If the son was dead, then where would the descendants come from through whom the Messiah would eventually arise to bless the world? Absorbed in these deep and troubling thoughts, the three day trip was a quiet one for the little band of travelers.

"Then on the third day Abraham lifted up his eyes, and saw the place afar off." The mountain upon which Moriah is situated is more than 2500 feet above the plain, so would be visible from a distance of a few miles. With the mountain in sight, the awful moment also loomed imminently before him. Time was running out for him to change his mind about giving up his only son to the LORD.

"And Abraham said unto his young men, Abide ye here with the donkey; and I and the lad will go yonder and worship, and come again to you."

There it is. There is the final decision, "I *and the lad will come again to you.*" Abraham could not at that point entertain the notion that Isaac would not come back down that mountain with him. *How* he was going to follow through with his decision to obey God's request and kill Isaac, and yet still bring the young man home to his mother was unfathomable, but he *was certain* that he would be able to do it. His assertion to his servants was made in faith that somehow God was able to accomplish His will through Isaac, no matter what.

God is the God of love, and hope against hope meant that somehow God would work this out for him. Faith must take the word of God as it is stated. "I will make of thee a great nation, and in thee shall all the families of the earth be blessed." No, it would not be him that pulled this off, but *God would do it.* Isaac's continued existence was necessary for this promise to be fulfilled and that meant that somehow God would solve this terrible dilemma for him.

"And Abraham took the wood of the burnt offering and laid it on Isaac his son. And he took in his hand the fire and the knife. So they went both of them together."

44

Total Commitment

Genesis 22:6-8

Abraham took the wood of the burnt offering and laid it on Isaac his son. And he took in his hand the fire and the knife. So they went both of them together. And Isaac said to his father Abraham, 'My father!' And he said, 'Here I am, my son.'"

Now had arrived the time and the question that Abraham had been dreading for three days. Silence along the journey had not made this question disappear nor minimized its horror. It was inevitable. It had hung in the air like a heavy choking fog that Abraham could not see through. When Isaac spoke, a stab of dread and fear went though Abraham's heart as he answered the tenderly voiced opening address, "My father ..."

Perhaps even in the heat of the midday, an icy chill ran down Abraham's spine as he answered, "I'm here, son. Yes? What do you want?" He knew what the question would be.

And Isaac replied: "Look, Father, I know we have the fire and the wood, but where is the lamb for the burnt offering?" I've been wondering all the time we've been walking and just have to ask you this. Did you overlook something when we left camp three days ago? We did leave in kind of a hurry that morning, before dawn, even. Maybe you forgot to stop by the flock and pick out a lamb?

"Abraham said, 'God will provide for Himself the lamb for a burnt offering, my son.' So they went both of them together," walking toward the mountain rising ominously just before them.

Abraham's answer was a true statement. God had provided Isaac for Himself. Isaac was to fulfill the promise that through his descendants would come the Messiah who would save people from their sin and rebellion against Him (Genesis 3:15; Matthew 1:21).[1] All of his life Isaac had known that he was the special promised child, born of a miracle pregnancy that only God could have produced when his elderly mother and father finally fully believed in the power of God to do what He said He would do.

And so they hiked on, climbing higher up the side of the mountain. There was no clear path. They had to make their way through the brush and around the trees, picking their steps carefully on the rocky slope to avoid losing their footing. As they climbed higher, nearer to the slaughtering place, the knife in Abraham's belt seemed so heavy, pulling him downward as it slapped against his thigh with each step. The bundle of wood on Isaac's back, scratching and scraping as he stumbled along reaching here and there for a foothold.

Finally, they arrived at the summit, and "they came to the place which God had told him of." This was it. Time had run out. They were there, at the place where he was going to kill his son. We can almost feel the shudder than must have passed over Abraham's body as he looked around that place, so desolate, so high and windswept. Even though Isaac was standing beside him, he felt very alone.

And he was praying, seeking God, reaching out to the only One who could help him, who alone could rescue him from this desperate situation. Will you take this task from me? Will You now intervene so I don't have to do this awful thing? Is there some other way? These questions evoke the words and experience of Christ in Gethsemane. "My soul is exceedingly sorrowful, even unto death ... O My Father, if it be possible, let this cup pass from Me!" (Matthew 26:38, 39). "And being in an agony He prayed more earnestly: and His sweat was as it were great drops of blood falling down to the ground." (Luke 22:44).

With bitter acid rising in his throat hindering his words, Abraham now had to explain to Isaac exactly what God had told him in the night four days ago.

---

1. "And I will put enmity between thee and the woman, and between thy seed and her seed; He shall bruise thy head, and thou shalt bruise His heel. (Genesis 3:15). "And thou shalt call His name JESUS: for He shall save His people from their sins." (Matthew 1:21).

Turning toward his son, he looked Isaac in the face. What he saw was a virile 17 year old innocent young man, who had been obedient all of his life to his mother and father's wishes. Abraham was now 120 years old, and though he was by no means decrepit, he was an elderly man and would be no match, if the situation developed into a physical struggle. Abraham did not fear his son; he knew the goodness of Isaac's heart. No violence had ever been exhibited in his character. But this was a situation of life and death for the young man. No young person wants to die! Resistance would be a perfectly natural response from Isaac when his father told him he was going to kill him.

And then, what would Abraham do? He had made up his mind to fulfill God's request to offer up his son. It was time for another serious decision: to follow God, or heed the pleas for mercy from his son when he told him what he was about to do to him.

We can hardly imagine how the conversation went; can barely fathom how a father would tell his son that he was about to kill him because God had told him to do it. Isaac had been raised in a family of faith. From his earliest experience, as an eight-day old baby, Isaac had been participating in the covenantal conditions stipulated by the Creator God who rules heaven and earth. He had witnessed many animals offered as whole burnt offerings, and as thank and peace offerings. He had been instructed that each and every one of those animal offerings pointed toward the coming Messiah who would give up His own life to save the human race from the punishment for sin. From the gate of Eden, the covenant promise had always been stated by God in the simple phrase, "*I will do this.*" I will fulfill My promise to you to save you from sin, to be everything you need in this world and the next.

Abraham believed this promise, handed down to him from Adam through Noah to Seth, and then from Seth to Shem, and then to himself when he still dwelt in the land of Ur, so many years before.[1] He had believed the promise enough to pull up stakes, giving up everything he had in that prosperous city, and move to this land where they now lived as nomadic shepherds, owning nothing but the tents and trappings of shepherds and herdsman.

---

[1]. Noah was still alive when Abraham was born. Noah's son Shem and Abraham were contemporaries. Shem was alive when Isaac was born, and Abraham died about thirty years *before* Shem died. Truth of creation, the fall of Adam, and the world-wide Flood was passed from one generation to another until Moses composed his five books.

And so, Abraham sat down there on the rocky hilltop and reminded Isaac of all the times when he had witnessed those offerings being made. He explained again the meaning, and told of the love of their heavenly Father toward all people. Then he told Isaac that God had not commanded him to kill his son, but had *asked* him to do this thing, and that after many days of agonizing prayer, he had decided that God knew what was best. God had never failed him before; God had always provided what was needed, just at the right time.

Then Abraham, perhaps with tears choking his words as they tried to exit his mouth, repeated what he had said earlier, "My son, God has provided here, too. You are the child of that promise, given to me and your mother when we were well past childbearing age." The God of the universe, Creator of all that exists and ever will exist, provided for Himself by giving you to us. For seventeen years I have cherished you as my only son. Now God is asking that I give you back to Him. But let us not forget: He also promised that through you would come descendants without number, and that from one of those descendants of *yours* would come the Messiah. We may not understand, but we must believe His word. God's word never fails.

And Isaac believed, too. He didn't understand, but he was willing to submit to what God had asked his father to do. And the two of them "built an altar there, and laid the wood in order," and then Abraham "bound Isaac his son, and laid him on the altar upon the wood. And Abraham stretched forth his hand, and took the knife to slay his son."

Both father and son were fully dedicated to the will of God, even though they did not understand this strange request. Nonetheless, they were going to be faithful, no matter what, both believing against all hope that both of them would return down the mountain to the waiting servants, and then return all the way back home to their wife and mother.

45

The Lamb of God

Genesis 22:9-14

Abraham stretched forth his hand, and took the knife to slay his son. And the Angel of the LORD called unto him out of heaven, and said, Abraham, Abraham: and he said, Here am I." Here I am, doing what you asked me to do! Yes, LORD, here I am! The promised son is on the altar and the knife to slay him is in my uplifted hand.

And the Angel said, "Lay not thine hand upon the lad, neither do thou any thing unto him: for now I know that thou fearest God, seeing thou hast not withheld thy son, thine only son from Me." The Angel of the LORD here is the same Being who spoke with Abraham all along the way, through every interaction and test of Abraham's character. He is Christ in His pre-incarnate form, and therefore, because He is God, He identifies Himself as God—the God for whom Abraham willingly chose to give up everything, including his only son.

Do not misread the words of the LORD here. God is omniscient. He knows all things past, present and future. Nothing is hid from the LORD. "All things are naked and opened unto the eyes of Him with whom we have to do." (Hebrews 4:13). "Shall not God search this out? for He knows the secrets of the heart" (Psalm 44:21). King David wrote, "LORD, You have searched me and known me. You know when I sit down and when I stand up; You understand my thoughts from far away. You observe my travels and my rest; You are aware of all my ways. Before a word is on my tongue, You know all about it, LORD. (Psalm 139:1-4).

Why then, did the LORD tell Abraham, "Now *I know* that you love Me, and honor Me above all things"? If, because He is omniscient, it was *already known* to Him that Abraham loved him so much that he would choose to slay Isaac simply because He *asked* him to do it, why did He need to test Abraham in such a mentally and spiritually traumatic manner? Why did this demonstration of Abraham's (and Isaac's!) faith need to take place?

Yes, this incident was also a test of Isaac's faith. We overlook that significant part of the story. Isaac was not a small, helpless baby, like the children sacrificed to Molech. He was seventeen at the time, and physically strong and very capable of defending himself against someone who tried to murder him. But Isaac did not resist. He did not run back down that hill away from his father's apparently crazy commitment to do the thing that God had requested of him—slay your only son as a whole burnt offering to Me (Genesis 22:2). When the situation was explained to him, Isaac, without questioning God's motive, also made the free choice to submit to the will of God. This commitment shaped his character for the rest of his life.

But, why was this demonstration of their characters and commitment to God necessary? Because the watching universe are not omniscient. They cannot read the hearts and minds of men. And neither can our great adversary, Satan. Though the Godhead knows all things, their creatures do not.

Centuries later, another man would be tested in a similar manner when Satan accused God of specially protecting the patriarch Job from Satan's power to destroy him. That incident was also a demonstration for the watching universe, as one man stood the test against all the evils Satan could throw at him. In that test, Job vindicated the loving character of His God. In the end of the story, it was God's character that was proven to be immutably holy, wise and loving.

Satan's accusations against God, from the beginning of his rebellion in heaven, have been that God is an ogre who demands unconditional and unquestioning obedience from His creatures, and if obedience is not rendered, He will destroy the disobedient. Satan's basic premise, presented to the heavenly angels when he fomented his rebellion in heaven (Revelation 12:7-9; Isaiah 14:12-15), included the accusation that God's commands are impossible to obey, and therefore, it was Satan's claim that God set up a situation where no one can "win."

Satan continues to make this claim that under God's government sin is inevitable, unavoidable, and yet punishable by eternal torment in a never-ending fiery hell. This is the god that Satan presents to the world, but it is a false god—not the true God of the Bible.

Since the fall of Adam, God has been on trial before the watching unfallen universe. Our world is the proving ground, human beings are the test case participants. The entire Bible contains evidence that proves Satan's accusations are unfounded, malicious, and designed to destroy confidence in God's everlasting, superabounding love.

But Abraham and Isaac chose not to accept the doubt concerning God's character that Satan attempted into instill in their minds as they stood on that rocky mountain top. That long three day walk gave Satan plenty of opportunity to turn Abraham's mind. After all, God only *asked* him to sacrifice Isaac, He didn't *demand* that he do it. There was a loophole through which he could circumvent this terrible deed, and even justify himself for avoiding the will of God.

As that small party plodded along toward Mount Moriah, Satan was recalculating how he could use Abraham's actions to prove that God is an ogre, who now was demanding human sacrifice just like all those pagan gods inspired by Satan himself. Either way, whether Abraham killed Isaac or not, Satan could use the outcome against God. If Abraham killed his son, then God was vicious in demanding human sacrifice. If Abraham refused to kill Isaac, then "faith" in God did not really "work" to produce obedience from a heart committed in love to God (see Galatians 5:5, 6; Romans 10:10).[1]

However, there was another outcome that Satan had not foreseen. God Himself would give the sacrifice. As they walked along the road Abraham had made the statement several times, but the meaning was not fully revealed to Abraham or to Satan until that awful crisis moment on Mount Moriah. "And Abraham lifted up his eyes, and looked, and behold behind him a ram caught in a thicket by his horns."

The ram was *behind* him, out of his view as he faced the altar laden with the precious sacrifice that he was about to slay. But a sheep that is caught in snare is not a *silent* sheep. If that ram had been there

---

1. "For we through the Spirit wait for the hope of righteousness by faith. For in Jesus Christ neither circumcision availeth any thing, nor uncircumcision; but faith which worketh by love." (Galatians 5:5, 6). "For with the heart man believeth unto righteousness; and with the mouth confession is made unto salvation." (Romans 10:10).

the whole time, he would have been thrashing around attempting to free his horns from the thicket's brambles, bellering loudly for all to take notice of his distress and come to release him.

However, this ram was not your typical ram. This ram caught in the thicket on Mount Moriah represented the Lamb of God who, nineteen centuries later, made no complaint about being handed over to evil men to die on that Roman cross.

"Now is My soul troubled; and what shall I say? Father, save Me from this hour? But for this cause came I unto this hour." (John 12:27). "He was oppressed, and He was afflicted, yet He opened not His mouth: He is brought as a lamb to the slaughter, and as a sheep before her shearers is dumb, so He opened not His mouth." (Isaiah 53:7).

Just as God always responds at the point when we most need whatever it is we desperately need from Him, so Abraham was given the substitute sacrifice just at the point when he was about to slit Isaac's throat with the knife held in his trembling hand. By a miracle, the Creator God gave a perfect ram for the sacrifice, and stuck him in a bramble thicket so he could not run away when Abraham approached him.

Hearing the animal rustling in the bushes behind him, Abraham turned around and saw the sacrifice he confidently told Isaac that God would provide. Rejoicing and crying with relief, Abraham untied Isaac's limbs, allowing his son to climb down from the pyre on the altar. "And Abraham went and took the ram, and offered him up for a burnt offering in the stead of his son."

Both father and son bowed before the LORD in humble, thanksgiving prayer. "And Abraham called the name of that place *Jehovah-jireh*: as it is said to this day, In the mount of the LORD it shall be seen."

The LORD knows our human distress as we suffer under the burden of sin that Satan has caused, and from the foundation of the world, He gave the perfect Sacrifice to take away our sin (Revelation 13:8; Hebrews 4:1-3; 1 Peter 1:18-21).[2]

The incident that took place that day on Mount Moriah was a prefiguring of the event that God would enact on the same mountain nineteen hundred years later when He gave *His only* Son to save the

---

2. "And all that dwell upon the earth shall worship him [the beast], whose names are not written in the book of life of the Lamb *slain from the foundation of the world.*" (Revelation 13:8). "Forasmuch as ye know that ye were not redeemed with corruptible

world from sin. "For God so loved the world, that He gave His only begotten Son, that whosoever believes in Him shall not perish, but have everlasting life. For God sent not His Son into the world to condemn the world; but that the world through Him might be saved." (John 3:16, 17).

The lessons from the life of Abraham are for us who are living at the very end of this world's history. "Now all these things happened unto them for examples: and they are written for our admonition, upon whom the ends of the world are come." (1 Corinthians 10:11). The lessons Abraham learned are the very same ones we must learn. Abraham is the "father of the faithful," the spiritual father of all who will walk with Christ in complete obedience and faithful submission to our Good Shepherd who came looking for His lost sheep.

"Seeing then that all these things shall be dissolved, what manner of persons ought ye to be in all holy conversation and godliness, looking for and hasting unto the coming of the day of God, wherein the heavens being on fire shall be dissolved, and the elements shall melt with fervent heat? [the whole earth burning in the lake of fire, Revelation 20:14, 15]. Nevertheless we, according to His promise, look for the new heavens and a new earth, wherein dwelleth righteousness. Wherefore, beloved, seeing that ye look for such things, be diligent that ye may be found of Him in peace, without spot, and blameless." (2 Peter 3:11-14).

---

things, as silver and gold, from your vain conversation received by tradition from your fathers; but with the precious blood of Christ, as of a lamb without blemish and without spot: Who verily was *foreordained before the foundation of the world*, but was manifest in these last times for you." (1 Peter 1:18-21). "Let us therefore fear, lest, a promise being left us of entering into His rest, any of you should seem to come short of it. For unto us was the gospel preached, as well as unto them [the ancient Israelites]: but the word preached did not profit them, not being mixed with faith in them that heard it. For we which have believed do enter into rest [God's eternal rest symbolized by the seventh-day Sabbath, see verses 9, 10], as He said, As I have sworn in My wrath, if they shall enter into My rest: although the *works were finished from the foundation of the world*." (Hebrews 4:1-3). God's "work" in the everlasting covenant was "foreordained" and "finished" from the "foundation of the world." There is nothing that can be added to it by man.

www.ingramcontent.com/pod-product-compliance
Lightning Source LLC
LaVergne TN
LVHW091535060526
838200LV00036B/611